Nine Keys to World-Class Business Process Outsourcing

Nine Keys to World-Class Business Process Outsourcing

Mary Lacity and Leslie Willcocks

BLOOMSBURY
LONDON • NEW DELHI • NEW YORK • SYDNEY

First published in the United Kingdom in 2015

Copyright © Mary Lacity and Leslie Willcocks, 2015

Bloomsbury Publishing Plc
50 Bedford Square
London
WC1B 3DP
www.bloomsbury.com

London, New Delhi, New York and Sydney

A CIP record for this book is available from the British Library.

ISBN: 9781472918482

Design by Fiona Pike, Pike Design, Winchester
Typeset by Newgen Knowledge Works (P) Ltd., Chennai, India
Printed and bound in the United States of America

Contents

List of figures

List of tables

Professional credits

The nine keys were initially introduced in Lacity, M. and Willcocks, L. (2014), 'Nine Practices for Best-in-Class BPO Performance', *MIS Quarterly Executive*, 13(3). We've also published dedicated articles on Key 9: Prioritize and incent innovation in Lacity, M. and Willcocks, L. (2014), 'Business Process Outsourcing and Dynamic Innovation', *Strategic Outsourcing: An International Journal*, 7(1), 66–92; Lacity, M. and Willcocks, L. (2013), 'Beyond Cost Savings: Outsourcing Business Processes for Innovation', *Sloan Management Review*, 54(3), 63–69.

Acknowledgements

Since 1989, we have interviewed thousands of private and public sector clients, providers and advisors in North America, Europe, Australia, Asia and Africa on the topic of sourcing business and information technology services. We therefore first and foremost thank the now over 2,500 executives across the globe who have participated in our research over the past 23 years. Without them, our work just would not have been possible. Due to the sensitive nature of outsourcing, many participants requested anonymity and cannot be individually acknowledged. Participants who did not request anonymity in our most recent studies of world-class BPO are acknowledged in the appropriate places throughout this book.

For the present book, we would very much like to thank all the interviewees and people who have so generously contributed their time and information so willingly. We only have limited space to name anyone specifically but we do owe some enormous debts and would like to acknowledge them here.

First, we thank the 65 client and provider executives from world-class BPO relationships who participated in the formal interviews conducted for this book. These leadership pairs are driving results and enabling all the other key practices of world-class performance. We thank the International Association of Outsourcing Professionals (IAOP) for working with us on administering surveys on partnering, innovation, cloud services and leadership pairs. In particular, we thank Debi Hamill, Michael Corbett and Matt Shockley of the IAOP. We thank The Everest Group, particularly Eric Simonson, for the 265 surveys on high-performance BPO, and Craig Mindrum for collaborating on the initial reports that served as a launching point for this book. We thank Accenture, the major sponsor for the foundations of this research, and their assistance in opening up so many research opportunities on this subject; also BPeSA for facilitating access to some major case studies. A particular debt is owed to John Hindle of Knowledge Capital Partners whose thought leadership led us into this study, and who generously supported our efforts throughout. It is only right that his founding idea of the future of outsourcing should inform Introduction of this book.

We thank the supportive research environments of our respective institutions. Mary thanks Vice Chancellor Nasser Arshadi, Dean Charles Hoffman, Dr Shaji Khan, Dr Maurice Dawson, Dr Joseph Rottman, Dr Dinesh Mirchandani, Dr Ashok Subramanian, Dr Kailash Joshi, Dr Vicki Sauter and Karen Walsh at the University of Missouri – St. Louis. Leslie thanks his great colleagues at London School of Economics and Political Science for their patience, kindness and moral and intellectual support over 8 years now.

Work is pleasurable only in the context of a fuller life. Mary thanks her parents, Dr and Mrs Paul Lacity, and her three sisters: Karen Longo, Diane Iudica and Julie Owings. She thanks her closest friends, Jerry Pancio, Michael McDevitt, Beth Nazemi and Val Graeser. Finally, her son, Michael Christopher, to whom this book all things in her life are dedicated. Leslie would like to thank his circle of family and friends for their forbearance and humour, and especially George, Catherine and Chrisanthi, not least for the getaway nights at the opera, Mary for being the other (better) half of his brain for over 20 years now, and Andrew for persisting with the tennis, against the odds. Above everything, love to his beloved wife Damaris, who brings joy to all life holds.

Finally, many thanks to everyone at Bloomsbury Press for supporting the development and production of this book including Alana Clogan, Stephen Rutt, Rosie Bick, Srikanth Srinivasan, R. S. LakshmiPriyah and P. S. Gajalakshmi.

Foreword

Peter Samuel-Bendor and Eric Simonson

Raising BPO aspirations beyond mediocrity

Outsourcing is an uncomfortable word. This is a common view in society, business circles and even in much of the outsourcing industry itself. But why?

Of course, potential loss of jobs makes discussions about outsourcing emotionally charged. But we think the mixed connotations arise from more than that. The reality is that outsourcing efforts typically deliver the expected cost and efficiency savings – but little beyond that. Because the model is difficult to change, commonly under-invests and is prone to misalignment between the client and service provider, there's often little to be excited about.

Despite the negatives related to outsourcing, few decide to reverse their decision and insource the work, suggesting the new state – underwhelming as it might be – is still better than the alternative. Further, there are true success stories of outsourcing delivering powerful value and realizing its potential. The difference between these initiatives and those stuck in mediocrity is not a better solution design or a more balanced contract (the traditional focus of the industry), but rather how the efforts are managed to ensure the initiative thrives.

The barriers to success are largely human factors and both buyers of outsourcing services and their service providers play a role in poorly managing their joint initiative. The uncomfortable reality is that those reading this book (yes, you!) are probably the same people who are unable to properly manage outsourcing – either directly or through those you manage and coach.

The case for change in business process outsourcing

The business process outsourcing (BPO) segment of the outsourcing market is arguably not even 20 years old – and certainly most enterprises have only adopted it in a meaningful manner since the year 2000. Given that the average contract term is 6 years, this means that most organizations are either in the first or second generation of their initiatives – with some being in their third generation.

In our research into the adjustments made to outsourcing contracts during end-of-term decisions, we generally see organizations increasing the scope of services. Sometimes, this takes the form of adding more geographies or businesses. Frequently agreements add new areas of service – often moving from a core of transactional services to include more judgement-intensive services. Although sometimes scope is removed, on balance, scope is increased.

That is the good news and generally suggests there is enough satisfaction with BPO to continue investing in expanding the model. Service providers' increased efforts to adopt new pricing models and increased technology capabilities are also cause for optimism.

The bad news is that we have recently seen a notable increase in the portion of deals which are not renewed, but rather transitioned from one service provider to another.

Our recent data shows that 55 per cent of the finance and accounting outsourcing (FAO) agreements up for renewal in 2013[1] were not renewed with the original service provider (most transition to a new provider). This is an increase from 21 per cent in the previous 2 years. Although less dramatic, our data shows similar trends in other BPO markets such as human resources, procurement and others.

This is a startling change in the market and in the big picture it is not good for neither the buyers of outsourcing services nor their service providers.

What needs to change

Although some of the motivation for switching is to align to a service provider with more attractive capabilities and investments, our
work across the market indicates that much of the switching is simply
because the original provider is viewed as 'okay' and the buyer hopes to
find a better relationship with a new provider.

This is understandable, but misses the point that true satisfaction
in BPO comes from successfully working together with the service
provider. In our view, *the success of an outsourcing relationship is measured
not by the absence of problems, but rather by the ability to constructively solve
problems together.*

By working together, both parties need to orient their mindset towards
the reality that a BPO initiative[2] cannot be static, but rather is always
evolving. As such, it needs both sides to engage and guide the initiative
versus hoping a 'fire-and-forget' approach will lead to satisfaction.

What needs to change is the mindset and commitment by both the
buyer and service provider to successfully managing their joint initiative – success is unlikely to come from simply switching providers.

How this book helps

Drs Leslie Willcocks and Mary Lacity are the pre-eminent academic
minds focused on the outsourcing domain. They have chosen to take a
pragmatic view of how to develop meaningful insights on outsourcing
success. Instead of sitting in an ivory tower looking at spreadsheets of
macro-environment trends, they have walked the streets and engaged
with people doing outsourcing. They have done that consistently over
many years as ongoing members of the outsourcing community.

This book reflects a culmination of their knowledge into what makes
BPO successful – not just okay, but world-class success. It draws on
many research initiatives and explains the path to success in nine key

practices. These nine practices cover three time horizons – launching, staying on target and exploring new frontiers – which are vital to every outsourcing initiative. Further, most of the nine key practices focus on the heart of what makes a difference between mediocre BPO and world-class BPO – the human side of managing the initiative.

Everest Group had the privilege of conducting some of the research utilized in this book and is excited to see those findings and other insights combined into such a clear and powerful guide to improving BPO success.

Best wishes to you and your organization on the journey to reach world-class BPO success. We look forward to hearing you excitedly talking about your BPO successes!

Peter Bendor-Samuel, CEO and Founder
Eric Simonson, Managing Partner of Research
Everest Group
Dallas, TX
September 2014

---

[1] Gupta, S., Khandelwal, V. and Menon, A. (2014), Finance and Accounting Outsourcing (FAO) Annual Report 2014 – Transformational Agenda to Combat Reducing Stickiness, Everest Group report, Dallas.

[2] Note that we use the concept of 'initiative' instead of 'contract', 'agreement', or 'relationship'. 'Contract' and 'agreement' suggest something which is a static point in time, whereas 'initiative' is an ongoing effort that anticipates the need to evolve. 'Relationship' is what enables successful management of an 'initiative' – but it is the enabler versus being the first-order objective. A good relationship is required for a successful BPO initiative.

Introduction: Outsourcing as evolution

Dr John Hindle

Outsourcing is disruptive. It's a fist in the solar plexus – a violation of the body politic – a shock to the system that ripples throughout an organization, generating multiple aftershocks and dislocations. While 'selling the mailroom', as Peter Drucker enjoined, or even the office building itself may not be that traumatic, when outsourcing is extended into the fundamental business processes that enable the enterprise to operate, its effects are more visible and personal, disrupting relationships and ways of working that, however imperfect, have supported operations and sustained lives and livelihoods in what was previously a unitary entity.

Anticipating and preparing for these first- and second-order effects is critical to successful outsourcing, but is all too often ignored or forgotten in the rush to conclude a deal and seal the anticipated gain. As our authors note, the record is not that great. In a 2012 study by Everest Group, 60 per cent of BPO engagements were struggling to meet what might be considered the 'basics' of any BPO engagement: achieving cost targets, service levels and service reliability. In a more recent study from HfS Research, 49 per cent of buyers describe their current engagements as 'mainly lift and shift' of people and existing processes, with little or no transformation. Measured against the vaunted promise of BPO to radically improve enterprise services, these can only be seen as underwhelming results, and remind us of Dr Johnson's eighteenth-century observation about women preachers: 'Sir, a woman's preaching is like a dog's walking on his hind legs. It is not done well; but you are surprised to find it done at all'. (Of course by the twenty-first century women preachers have become very common. One only hopes that BPO will not need two centuries to evolve more sensible practices!)

Yet this is only half the picture. The other half looks quite different – a mix of engagements with decent performance and satisfied clients, distinguished by a smaller group of exceptional engagements delivering what our authors term 'world–class' results – creating new and sustainable business value for both buyers and providers. How are we to interpret this mixed record? Why do some BPO engagements succeed where others fail? Why are there so few standouts? And why do buyers keep buying in the face of significant risk? Is it simply what Dr Johnson called 'the triumph of hope over experience?' Or are there larger forces at work that determine success or failure in BPO, whose lineaments can only be perceived and understood from a distance and in a wider context? That is the aim of this volume – to collate and interpret the best available data on BPO, and, through analysis and interviews, to identify and explicate the path to higher performance.

To state the obvious, BPO is a complex commercial engagement between two principal agents – a buyer and a service provider – involving myriad moving parts that interact dynamically and constantly. Within the organizational systems of both principal agents are many sub-agents, 'nested' sub-systems and third parties providing 'ingredient' elements to the contracted service, each of which operates semi-independently. The interaction among all these systems – the collective actions and behaviours of all the various service contributors – can radically influence performance of the contracted service for better or worse. BPO looks very much the epitome of a complex adaptive system, in other words.

At the heart of any BPO engagement is a fluid matrix of business imperatives (competition and profit), human needs and aspirations (skills, jobs and careers) and fast-moving technologies (cloud, automation, analytics). Getting this confluence of people, process and technology right, and identifying, educating and securing alignment on the part of all the actors involved around desired outcomes is no small undertaking – which makes it all the more important to understand how those who get it right got it right. A little history and perspective is in order.

Following on from earlier experience with information technology outsourcing (ITO), enterprises began externalizing back-office functions in the early 1990s as they sought to identify and focus on the core competencies that gave them competitive differentiation. Indirect support functions such as accounting, payroll and often procurement were seen as prime candidates for externalization, and the earliest engagements arose in these internal service functions. Barely 20 years later, BPO is still fairly early on the services learning curve compared to manufacturing, where decades, even centuries, have advanced the state of practice we take for granted today, with high-quality mass customization and ever-shrinking costs. So perhaps the current state of play is all we can reasonably expect. Research does suggest, however, that while it is early days yet, BPO performance is on a path of steady improvement as buyers and providers gain, share and apply their experience. That improvement path begins with an understanding of the power – and the limits – of industrialization.

In a seminal 1976 article entitled 'The Industrialization of Service', Ted Levitt argued that businesses should take a manufacturing approach to improving service industries, an approach characterized by 'applied rationality', 'hard', 'soft' and 'hybrid' technologies, and the division of labour at scale. 'The managerial rationality we see embodied in the practical imagination we see exercised everywhere so effectively in manufacturing', he wrote, 'can, given the effort, be applied with similarly munificent results in the service industries'. Taking a manufacturing approach to service, he explained, involves breaking a task down to its irreducible inputs and activities, eliminating unnecessary or redundant steps, and then re-designing processes and systems to standardize and replicate each performance 'unit' precisely, using the most cost-effective source of labour.

It's an approach that mirrors the eighteenth-century Newtonian 'universe-as-machine' paradigm from which it sprang. As the Industrial Revolution demonstrated, it has been a powerful means of raising output and creating wealth. Productivity in manufacturing has improved massively over 250 years through the continual application of this approach, first by the use of steam as a source of power, then in Henry Ford's assembly line and Frederick Taylor's time and motion studies (under the rubric of 'scientific management'), and more recently by the application of computing and robotics and just-in-time supply chains.

Levitt's call to arms around improving services through specialization, scale and the application of technology frames the context for BPO as a management practice, and helps us understand why some engagements perform better than others. Where it has succeeded in delivering good service, BPO has responded to Levitt's call for industrialization applying the same methods that enabled manufacturing to reduce risk, drive standardization, increase productivity and improve reliability and predictability. Where it has failed – the 'lift and shift' approach – it has done so because it has focused exclusively on one dimension – the cost of labour – instead of applying the full transformation suite of people, process and technology. Industrialization, then, properly applied, is an essential transformational approach that marks the difference between poor and good performance. But industrialization alone cannot explain the difference between good and world class performance – it is a necessary but insufficient condition. Something more is required. That something becomes clear when we take a systems view.

By itself, the industrialization approach – atomizing processes, re-organizing and relocating them for greater efficiency – treats the organization as a machine whose parts can be arranged in a more efficient, elegant and reliable fashion through intensive activity measurement and process re-engineering. It helps explain the preoccupation with service level agreements (SLAs) in BPO contracts, which measure the parts of a process rather than its end-to-end performance, and inputs rather than outcomes. Where industrialization falls short, however, is against the obvious fact that the act of outsourcing fractures patterns and places of work, disrupts relationships and introduces new actors and ways of working, and the act of process re-engineering multiplies these effects exponentially. While industrialization is a necessary condition for raising service productivity, reliability and efficiency and delivering a 'good' level of performance, a pure machine approach is insufficient by itself to deliver world-class performance.

We have observed that industrialization grew out of an eighteenth-century Newtonian world view. In the twentieth century, however, the study of quantum physics disrupted the prevailing Newtonian paradigm, and gave rise to a new scientific theory in which the world is more organic and less mechanistic than had been previously thought – a more dynamic world, where change is constant and structures are continually evolving in response to their environment. Applied to organizations, this new perspective has encouraged the development of a systems view of the enterprise. Whereas the Newtonian view of the organization gives primacy to understanding the parts that make up the enterprise and organizing them for maximum efficiency, the quantum or systems view gives primacy to the organization as a whole – to understanding the relationships among the parts, the rules that govern their interactions and the ways in which those relationships are established or can be re-established and optimized for maximum value. As Peter Senge puts it succinctly: 'The world is made of circles and we think in straight lines'. Or as Margaret Wheatley describes it in more detail:

> Every time we go to measure something, we interfere. . . . Every act of measurement loses more information that it obtains. . . . Since there can be no definitive measurement, what is important . . . is to note the *quality* of the system – its complexity and distinguishing shapes. . . . If we ignore these qualitative factors and focus on quantitative measure, we will always be frustrated by the incomplete and never-ending information we receive. . . . [W]hat we *can* know, and what is important to know, is the shape of the whole – how it develops and changes, or how it compares to another system. (*Leadership and the New Science: Discovering Order in a Chaotic World*, 129)

(Note: This observation explains at least in part the common buyer experience of 'SLAs green, service red', in which the service level performance indicators established for a given business process are being met, but the client is unhappy with the business result, and hungers for the 'something more'.)

If we take a systems view to the establishment of a BPO relationship, it is surely worth noting that six of the nine keys that unlock world-class BPO performance identified by Willcocks and Lacity are explicitly focused on ways in which world-class engagements structure the relationship between provider and buyer, from assigning leadership pairs to driving change management, to adopting a partnership approach to governance, to aligning the retained organization around the new processes, to resolving conflicts fairly and ultimately to incentivizing both parties for innovation.

The critical importance of focusing on relationships as well as processes – both the overall buyer/provider relationship as well as the day-to-day relationships involved in service execution – is manifested by a fundamental principle of complex adaptive systems: that a small change in initial conditions produces ever-increasing effects over time. Establishing a BPO relationship correctly at the outset – with the right leadership, partnership attitudes, outcomes, incentives and governance structures – is itself the single most important meta-variable in enabling world-class performance. It is with this goal in mind – helping buyers and providers optimize their chances for success – that Knowledge Capital Partners engages in research, education and advisory services in the field of services sourcing. Especially as digital and cloud technologies are poised to disrupt traditional service delivery – from busy hands transacting repetitive processes to intelligent, self-aware systems that enact processes directly – getting it right at the outset has never been more important.

John Hindle
Founding Principal
Knowledge Capital Partners

Chapter 1

Introducing the nine keys to world-class BPO[1]

What's inside: This chapter reviews the BPO report card, points to foundational practices that lead to good performance and introduces the nine key practices that lead to world-class BPO performance.

1.1. Introduction

Organizations source many of their business processes through external service providers, a practice known as BPO. Growing from about a $150 billion global market in 2000 to $304 billion by 2013,[2] BPO growth shows no sign of slowing down. But despite its long history and escalation, BPO performance has a mixed report card. Some clients achieve superior results from BPO, while other clients experience grave disappointments. What accounts for such disparities in performance?

Our research sought to find the key practices that distinguish world-class BPO performance. We wanted to understand how some BPO relationships achieve more than just minor cost savings and meet SLAs. We wanted to know how some BPO clients extract additional sources of value from their BPO relationships. World-class performers deliver much greater business value to clients. Providers in our study helped clients implement shared services on a global scale, enabled rapid growth, delivered products faster and increased the clients' bottom lines by, for example, capturing more discounts and by reducing errors. Based on the results of five surveys and on interviews with client and provider executives leading 32 BPO relationships (see Appendix A for details about the research method), we identified nine key practices that contribute to world-class BPO performance. We organized the nine practices along a journey to world-class performance. Three practices

Table 1.1 The nine keys for world-class BPO performance

Launch the mission	⌘ 1. Assign a great leadership pair
	⌘ 2. Focus on business and strategic benefits beyond cost efficiencies
	⌘ 3. Drive strong transition, transformation and change management capabilities
Stay on target	⌘ 4. Adopt a partnering approach to governance
	⌘ 5. Align the retained organization, outsourced processes and provider staff
	⌘ 6. Resolve issues together and conflicts fairly
Explore new frontiers	⌘ 7. Use technology as enabler and accelerator of performance
	⌘ 8. Deploy domain expertise and business analytics
	⌘ 9. Prioritize and incent innovation

launch BPO relationships in the right direction, three practices keep the BPO relationship on target and three practices explore new frontiers (see Table 1.1).

Key practices around establishing a relationship should happen first. These practices include assigning strong leaders, seeking business value beyond cost and managing the transition. Practices to keep relationships on target include governing end-to-end performance as partners, deeply involving the provider's staff and solving inevitable service issues together. Once relationships are stable and delivering the anticipated business and strategic benefits, world-class performers unleash the power of technologies, analytics and innovations to deliver new value.

We think practitioners would benefit by adopting the practices in the order suggested in Table 1.1. Reality, of course, is messier. In our research, no best-in-class performers enacted the nine practices in precisely this sequence. Some BPO clients initially assigned lousy leaders, contracted too rigidly for cost efficiencies at the sacrifice of business benefits and failed to align their retained organizations with outsourced processes and provider staff. The consequences were poor to marginally acceptable performance. To rescue these BPO relationships, the partners in our study who enacted even some of the nine key practices dramatically improved performance. The very top BPO performers – those in the upper 20 per cent of performance – adopted seven or more of these practices. Our most powerful message is that it is never too late to improve BPO performance.

1.2. The BPO report card

There are many surveys that assess BPO performance, including our own academic review[3] and the BPO survey conducted by Everest (see Appendix B for details on the survey).[4] The academic review assessed three levels of performance: positive (56%), no change (33%) and negative (11%). The Everest survey assessed three levels: best-in-class (20%), potential best-in-class (20%) and typical (60%). Although the performance levels and rates vary depending on which survey is consulted, all of the evidence suggests that BPO performance varies widely across companies and industries. Our in-depth case studies conducted over the last 12 years find that BPO performance is best differentiated by four levels of performance: poor, doing okay, good and world-class (see Figure 1.1). We estimate that approximately 15 per cent of BPO relationships have poor performance, 40 per cent are doing okay, 25 per cent are good and 20 per cent are world-class performers.

Poor BPO performance is characterized, from the client's perspective, by lack of cost savings (or worse – cost escalation after outsourcing), poor service performance and low client satisfaction. Poor BPO performance can result from failure to execute foundational processes, including a flawed business case, a tough-minded procurement process more suitable for the purchase of products rather than BPO services, lack of in-house client retained capabilities to integrate the provider successfully in the organization, poor knowledge transfer or poor provider staffing. Sometimes poor performance is only temporary (such as during a rocky transition), while sometimes poor performance lasts until the relationship terminates.

Doing okay performance is characterized, from the client's perspective, by some cost savings and acceptable service performance, and mixed client

Figure 1.1 Levels of BPO performance

satisfaction. The relationship struggles with some service lapses while other services are performing fine.

Good performance is characterized by cost savings delivered, by service levels that are 'green' (i.e. meeting contractual SLAs) and by good client satisfaction. These relationships are humming along, and partners are usually keen to ask 'What's next?' What's next is, potentially, world-class performance.

World-class performance is characterized by continual improvements in productivity (cost) and/or quality (service) for baseline services. Beyond baseline, the partners focus on continually improving the client's key performance indicators (KPIs), not just improving SLAs. World-class relationships are also characterized by the high client satisfaction, continual rounds of innovation delivered and business benefits delivered.

BPO performance is not stationary – it can get better or worse over time (see Figure 1.2). During the life of a BPO relationship, one common pattern we found is that performance was often temporarily poor during the transition (1 to 3 months), and then proceeded to doing okay or good performance as the relationship stabilized. The quote from one client is representative of the trajectory of BPO performance and of the importance of communicating realistic expectations, 'Communication is absolutely key. Tell the organisation what's going to happen. Be realistic and tell the organisation, particularly the senior management of the organisation, that things will get worse before they get better. But give them a date. Tell them how long that pain is going to last. And of course, having told them, deliver to that timescale'. – BPO client

This book aims to help practitioners improve BPO performance by adopting the key practices that lead to world-class performance. Much like long-term, happy marriages, both partners have to stay engaged, enthusiastic and willing to execute the practices that deliver continually excellent results.

Although the four levels of performance – poor, doing okay, good and world-class – are described from the client's perspective, data show that client performance is highly coupled with provider performance. In our prior outsourcing research, we investigated the relationship between client-reported performance and provider-reported performance in 85 client–provider matched pairs. Among the 85 reported relationships, 60 per cent had positive outcomes from both the client and provider perspectives – this is compelling evidence for the win–win (see

Figure 1.2 BPO performance can get better or worse over time

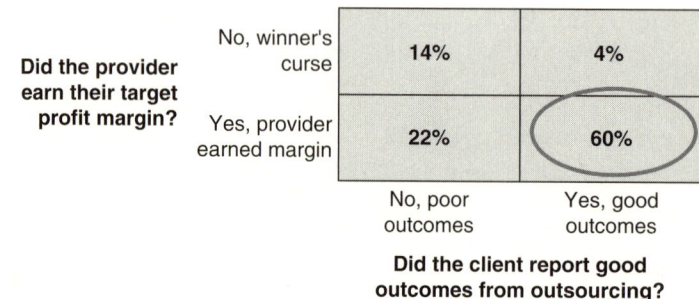

Figure 1.3 Client and provider outcomes: The evidence for the win–win (Source: Adapted from Kern et al. 2002)[5]

Figure 1.3). There was also a strong connection between provider's failing to earn their target profit margin on a deal and the client's reporting of poor outcomes. In many poor-performing deals from a client's perspective, the deals were bad for the provider as well. Specifically, in 18 per cent of the relationships, when the provider failed to earn their target margins, 14 per cent of clients reported poor outsourcing performance and only 4 per cent reported good outcomes. In contrast, providers met their target margins in 82 per cent of the deals, and only 19 clients (22%) reported poor outsourcing performance. This data is actually quite powerful because it shows that it is in the best interest of both parties to ensure a mutually beneficial relationship. The win–win relationship is not a nice-to-have, but a must-have.

1.3. Sourcing practices that lead to good performance

One [foundational practice] is to baseline your performance, otherwise when the BPO starts working, people only notice what's getting worse than before not necessarily when it is getting better. Also the business tends to have a very pink vision of how their life was in the past. So having a few baseline surveys is quite useful when it comes to showing if we are making progress or not making progress with facts rather than perceptions. – Global

Procurement Manager

The majority of client firms, about 65 per cent of them, achieve BPO performance in the doing okay/good performance range. These clients often pursue outsourcing to reduce costs, to focus in-house staff on more strategic activities and to access provider skills. They expect the provider to deliver good services as defined, measured and reported on in SLAs. The fundamental practices to achieve cost savings, solid delivery on SLAs and good client satisfaction ratings are thoroughly covered in another book, *Outsourcing: All You Need to Know*.[6] That book is designed to help practitioners learn about the foundational practices to investigate, target, strategize, design, select, negotiate, transition, manage and regenerate good outsourcing relationships. Figure 1.4 depicts the foundational model.

Clients who master the foundational practices are ready for the nine keys to world-class performance.

1.4. The nine keys to world-class performance

BPO relationships should be launched with the right people, the right mission and the right hand-off. World-class BPO performers stay on target by deploying practices that adapt to change and by systematically exploring new opportunities, often with the assistance of new technology, business analytics and other innovations. The sequencing of the nine practices is prescriptive – it is our best advice based on all the evidence from all our other cases. We begin with the three keys for launching a world-class BPO relationship.

1.4.1. Three keys to launching a world-class BPO relationship

BPO relationships are best launched by assigning a strong leadership pair, focusing on business benefits, and driving strong transition, transformation and change management. The three key practices to launch

ARCHITECT PHASE				ENGAGE PHASE		OPERATE PHASE		REGENERATE PHASE
BUILDING BLOCK 1 INVESTIGATE	BUILDING BLOCK 2 TARGET	BUILDING BLOCK 3 STRATEGIZE	BUILDING BLOCK 3 DESIGN	BUILDING BLOCK 5 SELECT	BUILDING BLOCK 6 NEGOTIATE	BUILDING BLOCK 7 TRANSITION	BUILDING BLOCK 8 MANAGE	BUILDING BLOCK 9 REFRESH
OUTCOME Acumen	**OUTCOME** Focus	**OUTCOME** Long-term strategies	**OUTCOME** Detailed future	**OUTCOME** Best value for money	**OUTCOME** Sealed deal	**OUTCOME** Adept start	**OUTCOME** Results	**OUTCOME** Better, faster
Key Actions ↗ Understood lifecycle ↗ Core expertise ↗ Insight form others ↗ Tested expectations ↗ Market intelligence	**Key Actions** ↗ Sourcing map ↗ Prioritized scope ↗ Rollout approach ↗ Profiles	**Key Actions** ↗ Configuration strategy ↗ Business case & approach ↗ Tender approach ↗ Transitions (in & out) strategy ↗ Contract mgmt & retained org strategy ↗ Lifecycle communications plan	**Key Actions** ↗ Contract scorecard ↗ Contract blueprint ↗ SLA ↗ Financial schedule ↗ Governance charter ↗ Mobilization & exit schedules ↗ Conditions of contract	**Key Actions** ↗ Evaluation team ↗ Selection criteria ↗ Market package ↗ Facilitated bids ↗ Evaluation ↗ Due diligence	**Key Actions** ↗ Negotiation team ↗ Analyzed issues ↗ Negotiation strategy	**Key Actions** ↗ Final plans ↗ Transition team ↗ Managed staff ↗ Transfers ↗ Re-engineered & integrated practices ↗ Acceptance	**Key Actions** ↗ CM network ↗ Compliance audits ↗ Continuous improvement ↗ Controlled finances ↗ Performance mgmt ↗ Ongoing forecasts ↗ Relationship mgmt ↗ Remain informed ↗ Managed issues, variations & disputes ↗ Record keeping & reporting	**Key Actions** ↗ Next gen capability ↗ Outcomes & lessons ↗ Next gen decision ↗ Next gen lifecycle roadmap

Figure 1.4 Foundational practices (Source: Cullen et al. 2005)[7]

relationships all contribute to world-class BPO performance, but the leadership pair is the one master key that unlocks the power of all the other keys.

🔑 Key 1: Assign a great leadership pair

We have very good individuals on this account. We have good people who are interested in doing these things together. – Senior Director

Pick up any business periodical and one will likely find an article on leadership. We dare to say nearly all leadership research[8] focuses on a *single* person. Leadership is almost always conceived of as a social process in which *one person* enlists a group of people to achieve a common goal. We think this view of leadership is passé. In today's economy, business value is increasingly created by close, *interorganizational* collaborations. How can we expect a single leader to move many organizations towards one common goal?

Instead of a single leader, we found that an effective leadership *pair* is the master key to achieving world-class BPO performance. An effective leadership pair – one person from the client organization and a counterpart from the provider organization – must work collaboratively to implement the other eight practices associated with world-class performance.

What do these leadership pairs do? During our interviews, we found that effective leadership pairs focused on where the outsourcing relationship should go, not where the relationship was in the past. Each leader was transparent by being open and honest about all operational issues with his/her counterpart. The leadership pair acted swiftly to remove or work around obstructions stemming from people, processes or contracts. The leaders never talked poorly about the other party. (They admitted that they frequently disagreed, but they resolved these issues behind closed doors and presented a united front to their respective organizations.) Each leader had high levels of credibility, clout and power within his/her own organization. Also, it was clear that each leader enjoyed working with his/her counterpart. In Chapter 2 of this book, we describe effective leadership pairs in great detail. Appendix B presents a diagnostic tool to assess leadership pair effectiveness. Our research finds that if the current leadership pair is performing poorly, changing one or even both leaders can significantly improve performance.

⚷ Key 2: Focus on business and strategic benefits beyond cost efficiencies

You need to know what you are trying to accomplish with outsourcing. You have to be thinking way beyond cost. Labor arbitrage is a one-time gain. You want to be thinking about what you will do in your own company and what you will not be doing. Strategy emerges from that. – Manager of Global Workshare, Manufacturer

World-class BPO relationships consider the cost benefits of outsourcing to be table-stakes. Sure, costs will be part of every business case, but the highest performing BPO relationships focused more of their attention and resources on achieving benefits like getting products on store shelves faster, bringing about large-scale changes in the client's retained organization, leveraging the provider's widely sought after but scarce subject matter expertise (SME) and increasing customer satisfaction or resolving customer issues better and faster. Insightful clients include business and strategic benefits in the business case, setting the tone for attracting the right provider. As explained in Chapter 3, clients from world-class BPO relationships understand that they need to invite providers into 'the strategic tent' to achieve benefits beyond costs.

⚷ Key 3: Drive strong transition, transformation and change management capabilities

There's a tremendous temptation to push it over the fence to the outsourcer and immediately kill off your retained organisation. What we did was consciously over-resource the retained organisation at the beginning, knowing that we'd ramp it down later. And I think that's very, very important. – BPO Client

The journey to achieve world-class performance requires expensive, politically charged and painful transformation levers such as centralization of budgets, standardization and optimization of processes, automation and technology enablement and often labour relocation. In some world-class BPO relationships, the client leaders transform the retained organization themselves and then engaged a provider to help operate, expand and improve the transformed services organization. In other world-class BPO relationships, client leaders engaged a provider to deploy some or nearly all of the transformation levers in a model called 'transition–transform–continually improve'. Regardless of the approach, strong transition and change management capabilities are vital.

Many clients fail to invest in enough resources during the transition because they do not want to erode the financial business case.[9] Yet, service excellence cannot happen without investing in an excellent transition team, managing all the stakeholders affected by outsourcing and transferring knowledge (e.g. shadowing, mentoring and training). We also know from the BPO survey and other research that the client's change management capability is crucial for continuing outsourcing success.[10] On most accounts, performance actually gets worse during the initial handover. Strong transition, transformation and change management capabilities are needed to stabilize the relationship and set it on a path to world-class performance (see Chapter 4).

1.4.2. Three keys to keep world-class BPO relationships on target

Adopting a partnering approach to governance, aligning the retained organization with outsourced processes and provider staff and resolving issues together fairly keep BPO relationships on target for delivering world-class performance. Essentially, these key practices help BPO partners adapt to the inevitable, pervasive and sometimes 'wicked' problems of the world of change.

🔑 Key 4: Adopt a partnering approach to governance

I don't think you should manage providers with the stick approach and say, 'we'll let you figure out how you want to manage your business and we'll just beat you every time you miss your numbers'. I don't believe in that. – Marketing, Acquisition and Retention Director

When most people think of a partnering or collaborative approach to BPO governance, they think of governance *structures*, such as joint operating, management and executives committees. While our research confirms that these governance structures are foundational, they are pervasive practices present in all substantially sized BPO relationships. Governance structures are thus a 'hygiene' factor, because the absence of such structures may result in poor performance, but the presence of governance structures does not in itself necessarily lead to world-class performance.

In world-class BPO relationships, a partnering approach to BPO governance is much more than a set of committees; it also comprises embedded partnership *attitudes* and *behaviours*. A partnering approach to BPO governance begins with an *attitude*, we call the 'Partnership View' in which a client regards the provider as a strategic partner rather than as an opportunistic vendor. The partnership view manifests itself in partnership *behaviours* regarding communication, planning and establishing boundaries. As discussed in Chapter 5, top BPO performers include the provider in 'the whole picture' of the end-to-end business process, even when the provider is only directly accountable for discrete sub-processes defined by SLAs.

🔑 Key 5: Align the retained organization, outsourced processes and provider staff

I challenge my own leadership team members by saying 'you don't just have 20 people here you actually have 120 because 100 of your people are over in Bangalore with the provider'. You can't run a process without including your team over in Bangalore as part of your operation. – Head of Shared Services

In Chapter 6, we focus on the resulting shape of a client's retained organization and three key stakeholders – internal business clients, employees in the business services organization and BPO providers. Transitioning to a BPO relationship can be tough on workers in the retained organization if steps are not taken to help them succeed in the new environment. Their roles will often shift and they will find themselves charged with managing and coordinating the outsourcing service relationship rather than simply managing others executing tasks. From the interviews, we learned that clients from high-performing BPO relationships transformed their internal business 'users' into educated 'customers'. Whereas 'users' consume resources with little thought to costs, educated 'customers' make informed choices about service levels, functionality and costs they incur. Finally, clients from world-class relationships treat the provider's remotely located staff as part of the global delivery team by collaborating virtually and physically with them. This includes engaging the provider's remote delivery teams located in places like India, the Philippines, Brazil and Eastern Europe. Effective client leaders visit remotely located provider staff once or twice a year even after the relationship has stabilized. As further discussed in Chapter 6, world-class BPO partners align the retained organization, outsourced processes and provider staff.

Key 6: Resolve issues together and conflicts fairly

A problem is not a Microsoft problem or an Accenture problem; it's our problem so we have to work TOGETHER. TOGETHER is capitalized. . . . The reason why it is capitalized is that you want to enforce the theme or the basic principle that we have to work TOGETHER. – Microsoft Senior Director

Even in world-class BPO relations, problems like service issues that harm performance, relationship traumas that hurt rapport and commercial conflicts that financially damage one or both parties occur.

A collaborative approach that resolves problems together and conflicts fairly is a distinguishing characteristic of world-class BPO performers. In contrast, partners from poor-performing relations assumed an aggressive approach to problem-solving and ended up with results that weakened the relationship, with partnership dissolutions, or lawsuits.

We identified six principles of collaborative problem-solving. The parties (1) behave appropriately (or are replaced), (2) never assign blame, (3) treat all problems as jointly owned, (4) are transparent about all relevant data, (5) seek solutions that both parties can live with and (6) protect each other's commercial interests. Chapter 7 explores these principles in 15 storylines of actual problems and how parties aimed to resolve them. Problems span the spectrum from minor skirmishes caused by obstructionist behaviour to the most serious of commercial conflicts caused by poor pricing models, drastic drops in service volumes and inequitable allocations from gain-sharing/pain-sharing clauses. For other partners facing these problems, the chapter offers detailed guidance.

1.4.3. Three keys for exploring new frontiers

World-class BPO performers not only stay true to the core mission, they systemically seek out new opportunities to improve the client's business performance. Top performers use technology as enabler and accelerator of performance, deploy domain expertise and business analytics and prioritize and incent innovation.

⊶ Key 7: Use technology as enabler and accelerator of performance

BPO buyers are much more likely to see value when the engagement was designed around a technology enabled transformation – Phil Fersht, Founder and CEO, HfS Research[11]

World-class BPO relationships leverage technology for business outcomes. Indeed, many people conceive of BPO in terms of people, processes and *technology*, thus placing technology as one leg of a three-legged stool. Many clients commend their BPO provider's deployment of self-service portals, automation, business analytics, forecasting tools, workflow tools, governance tools and cloud services because these technologies enable lower costs, better service and tighter controls. A 2014 survey by HfS research placed an even greater importance on technology for achieving business value from BPO and many people are talking about the role of robotics in BPO. These and other BPO technologies are covered in Chapter 8.

⚷ Key 8: Deploy domain expertise and business analytics

Whoever you select as a provider, within one year, the SLAs are going to be green. That's just going to happen. The business case, that's mostly labor arbitrage. So one year in, everything's green, you're going to ask, so where do I get my additional value? The only way you drive that out is through the analytics that look at processes end-to-end. – Accenture Account Manager

In world-class BPO relationships, clients leverage the combined process and industry expertise of their service providers. Providers apply domain expertise to launch rigorous analytics processes that measure the right KPIs, deploy tools and techniques to measure and report on KPIs and deploy algorithms, models and sophisticated statistics to identify weaknesses and opportunities. Then, the partners redesign processes to deliver measurable business outcomes. Chapter 9 provides several in-depth examples.

⚷ Key 9: Prioritize and incent innovation

If I run a project together with the provider that takes a person away, then the provider loses the revenue. That would be stupid of the provider to do. So what we then did was look at those projects to make sure we have a split of the gain-share to make it attractive for both of us. – Senior Director

Clients in world-class BPO relationships understand that they need to incent providers if they seek innovation.[12] Most outsourcing deals that we have studied are not designed for innovation, even though the parties may devote a lot of rhetoric to innovation. At the beginning of most deals, the usual sticking point is: *Who will pay for innovation?* Sometimes, clients volunteered an innovation fund against which approved client/provider proposals could draw. However, when confined inside a traditional cost-focused contract, innovations were rarely realized because the provider's attention was focused on urgent operational issues. Risk-sharing, gain-sharing, strong partnering behaviours and a provider seat at the strategy table are critical components in any outsourcing arrangement that is going to deliver meaningful innovations.[13] In Chapter 10, we present an entire framework to manage dynamic innovation in BPO relationships.

1.5. Lessons learned

BPO clients have a number of things to learn from the research:

It is never too late to improve BPO performance. We studied many clients who enacted the key practices well after the initial contracts were signed to reclaim or to establish world-class performance. Furthermore, BPO relationships can be improved or reinvigorated by adopting just some of these practices. One client achieved strong results by adopting just four of the practices. Although all of the practices complement and reinforce each other, a strong leadership pair is the single best performance improver. This is because – despite the promise of BPO robotics – most BPO relationships are heavily people-dependent. Some BPO relationships we studied had over 1,000 provider employees devoted to the clients' accounts. A leadership pair is needed to guide the teams towards top performance.

There is a big deal about big deals. Although the Everest survey did not find size to be a significant factor that influenced BPO outcomes, we learned from the interviews that size *does* account for a number of important benefits. For clients, the major advantages that the large BPO deals have over smaller ones include attracting the attention of top providers AND the attention of the providers' C-suite; spreading transaction costs over a large volume of work and really allowing deeper strategic focus on the retained organization. Many clients from large accounts also praised the ease at which they can scale up resources. For providers, growing client accounts also helps the BPO provider compete successfully within the global provider firm for more resources and top talent. Large and growing deals keep the relationship vibrant, as partners tackle new challenges.

---

[1] The nine key practices were first published in Lacity, M., and Willcocks, L. (2014), 'Nine Practices for Best-in-Class BPO Performance', *MISQ Executive*, 13(3), 131–146.

[2] Presentation by Avasant at the Service Provider Summit in London, September 2013.

[3] Our most comprehensive data comes from the review of 1,356 findings from 254 academic research studies. Aggregating results across all BPO empirical studies reveals that 56 per cent of outsourcing engagements resulted in positive outcomes, 11 per cent of engagements resulted in negative results and 33 per cent of the engagements did not result in any change in performance for the clients. (ITO clients, by comparison, reported positive outcomes from outsourcing 63% of the time.)

[4] Mindrum, C., Hindle, J., Lacity, M., Simonson, E., Sutherland, C. and Willcocks, L. (2012), 'Achieving High Performance in BPO: Research Report', available at http://www.accenture.com/Microsites/high-perfbpo/Pages/home.aspx

[5] Kern, T., Willcocks, L. and Van Heck, E. (2002), 'The Winners Curse In IT Outsourcing: Strategies For Avoiding Relational Trauma', *California Management Review*, 44(2), 47–69.

[6] Cullen, S., Lacity, M. and Willcocks, L. (2014), *Outsourcing: All You Need to Know*, White Plume Publishing, Melbourne.

[7] Cullen, S., Seddon, P. and Willcocks, L. (2005), 'Managing Outsourcing: The Lifecycle Imperative', *MISQ Executive*, 4(1), 229–246.

[8] One notable exception looks at leaders from multiple organizations: Davis, J. and Eisenhardt, K. (2011), 'Rotating Leadership and Collaborative Innovation: Recombination Processes in Symbiotic Relationships', *Administrative Science Quarterly*, 56(2), 159–201.

[9] Carmel, E. and Tjia, P. (2005), *Offshoring Information Technology: Sourcing and Outsourcing to a Global Workforce*, Cambridge University Press, Cambridge. Dibbern, J., Winkler, J. and Heinzl, A. (2008), 'Explaining Variations in Client Extra Costs between Software Projects Offshored to India', *MIS Quarterly*, 32(2), 333–366.

[10] Ranganathan, C. and Balaji, S. (2007), 'Critical Capabilities for Offshore Outsourcing of IS', *MIS Quarterly Executive*, 6(3), 147–164. Lacity, M., Khan, S., Yan, A. and Willcocks, L. (2010), 'A Review of the IT Outsourcing Empirical Literature and Future Research Directions', *Journal of Information Technology*, 25(4), 395–433.

[11] Fersht, P. and Sutherland, C. (2014), 'BPO on the Brink of a New Generation: Technology Transformation', HfS Research White Paper, Boston, MA.

[12] Lacity, M. and Willcocks, L. (2013), 'Beyond Cost Savings: Outsourcing Business Processes For Innovation', *Sloan Management Review*, 54(3), 63–69.

[13] Willcocks, L., Cullen, S. and Craig, A. (2011), *The Outsourcing Enterprise: From Cost to Collaborative Innovation*, Palgrave, London.

Chapter 2

⚷ Key 1: Assign a great leadership pair

What's Inside: This chapter focuses on the extraordinary people who enact the practices that lead to world-class BPO performance. It includes a description of ten attributes of effective leadership pairs, case studies on how leadership pairs affect BPO performance and advice on building the teams that support the leadership pairs.

2.1. Introduction

Leadership is defined by results. – Peter Drucker

An effective leadership pair – one person from the client organization and a counterpart from the provider organization – must work collaboratively to implement the other eight key practices associated with world-class performance. We think top BPO performance requires an effective leadership pair because BPO is a people business. Considering that most of the costs of BPO come from globally dispersed labour and that the services are delivered by people from two different companies with two different cultures, merely 'managing' a BPO relationship would not produce the results we witnessed in world-class BPO relationships. Even BPO relationships that were initially performing poorly have been transformed into great or world-class performance under the right leadership pair.

So what does an effective leadership pair look like? In our case study and survey research, we identified ten attributes of effective leadership pairs:

1. Focus on the future
2. Transparency

3. Problem solve
4. Put the customer first
5. Spirit of togetherness
6. Clout
7. Action-oriented
8. Trustworthy
9. Empathetic
10. Chemistry with counterpart

Next, we explain each attribute, and present data that looks at the perceptions of their relative importance.

2.2. The ten attributes of effective leadership pairs

The ten attributes of leadership pairs initially emerged from the interviews. First, we looked at client leadership behaviours and provider leadership behaviours individually. For clients, we began to notice that client leaders from top-performing BPO relationships saw the BPO provider's role as one of enabling their own vision for world-class services – putting the internal customer first. These client-side leaders focused on improving BPO performance by switching the conversation from 'where we are' to 'where we want to be'. They forgave past outsourcing sins by waiving penalties, switched the conflict resolution process from finger-pointing to problem-solving and considered the provider's commercial interests in moving forward. They aligned incentives between client and provider organizations, motivated and empowered people in their chains of command and integrated the provider deeply and meaningfully into their organization. Provider leaders were equally important in driving top BPO performance. Provider leaders who switched behaviour from selling to advising, cued in early to client signals, built trust by making decisions in the best interest of client, went beyond just meeting SLAs and advocated innovations that benefited both parties significantly improved BPO performance. We began to see how the behaviours of both influenced each other until a cohesive set of ten leadership pair attributes emerged.

Next, we sought to more rigorously explore the attributes. To what degree do client and provider leaders exhibit these attributes? Are certain attributes more important than others? Do clients and providers share similar perceptions about leadership pair attributes? To answer these questions, we surveyed delegates during the customer only and provider/advisor only networking sessions at the 2014 IAOP Outsourcing World Summit.[1] The sample of 139 completed surveys comprises 72 clients, 51 providers, 6 advisors and 10 providers/advisors.

Based on the survey results, we dropped one attribute (individual performance) and added the attribute empathy. The ten final attributes are:

1. *Focus on the future*: *Each leader focuses on where the outsourcing relationship should go, not where the relationship was in the past.* This was a particularly important leadership pair attribute for BPO relationships that needed to improve performance. Letting go of the past frees the pair to focus on moving ahead. At one bank, BPO performance was very poor initially. The provider explained that the relationship only improved after the client stopped harping on the distant past. He said, 'I think their ability over the past few years to let [past performance] go has been very important. That might sound completely irrelevant but I think their ability to let the past be the past and focus on the future of the service has been very successful'. On another account, a client leader described how he and his counterpart forget the past. Although his contract entitles his organization to service credits when the provider misses SLAs, he doesn't invoke this clause because he wants the leadership pair to focus on moving the relationship forward.

2. *Transparency*: *Each leader is open and honest about all operational issues.* In one open-ended survey we conducted (see Appendix A), transparency was among the top three things clients and providers wanted from each other. Clients wanted providers to be more transparent about their profit margins, costs, subcontracting practices, risk profile and true attrition rates. One client wanted to ask the provider, 'Why is your cost structure a secret?' Clients also wanted to better understand how provider organizations allocate resources to staff client accounts. The survey also found that providers wanted clients to be more transparent about their actual average baseline service levels – not about their most

optimistic guesses or their most favourable performance. Providers wanted clients to be more forthcoming about process complexity, process exceptions and process volumes. Providers had a difficult time assessing these issues during due diligence, causing many surprises during the early months after transition.

In world-class BPO relationships, the interviews revealed that leadership pairs are transparent about all relevant operating issues. Beyond operations, many client leaders also kept their provider counterpart abreast of new strategic directions that might affect the BPO relationship. Examples from the interviews include a client informing a provider about a likely merger which would dramatically increase service volumes and a likely divestiture which would decrease volumes. Providers also share news with clients that might affect the relationship. One client lead said of his counterpart, '[He] certainly flags future risks in their business with me regularly'.

3. Problem solve: Each leader seeks to diagnose and fix problems; he/she does not seek to assign blame. No service organization has a crystal ball to precisely predict demand and certainly no business service runs perfectly – there will be occasional outages and pieces that fall through the cracks that cause slippages in performance. In world-class BPO relationships, the leadership pairs make sure that there is an infrastructure up and down the chain of command to swiftly solve problems. The sequence is always to: (1) find the cause, (2) fix the problem and (3) let the leadership pair worry about the commercial consequences later. One client account leader described the process this way: 'Our relationship is such that when something goes wrong, neither or us worries about whose fault it is, either as an individual or which organisation. We both worry first about fixing it and then second, about root cause analysis'. The aim is to resolve issues at the lowest possible level, only escalating problems when they are particularly severe or in need the leadership pair to re-establish commercial parity. This attribute is also a key practice discussed in Chapter 7: Resolve issues together and conflicts fairly. In the chapter, we will discuss many examples of problems that arose in BPO relationships and how effective leadership pairs resolved them.

4. Put the customer first: Each leader always does what is best for the customer organization, then, if need be, fairly compensates the adversely affected party.

In BPO relationships, the 'customer' may be an internal customer in the client organization who receives service from the BPO provider or the customer may be external, as is in the case of customer care or call centre outsourcing. In cases of procurement and invoice processing, the external 'customer' may be other vendors. In world-class BPO relationships, the focus is always on providing the customer with superior service, even if requests are slightly outside of the scope of the contract. Parties rush to service the customers and then determine equitable compensation.

On one legal services outsourcing (LSO) relationship, the client severely under-estimated the number of lawyers the LSO provider would need to staff for a document review. Although the client recognized that it was their fault for under-estimating the volume of work, both parties jumped into action. The provider could only meet the surge in demand by having existing employees work with overtime pay. The client and provider were sensitive about demoralizing and burning out the LSO provider's staff, so they made the overtime work voluntary. The client also paid for the employees' transportation, security personnel and facilities management costs for weekend shifts. Eighty per cent of the LSO provider's employees volunteered and the project was completed on time. The leadership pair did what was best for the customer organization and fairly compensated the adversely affected provider staff.

5. *Spirit of togetherness*: *Each leader does not talk poorly about the other party but instead presents a united front.* BPO relationships are difficult – there is no doubt. But effective leadership pairs address sensitive and controversial issues behind closed doors, bringing in key stakeholders as needed until the issue is resolved. During the closed door sessions, debates might get quite heated, but once a resolution is reached, the leaders emerge to present a united front as they seek buy-in for the proposed resolutions from their respective organizations. We have many examples of this attribute from our interviews. On one account, an effective leadership pair retold the story of fighting over a multi-million dollar invoice. It took quite a few rounds of deliberations before they decided to split the amount. The leaders left this acrimonious event behind them and went forward to jointly sell the decision to their organizations. As of 2014, the pair continues to work collaboratively on their top-performing account.

6. *Clout: Each leader has high levels of credibility, clout and power within his/ her own organization.* Both leaders, but client leaders in particular, must have credibility, clout and power within their own organizations. The path to world-class performance requires marshalling resources and people to all work towards a common vision. One provider describes the importance of his client's stature within the client organization: 'I think when you work with your client, it's very important your relationship person is respected within the client firm, has weight with them and is a very strong political operator. [Our client lead] is very experienced. He knows the business very well. He knows how relationships work and he's very politically aware. So the individual that is your counterpart has to be mature, has to be well-respected and should be very politically astute'. On another account, the client was initially pleased that the provider hired a new top gun to serve as the provider account lead. Although this person had great experience and was a customer-focused leader, he had no established relationships within the provider firm. He had trouble staffing temporary assignments with high performers and he did not get top priority when cold-calling key provider support people. As one interviewee said, 'He didn't know who to call when the lights went out'. (Please note this is just one example of an ineffective external hire; we provide counter examples in the case studies, Section 2.4.)

7. *Action-oriented: Each leader acts swiftly to remove or work around obstructions stemming from people, processes or contracts.* If clout is conceived of as a kind of potential energy, then the action-oriented attribute can be conceived of as its kinetic counterpart. Effective leaders are not afraid to expend their clout to get things done. One client lead of a supply-chain BPO relationship provided some examples. He said: 'One of the initial challenges was trying to remove roadblocks and get my organization to make sure they accept the provider as part of the operating model'. The functional groups within his organization were creating certain barriers, such as not giving the provider information, not treating them with respect and not giving them the attention they gave their other colleagues in the organization. His company did not let vendors have access to company software or data, which prevented the BPO provider from working effectively. He jumped into action: 'There are a couple of key things really that helped with success. One is removing

the roadblocks and the handcuffs to allow the service provider to do what they are required to do to provide a tier one type service. I made sure that our other functional groups in the organization understood that this provider works for me, it's not an external vendor. Treat them as another internal functional group within the organization'. He got the provider access to their IT, tools and data. He also had the provider employees assigned to his account change their email signatures to his company name. The results were tremendous – the leadership pair went on to improve significantly some of the client's KPIs.

8. *Trustworthy: Each leader is trustworthy and has good intentions towards his/ her counterpart.* Most of the academic research on trust in outsourcing relationships has focused on organizational trust.[2] Initially, organizational trust in outsourcing is the confidence that the other party will conform to one's expectations. Fair contracts help to build this initial view of trust. In the long term, however, organizational trust is based on behaviours. Client organizations trust providers that deliver promised services. Trust is also built by resolving conflicts fairly, rather than holding the disadvantaged party to a contractual clause that may have been negotiated based on shaky data or assumptions that no longer hold. Thus, organizational trust is ultimately about performance.

From the interviews, we found that individual trust within the leadership pair operates in much the same way. At first, trust is a hoped-for attribute. Leaders often initially adopt Ronald Reagan's position 'trust but verify', which he used when dealing with Soviet Russia. One provider account manager agreed that 'trust is built on transparency' – the so-called verification of truth. Deep trust is built slowly over time with repeated trustworthy behaviours. One client account lead said, 'Trust is probably the number one behaviour that leads to success. I can't stress enough how a trusting relationship drives success. If there is no trust between me and [my provider], then we would be only be managing to the very strict contractual obligations that we have'.

9. *Empathetic: Each leader understands, is aware of and is sensitive to the counterpart's feelings, thoughts and experiences.* Research finds that human beings are more able and willing to empathize with those most similar to themselves.[3] It is not surprising, then, to find that one of the best ways to build empathy is to find someone with prior experience in the opposite

role the person is now asking to lead. BPO has been around long enough for many individuals to have rich career paths in many areas of service as clients, providers and advisors. We interviewed several leaders who used to hold the counterpart's position. One client leader used to work for the provider organization. He was actually in-charge of a consulting project that pointed to BPO as part of the solution. He helped architect the BPO deal from the provider's side, and then was hired by the client (with full blessing from the provider) to serve as the client side lead.

The Leadership Pair Effectiveness survey also pointed to the importance of empathy. We found that clients rated the client leaders significantly higher than the provider leaders for eight of the nine attributes that were assessed. Similarly, providers rated the provider leaders significantly higher than the client leaders for six of the nine attributes. Neither community significantly rated the other higher on *any* attribute. We think respondents naturally empathize more with their own communities. On the open-ended question, one provider respondent wrote, 'Failure to empathize with the counterparty's issues inhibits leadership pair effectiveness'. Based on the findings from the survey and interviews, we added the attribute empathy to the list of leadership pair effectiveness.

10. *Chemistry with counterpart: Each leader enjoys working with his/her counterpart.* The client and provider leaders must have the right chemistry. In several cases, we found client–provider pairs who were both experienced and effective individual leaders, but the combination simply did not work. For example, at one world-class BPO relationship in Europe, the client leader requested a new provider account manager because the first person assigned – who was quite senior – had his own ideas for what needed to be done. The provider assigned a new account leader who was more junior and more compatible with the client lead. The client lead contrasted the two provider leads: 'The provider appointed a UK-based delivery account manager and through the initial period, the relationship did not work. I don't know whether it was chemistry or what; he was a more senior guy with the attitude: 'Well, I've done it, I know what I'm doing, I don't know why you're panicking, leave me alone to get on with it'. He may have been a very good person but I couldn't work with him. The provider bravely and ultimately was correct to say: okay, if that's the case, we'll pull him out. They put somebody else in who was actually more junior but was somebody with whom we could

work. The junior one was very engaged, very hard working, and took instructions a little better'.

The ten attributes of leadership pair effectiveness – focus on the future, transparency, problem solving, put the customer first, spirit of togetherness, clout, action-oriented, trustworthy, empathetic and chemistry with counterpart – emerged from our study of world-class BPO performance. We wondered the degree to which client and provider leaders exhibit these behaviours among the wider population of outsourcing arrangements. We also wondered if some of these attributes affect leadership pair effectiveness more than others. We now turn to our Leadership Pair Effectiveness survey results to answer these questions.

2.3. Rating the leadership pair attributes

We asked each respondent of the Leadership Pair Effectiveness survey to think of one particular leadership pair managing an outsourcing relationship with which they are familiar. We asked respondents to rate the extent to which they agree that the client leader exhibits each of the leadership pair attributes and the extent to which they agree that the provider leader exhibits each of the attributes. All questions used a 7-point scale, with 1 indicating strongly disagree and 7 indicating strongly agree that the leader exhibits the attribute.

Overall, one can see from the aggregated data in Table 2.1 that respondents rated nine leadership attributes rather highly. (Empathy was not assessed on the survey.) When including responses from the entire community (clients, providers and advisors), the average ratings for the leadership attributes of client leaders and provider leaders are over 5.0 on a 7.0 scale. Several other interesting inferences can be made from the ratings of leadership pair attributes. As indicated by the *orange cells* (or light grey cells if reading in black and white) in Table 2.1, the entire community rated the *client* leader's transparency, focus on outcomes, clout within the client organization and trustworthiness as statistically higher than the provider's ratings on these behaviours. As indicated by the *blue cells* (or dark grey cells if reading in black and white) in Table 2.1, the entire community rated only the *provider* leader's spirit of

Table 2.1 Leadership attribute ratings by clients, providers and advisors. The degree to which respondents agree that the client and provider leaders exhibit leadership attributes: 1 indicates strongly disagree and 7 indicates strongly agree that the leader exhibits this attribute

	Focus client	Focus provider	Transparent client	Transparent provider	Problem solve client	Problem solve provider	Customer first client	Customer first provider	Spirit client	Spirit provider	Clout client	Clout provider	Action client	Action provider	Trustworthy client	Trustwothy provider	Chemistry client	Chemistry provider
All respondents	5.2	5.2	5.4	5.0	5.1	5.2	5.7	5.0	5.1	5.3	5.6	5.3	5.4	5.3	5.7	5.4	5.5	5.4

	= client behaviour significantly greater than provider behaviour
	= provider behaviour significantly greater than client behaviour

Table 2.2 Leadership attribute ratings by clients OR providers

	Focus client	Focus provider	Transparent client	Transparent provider	Problem solve client	Problem solve provider	Customer first client	Customer first provider	Spirit client	Spirit provider	Clout client	Clout provider	Action client	Action provider	Trustworthy client	Trustwothy provider	Chemistry client	Chemistry provider
Client respondents only	5.4	4.7	5.7	4.4	5.4	4.8	5.8	4.4	5.2	5.1	5.6	4.8	5.5	4.8	5.7	4.8	5.3	5.1
Provider respondents only	5.0	5.7	5.0	5.6	4.6	5.7	5.6	5.7	5.1	5.7	5.7	5.8	5.3	5.7	5.7	6.0	5.6	5.7

	= client behaviour significantly greater than provider behaviour
	= provider behaviour significantly greater than client behaviour

togetherness as greater than the client's. Our case study research also found that providers are much less likely to speak poorly about a client's behaviours while many clients feel free to discuss a provider's shortcomings.

When including responses from just the clients or from just the providers, other interesting patterns emerged. From Table 2.2, the row of client responses shows that clients always rated client leaders *higher* than clients rated provider leaders for all nine attributes. These differences are statistically significant for eight of the nine attributes: focus on the future, transparency, problem solving, putting the customer first, clout, action-oriented, trustworthiness and chemistry. The row of provider responses also shows that providers always rated client leaders *lower* than providers rated provider leaders for all nine attributes. These differences are statistically significant for six of the nine attributes: focus on the future, transparency, problem solving, spirit of togetherness, action-oriented and trustworthiness. Where one stands depends on where one sits.

To assess which attributes contributed most to leadership pair effectiveness, we asked respondents to rate on a 7-point scale the overall effectiveness of this leadership pair at managing the outsourcing relationship. The vast majority of the entire community (client, provider and advisor respondents) chose to rate a relatively effective leadership pair (see Figure 2.1). The mean rating for the effectiveness was 5.27. Clients thought of slightly less effective pairs with an overall effectiveness rating of 5.04. Providers thought of slightly more effective pairs with an overall effectiveness rating of 5.47.

Once we had an overall effectiveness rating, we were able to assess whether particular attributes were more critical than others. We found

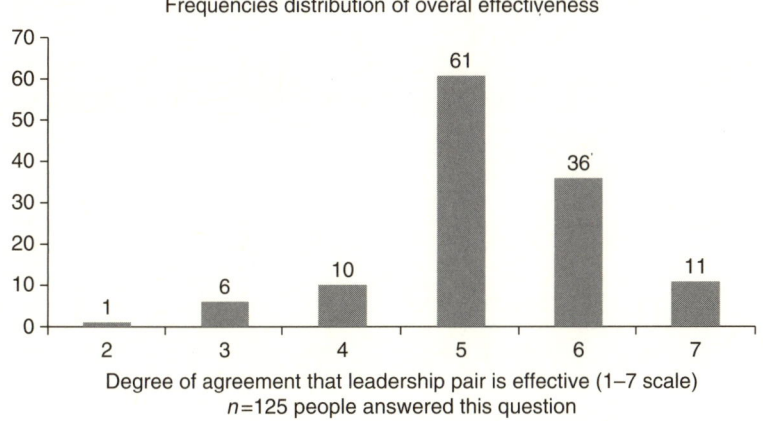

Figure 2.1 Respondents ratings of leadership pair effectiveness

that, once again, the results varied significantly based on whether clients or providers were answering the survey questions. When considering only client responses, four leadership attributes had the most significant effects on overall leadership pair effectiveness.[4] These were the provider leader's trustworthiness and chemistry and the client leader's clout and spirit of togetherness[5] (see Figure 2.2). When considering only provider responses, three leadership attributes had the most significant effects on overall leadership pair effectiveness. These were the provider leader's clout and the client leader's chemistry and transparency[6] (see Figure 2.3).

In the client respondent sample, client clout significantly affected leadership pair effectiveness but provider clout did not. In the provider respondent sample, provider clout significantly affected leadership pair effectiveness but the client clout did not. *Each community (client and provider) views their own stature within their organization as vital to effectiveness but did not place the same importance on the counterpart's stature.*

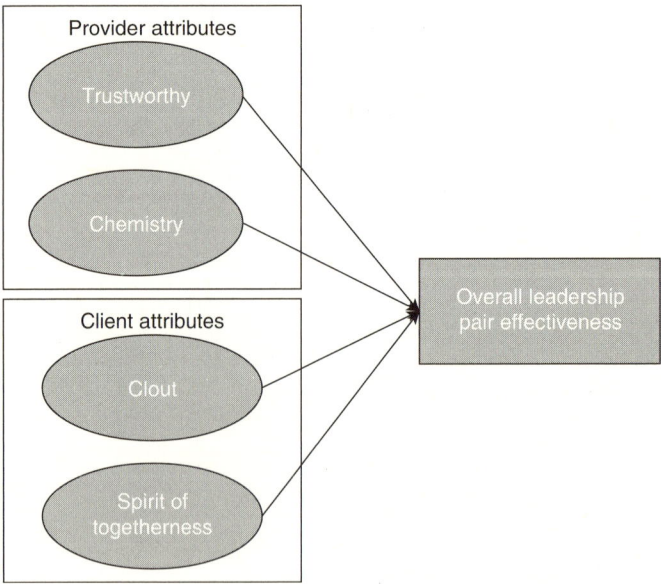

Figure 2.2 Most important leadership attributes (client respondents only)

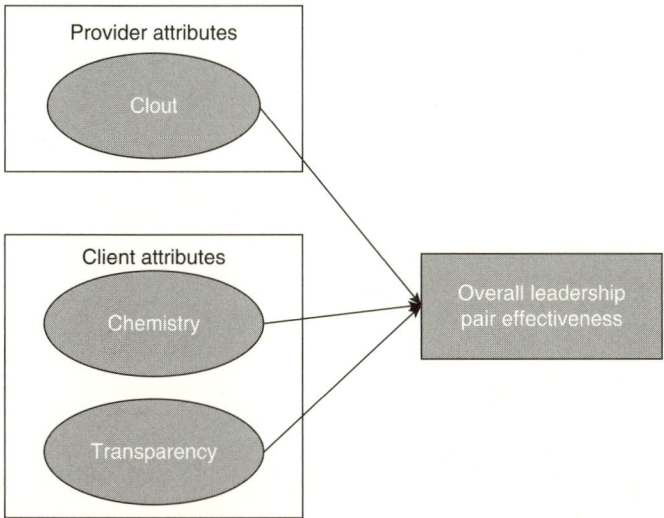

Figure 2.3 Most important leadership attributes (provider respondents only)

In the client respondent sample, provider chemistry significantly affected leadership pair effectiveness but client chemistry did not. In the provider respondent sample, client chemistry significantly affected leadership pair effectiveness but the provider chemistry did not. *Each community (client and provider) views the counterpart's chemistry as vital to success but did not place the same importance on their own community's chemistry.*

Thus, the interesting thing about this survey data is the differing perceptions when clients and providers rate leadership pairs, though we tended not to find this difference when looking at really top-performing leadership pairs in our case study research.

2.4. Case studies: How leaders transform BPO performance

In this section, we present cases of how leadership pairs affected BPO performance (see Figure 2.4). The most dramatic changes in performance

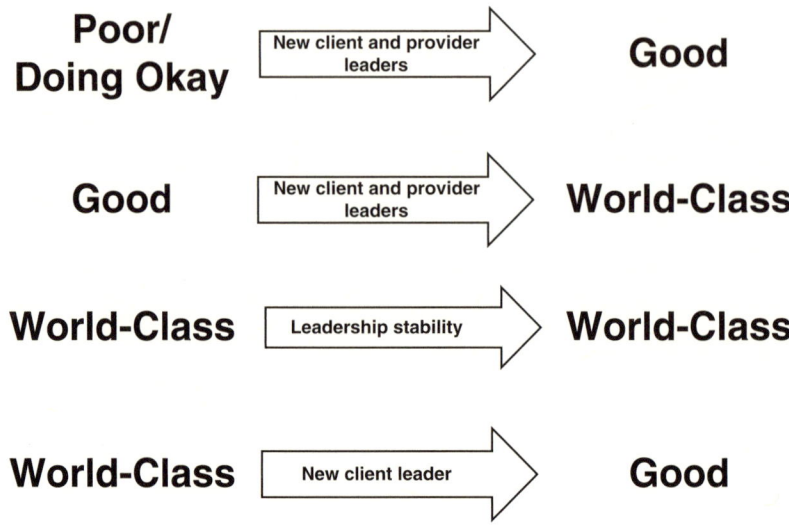

Figure 2.4 Cases on the effects of leadership turnover on BPO performance

were prompted by complete leadership turnover in the top-level client and provider organizations. When client organizations recruited an external person to take charge and the provider assigned a new provider account manager, employees up and down the chains of command in both companies were signalled strongly that transformation was going to occur. We provide one case example from a consumer products company.[7] Performance improved from poor to great. The second case shows that leadership stability can sustain world-class performance over a long period of time. The third case shows how turnover of the client-side CEO eroded BPO performance. The final case examines an interesting outlier, one we call 'an old dog learns new tricks'. It tells the story of how one leader completely transformed his behaviour after an acquisition.

2.4.1. From poor to good BPO performance

This consumer products company signed a BPO deal in 2007 for human resource outsourcing (HRO) services including recruitment, payroll, employee data, training and development. By 2010, the relationship was bordering on poor performance/doing okay. The provider assigned a new delivery manager and a few months later, the consumer products company recruited a new transformational leader from an external company. The new client leader described the BPO performance when he first arrived: 'When I got here, things were completely in the ditch. Our key service indicators were not being met'. The new leaders worked together to improve performance dramatically. The client said: 'Basically, we went on this very rigorous path to getting the wheels back on our service agreements. All the indicators went green for the first time'.

What leadership behaviours led to such an improvement? The new leaders focused their efforts on fixing problems rather than assigning blame. To help with root cause analysis, the provider implemented a business analytics tool – at no additional cost – to better diagnose service issues. The partners first identified service solutions that were best for the client, then worried about the commercial implications. The provider account delivery manager explained: 'What this client does extremely well is to raise an issue from their side and allow us to raise issues from our side so that we can deal with them openly and transparently, without doing fault-finding. What we do in those cases is a very rigorous root cause analysis and we look what needs to be better. We jointly approach how do we get the outcome the client is looking for and then ask: what does that mean for the relationship? The first focus is this is the outcome that we need to be going for and how do we jointly go about it? They work very collaboratively with us in doing that'. For instance, the client did not like the interface of one of the provider's proprietary tools. The partners agreed to use another vendor's cloud-based solution and reached an equitable commercial agreement.

As service levels went green, the partners also worked on more value-added innovations. For example, the consumer products company wanted to recruit engineers with demographics that better match their consumers. The provider helped by changing the recruitment strategy from reacting to current job openings to proactively building a pipeline of potential engineering candidates. The provider also bolstered the employee referral plan and implemented better metrics such as 'hiring manager satisfaction' with the pool of candidates sent by the provider.

The client now includes the provider in the end-to-end service and invites the provider to serve on Six Sigma teams aimed at improving end-to-end service performance. All of the nine key practices of world-class performance are now evident, prompted by the way the two new transformational leaders have treated the relationship. The client leader explains the difference in approach: 'We did some personnel changes on this side; they did some personnel changes on their side. Our new provider account representative was assigned to our account just a few more months before I got here. So I think we had a better sort of partnership. We got much more analytically driven around what were the areas of under-performance versus an overall number with a particular role that we had trouble with. We began to problem solve them. We were able to go in and really target where the issues were, rather than having a broad discussion of what is not working. We now operate in the spirit of a partnership'.

2.4.2. Maintaining world-class performance with leadership stability

In the case of the consumer goods company, changes in both client and provider leadership prompted a dramatic improvement in BPO performance. However, in other cases, we found that leadership stability was also a viable route for improving or maintaining high performance. It is really a matter of experienced leaders embracing the attributes of effective leadership pairs that move a relationship to high performance and keep it there. If the leaders are involved from the contract negotiation stage, a real benefit of leadership stability is confidence that the contract negotiated can be delivered.

The Microsoft–Accenture (see Chapter 11 for the full cast study) deal for global financial and accounting services has had the same leadership since its inception. The individual leaders at both Microsoft and Accenture are clearly transformational leaders who have been devoted to this partnership since the beginning. Microsoft partnered with Accenture in 2007. The initial 7-year agreement spanned 90 countries and 450 individual roles. Within 18 months, the partnership designed and implemented a global set of standardized processes across 92 countries, improved internal controls and compliance, improved scalability and reduced costs by 35 per cent. In 2009, the partnership was extended to include more accounts payable and buy centre processes. The contract was worth $330 million in 2012 and was extended until 2018. Five years into the BPO relationship, the partners continue to innovate Microsoft's financial, accounting and procurement processes. In 2010–2011, for example, the partners moved 25 international subsidiaries from manual invoicing to electronic invoicing. The partners implemented new tools that increased transparency by allowing Microsoft's business users to see every dollar spent and timely measures on performance. New transformation projects are planned and delivered each year.

During all this time, there has been a steady set of leaders managing the Microsoft–Accenture relationship, which is key for sustaining high performance in this relationship. However, transformational leaders will get bored without new challenges, so long tenures are also associated with growth of the BPO relationship in terms of scope of services, expansion to new locations and continual rounds of innovation.

2.4.3. New CEO shifts gears, moving world-class to good performance

Our recent BPO interviews were intentionally biased to focus on high-performance BPO relationships. Thus, most of the examples we have drawn on are from good or world-performance BPO relationships. We do note, however, that the reverse is also possible – BPO performance can erode over time. During our BPO case study research, we found examples where great performance slipped to good performance and good performance slipped to doing-okay performance because of leadership turnover. Much like long-term, happy marriages, both partners have to stay engaged and enthusiastic to prevent performance decline. The case below describes how a new CEO shifted gears, resulting in a slip in the strategic role of BPO.

As one government-owned utility became privatized, a new CEO prompted huge changes in strategy to focus more on customer sales, engagement and satisfaction. The new strategy required a complete uplifting of the employees' skill sets. The CEO needed assistance with the employee transformation. His company entered into a 5-year strategic alliance with a BPO provider to help transform the company's training programs. The BPO relationship was instrumental in developing over 1,000 new courses that retooled more than 90,000 employees. The partners worked together to increase efficiency and flexibility, cutting the time to develop courses by nearly a third and reducing scheduling time from quarterly to monthly. The BPO relationship won many awards for its performance. Then a new CEO came on board and the strategy shifted, resulting in the provider's contribution moving from a strategic role to an operational role. From the client's perspective, the provider had built up their internal capabilities to the point where they could bring the process back in-house. From the provider's perspective, this was initially seen as a body-blow. The new CEO values its provider relationship and it looking to engage the provider in completely new areas of the business.

2.4.4. An old dog learns new tricks

The cases described earlier showed that leadership turnover often affects BPO performance. We wondered, 'Can existing leaders transform a poor-performing relationship to a good or even world-class performance?' We did uncover one extraordinary example of a turnaround case involving the same leaders. Although this was not a typical pattern, it does illustrate that existing leaders can improve performance by embracing the attributes of effective leadership pairs. Here is their story:

On this procurement account, the client and provider leaders remained the same even after the provider firm was bought out by a larger competitor. What is fascinating about this leadership stability story is the fact that the performance went from poor to high after the acquisition. The root cause of poor performance was an aggressive interpretation of a gain-sharing clause by the first provider firm, resulting in outrageous, million-dollar invoices to the client. The parties escalated the conflict to a formal dispute. After the acquisition, the contract was favourably renegotiated. The acquiring firm reoriented the incumbent provider lead. The client lead was pleasantly surprised by the metamorphosis and said: 'Robert (a pseudonym) was on this account from day one. He was a VP of [the previous provider] and sort of disappeared from the account and only started showing up again during renewal. Robert was important to that because he was coming over and the other VP was not coming over. Now I see a completely different perspective of Robert since he's been at [the new provider] just a year. He's actually trying to solve my problems and not get money out of me . . . It's been very eye-opening'.

2.5. Leadership teams – the role of middle managers

The leadership pair has the primary responsibility for ensuring BPO performance, but the pair needs effective middle managers to make outsourcing work. Research shows that middle managers have a strong 'craft' commitment to their work but are also ambassadors between top management and the workforce, between the many teams that make an organization and its collaboration partners function effectively. They are the key resource for coordination, whether interfacing, scheduling or managing flow of materials, activity, funds and ideas through an enterprise or project.[8] We, along with our colleagues Catherine Griffiths and David Feeny, have studied the role of middle managers on the success of outsourcing. We've found that middle managers have considerable influence on the long road to implementation over interpreting, modifying and executing services. Middle managers from both client and provider organizations need specific capabilities to ensure world-class performance.[9]

Client middle managers need governance, business requirement elicitation, technical, process and provider management capabilities. These capabilities are more about managing the demand side of service delivery. From our interviews, we learned that it is not always easy to shift a client-side middle manager who used to be in-charge of performing the service to a middle manager in-charge of coordinating demand from customers with their BPO provider. Chapter 6 describes nine capabilities the retained staff need to help deliver world-class performance.

Provider middle managers need delivery, transformation and relationship capabilities. These require a careful orchestration of operational excellence on baseline services while exploiting opportunities to transform the service with better processes and tools. All this activity must be coordinated with client counterparts so that both parties benefit from innovations. Provider middle managers with these capabilities are in high demand. The providers' top performers were often assigned to the largest and most prestigious accounts. Smaller and less prestigious accounts were often assigned the providers' 'B team'. If clients demanded a new middle manager, the provider usually acquiesced.

From all the data, it is clearly evident that senior executive sponsorship and an effective leadership pair is not enough to reach world-class performance. Middle managers are also needed.

2.6. Conclusion

We are clear that leadership pairs DO make a critical difference in outsourcing. In this chapter, we said how this can be the case and gave many examples of leadership pairs in action. After reading this chapter, we hope readers are asking, 'How effective is my leadership pair at driving outsourcing performance?' or if the reader is part of a leadership pair, 'Am I an effective leader?' Our findings have been developed into a diagnostic tool to assess Leadership Pair Effectiveness (see Appendix B). If each person assesses the ten attributes independently, results can be compared and divergence of opinions will prompt an honest dialog about the state of the relationship and which behaviours need to be improved going forward. Initially an experienced coach or advisor might be needed to facilitate the dialog, but one of our findings is that leadership papers that are successful become quickly self-sustaining.

---

[1] Findings from the survey were initially published in Lacity, M., Willcocks, L. and Yan, A. (2014), 'Leadership Pairs Behind High Outsourcing Performance', *Pulse Magazine*, (9), 52–57.

[2] See Lacity, M. and Willcocks, P. (2012), *Advanced Outsourcing Practice: Rethinking ITO, BPO, and Cloud Services*, Palgrave, London.

[3] See Hoffman, M. (2000), *Empathy and Moral Development*, Cambridge University Press, Cambridge.

[4] Stepwise regression analysis was used to generate these findings.

[5] These four variables account for 61 per cent of the variation in the overall effectiveness rating.

[6] These three variables account for 43 per cent of the variation in the overall effectiveness rating.

[7] These examples were first described in Lacity, M. and Willcocks, L. (2013), 'Mastering High-Performance: Transformational Leadership', available at http://www.umsl.edu/~lacitym/LacityandWillcocksTransformationalLeaders2013.pdf

[8] Source: Osterman, P. (2009), *The Truth About Middle Managers*, Harvard Business Press, Boston, MA.

[9] See: Willcocks, L. and Griffiths, C. (2010), 'The Crucial Role of Middle Management in Outsourcing', *MISQ Executive*, September, 9(3); Feeny, D. and Willcocks, L. (1998), 'Core IS Capabilities For Exploiting Information Technology', *Sloan Management Review*, 39(3), 9–21; Feeny, D., Willcocks, L. and Lacity, M. (2005), 'Taking the Measure of Outsourcing Providers', *Sloan Management Review*, 46(3), 41–48.

Chapter 3

⌘ Key 2: Focus on business and strategic benefits beyond cost efficiencies

What's Inside: In this chapter, we compare the outsourcing aspirations of typical BPO performers to world-class BPO performers. World-class BPO performers focus more on business and strategic benefits. We provide examples of world-class BPO performers using outsourcing to gain business value beyond costs, for cost plus innovation and to enable global sourcing evolution, among other things. Achieving these additional benefits requires clients to invite providers into the 'strategic tent'.

3.1. Introduction

You need to know what you are trying to accomplish with outsourcing. You have to be thinking way beyond cost because that is only a one-time gain. Arbitrage is a one-time gain. You want to be thinking about what you will do in your own company and what you will not be doing; the strategy emerges from that. – The shared services manager for a manufacturing company

Focusing on business and strategic benefits beyond cost efficiencies was one of the most important practices associated with world-class BPO outcomes. As the BPO market matures, clients are expecting BPO outcomes beyond cost savings and meeting SLAs. Next-generation BPO clients want their service partners to transform their back-offices, to improve business performance, to support the client's shifting business directions and to deliver business outcomes not initially expected. Our study finds high performers shifting their priorities towards business and strategic outcomes, with cost savings and superior service

performance targeted as an automatic 'must-do' threshold requirement in most cases.

In world-class BPO relationships, both clients and providers acknowledge the importance of cost reduction, but do not see that as the prime
objective. This mindset manifests itself in several ways, one of them
being how the business case for the BPO programme is constructed. In
the Everest survey, two-thirds of high-performance businesses focus on
the potential value of business benefits beyond cost alone when creating
the business case, compared with only 26 per cent of typical performers.
High-performance businesses are also more willing to consider greater
functionality from the outsourced service, even if it costs more. Fifty-
eight per cent of high-performance businesses would consider service
options with greater value, even at higher costs, compared with 31 per
cent of typical performers.

The insight here is that cost reduction is a worthwhile, but not sustainable or most valuable benefit on its own. World-class BPO performance
is more driven by how outsourcing can create an organization capable of greater things – and cost reductions are just table stakes. Said
the director of financial shared services for a large consumer company:
'Going back to the objectives that we set out at the start, I think we
have used cost reduction as a stepping stone to being a more global
organization. Today we have 80 percent of our outsourced capabilities
operating from a global hub in the Philippines. That has helped us to
become more global as an organization and helped us to drive more
standard processes as an organization'.

Starting in the mid-2000s, there has been a marked change in how
BPO has been approached by an increasing number of organizations.
Realizing the huge amount of value being left on the table in their
back-office functions, the world-class organizations have sought to get
their own houses in order, leverage the rising capabilities offered by the
market and position their business platforms as an integrated set of
processes aligned with core business dynamism and global presence.
While most companies are still in their evolutionary stage, world-class
performance organizations are distinguished by being 6 to 8 years ahead
of the good and average BPO performers. In many cases, organizations
are just starting off on that path, driven by the 2008 financial crisis or
by subsequent recessionary times.

Next, we describe cost-focused, business-value-focused and strategic outsourcing aspirations and compare the outsourcing aspirations of typical BPO performers to world-class BPO performers. We provide many examples of world-class BPO performers that outsource for business value beyond costs, for cost plus innovation and to enable global sourcing evolution, among other things. Focusing on business and strategic benefits beyond cost efficiencies requires clients to invite providers into the strategic tent.

3.2. Outsourcing aspirations

Research on client organizations has uncovered a long list of motivations, expectations or as we call them, aspirations, that drive outsourcing decisions. The aspirations fall into four categories – cost-focused, business-value-focused, strategic and other (see the list in Table 3.1).

Four aspirations are cost-focused. Of these, *cost reduction is the most common BPO driver.*[1] Despite all the rhetoric of using outsourcing strategically, cost reduction has remained an important driver for a majority of client firms, from the earliest studies to more recent ones. The desire to use outsourcing to focus on core capabilities is the second most common reason cited by BPO clients besides cost reduction. The implication of this finding is that client firms do not outsource functions they consider among their core capabilities. The idea is that these activities are not strategic so clients can give them to providers. The further rhetoric attests that providers can perform these non-core capabilities much cheaper because of specialization and economies of scale. Thus, even though 'focus on core capabilities' *sounds* like a strategic-focused aspiration, it is usually part of the reasoning to justify why non-core capabilities can be outsourced more cheaply. Given that the biggest cost component of any business process is salaries and wages, two other related cost-focused aspirations have to do with avoiding headcount or shedding headcount. Finally, cost predictability is another cost-focused aspiration.

Clients with business-value-focused aspirations still care about costs, but they are willing to forego the lowest bid or pay slightly more than

Table 3.1 Outsourcing aspirations

Cost-focused	Business-value-focused	Strategic	Other	Outsourcing drivers	Description
√				1. Cost reduction	A client organization's need or desire to use outsourcing to reduce costs.
√				2. Access to expertise/skills	A client organization's desire or need to access provider(s) skills/expertise so they don't have to hire internally.
√				3. Headcount reduction	A client organization's need or desire to use outsourcing to reduce the number of staff.
√				4. Focus on core capabilities	A client organization's desire or need to outsource in order to focus on its core capabilities.
√				5. Cost predictability	A client organization's desire or need to use outsourcing to better predict costs.
	√			6. Business value	A client organization's need or desire to use outsourcing to improve business processes, even if it costs slightly more.
	√			7. Improve process performance	A client organization's desire or need to engage a provider to help improve a client's business, processes, or capabilities.
	√			8. Access to SMEs	A client organization's desire or need to access sought after and scare subject matter expertise (SME).

√	9. Technical reasons	A client organization's desire or need to gain access to leading edge technology through outsourcing.	
√	10. Scalability	A client organization's desire or need to outsource to be able to scale the volume of services based on demand.	
√	11. Flexibility	A client organization's desire or need to outsource to increase the flexibility of the use and allocation of resources.	
	12. Change catalyst	A client organization's desire or need to use outsourcing to bring about large scale changes in the organization. In our case studies, the desire to use outsourcing to help create and operate global shared services was a common example.	√
	13. Access to global markets	A client organization's desire or need to gain access to global markets by outsourcing to providers in those markets.	√
	14. Innovation	A client organization's desire or need to use outsourcing as an engine for innovation.	√
	15. Rapid delivery	A client organization's desire or need to engage in outsourcing in order to speedup project delivery.	√
√	16. Need to generate cash	A client organization's desire or need to generate cash through the sale of assets to the provider.	
√	17. Political reasons	A client stakeholder's desire or need to use an outsourcing decision to promote personal agendas such as eliminating a burdensome function, enhancing their career, or maximizing personal financial benefits.	

in-house costs as long as considerable business value is delivered. Business value includes the desire to engage a BPO provider to help improve the client's business, processes or capabilities or to access SMEs and leading edge technology through outsourcing. Scalability – the desire to use outsourcing to scale the volume of services based on demand – and the desire to outsource to flexibly allocate resources are two other business-value-focused aspirations.

Strategic aspirations all relate to partnering with BPO providers to help enable the client's strategic vision. Strategic aspirations include a client organization's desire to use outsourcing to bring about large-scale changes in the organization, gaining access to global markets by outsourcing to providers in those markets, using outsourcing as an engine for innovation or accelerating the delivery of new products or services.[2]

Given this list of cost-focused, business-value-focused, and strategic aspirations, how do typical BPO performers compare to world-class performers? It's not as simple as saying that typical performers focus only on costs while world-class performers focus only on strategy. Reality is a bit richer than that. From all the research we reviewed – over 1,300 findings – *we see that researchers have found strong empirical support that what drove typical outsourcing decisions was the desire to reduce costs on what is viewed as a non-core activity better provided by providers with superior skills, expertise and technical capabilities.* Thus typical performers focus on a combination of costs and business value.

In contrast to typical BPO performers, world-class performers have higher aspirations that include numerous business and strategic objectives. Most frequently among our world-class case studies, these aspirations materialized as the client's wish to find a BPO partner to help create and operate global shared services. These clients selected their BPO provider because of its global reach, its transformational capabilities to help created shared services and its ability to constantly innovate once shared services had been created and stabilized. Microsoft, BP and EMC all serve as examples (see Chapters 11–13 for their detailed stories).

Next we examine world-performance organizations that sought and received business value beyond cost savings, cost plus innovation and global sourcing evolution as examples for catalysts for change.

3.3. Business value

In previous studies we saw client organizations focusing primarily on cost reductions, making costs variable – or at least stable – and getting rid of the non-core back-office functions.[3] The world-class performers in the present study consistently position their back-offices and costs in a much larger business frame. Client senior executives realize that the fast-moving market requires them to transform their processes faster and more efficiently. They needed an operating organization that is nimble enough to support growth in a non-linear fashion and a structure that can efficiently adapt to the rapidly changing market conditions. With these larger strategic goals in mind, clients secure a collaborative partner to be able to deliver process innovation and support strategic positioning globally.

One electronics company outsourced its finance and accounting (F&A) functions to facilitate moving headquarters while retaining knowledge and achieving business process improvements. Another global pharmaceutical company outsourced its F&A functions to move away from a high-cost US location. This was primarily done to move from three regional operations to a more global delivery model and achieve variability in its cost base. Similarly, one imaging products company told us, 'Our business objective was actually to improve processes, to move to world class. . . . We could either re-engineer them ourselves or we could hire somebody who really knew how to do it and did it for a living. We thought that the second option now would be cheaper and quicker, particularly on something that was not core to our business – cash posting and cash receipt and accounts payable for vendors and vendor master data management. That's where it started. On the way, we didn't want that to cost us more money, but we weren't particularly looking for money savings'.

A major retailer provides an example of this more integrated business thinking. While cost was an important consideration in provider selection, the ability to improve performance was the client's main criterion. The client's Vice President of Replenishment explained, 'Outsourcing was more about service to our customers than about cost reduction. The outsourcing model is obviously woven potentially to save us money, but it wasn't our prime motivation'.

One executive from an imaging products company said that suppliers and retailers used to get frustrated at peak times as the accounting and finance systems struggled to deal with the escalation in business volumes. Due to process improvements in the outsourced F&A processes, accounts payable and receivable and monthly closing have now become a military operation. He commented, 'Labor arbitrage is temporary, but process improvement is permanent. Silent running was absolutely the main objective and it is not a problem for the organization any more. We achieved it more cheaply that we used to'.

The intimate relationship between provider performance and business outcomes is outlined by an executive of an engine manufacturer, 'I am not going to talk to you about labor arbitrage. We are way beyond this. But I will talk to you about how a critical mass of people working on a varied scope, and linking business processes together – kind of connecting the dots – is generating incremental value'.

One specific example of this incremental value can be found in the company's spare parts management process. The provider worked with its own proprietary tools to forecast demand in different regions across the world and recommended relocation of material across the regions to effectively meet demand. It positively impacted on-time delivery of spares for the engine manufacturing line, which led to improved service levels and greater customer delight.

These examples illustrate the way world-class performance organizations in our research all think and act to achieve results beyond cost savings alone. Their objectives are moving towards understanding how BPO can help them meet their business outcomes. This requires providers to possess greater business and domain expertise and the ability to identify and provide for emerging business needs. More than ever before, they need to be able to bring new capabilities and innovation to the table, and be sufficiently flexible to deliver a diverse range of business benefits to their clients.

3.4. Cost plus innovation

Innovation is so important to world-class performance that we devote all of Chapter 10 to describing HOW to incent and deliver innovations.

In the chapter, we will make the point that innovation begins with an aspiration.

World-class performance organizations are increasingly engaging BPO providers on a cost plus innovation agenda where cost savings are expected automatically across the lifetime of the contract. In some cases, we found those cost savings being used directly to fund innovation. Providers are selected because they bring distinctive capabilities and innovation capacity to bear explicitly on the areas outsourced, and beyond. As collaborative behaviour between the client and provider(s) becomes key,[4] providers must now remain highly attuned to business thinking and client imperatives.

A fundamental part of innovation is hiring a provider for their subject matter and transformation expertise. At a networking equipment company, there was certainly a focus on costs in a major FAO deal signed in 2007; however, the primary criteria was a partnership for transformation, flexibility and growth. This limited the choice of providers to those who could partner for transformation, rather than just deliver service at lower cost.

In a procurement deal at a major bank, a senior executive pointed out that the provider was actually a larger company than the bank, running a far tighter procurement process, 'We have actually taken a lot of learnings from them. They have a number of approaches that we would love to bring in', said a company executive, 'such as a "three strikes and you're out" procurement policy'.

Meanwhile in a procurement deal at a world leader in electronic design automation, one of their biggest outsourcing aspirations was to access the provider's procurement SMEs on legal spend and travel management, including airline, hotel and rental car negotiations. The client said, 'These are extremely complex and dynamic . . . You've got experts at the supplier team that go from company to company to company and they know the latest trends. They saw voice-over IP coming, they now know how to negotiate it'.

In world-class performance organizations, the innovation process is integral to the way the provider operates. Clients tend to continuously shape the governance and contractual context in a manner that enables innovation at every level. For instance, the supply chain service provider for a global retailer launched a host of continuous improvement initiatives targeted at improving the consistency of delivery. The provider team was responsible for a range of processes including forecasting based on seasonality and sales, setting purchase orders globally, overseeing shipping of products, allocating products to distribution centres and shipping them to stores. According to the vice president of replenishment, 'They have, in the last 18 months, placed a number of resources to spend time re-engineering and designing new or the right processes to drive the business functions all the way from initial category strategy to getting the product moving through the supply chain, which includes the vendor community, through our network, and eventually getting to those stores to support the sales plan'.

In a learning contract at a large bank, a client executive observed that the relationship with the provider had brought new ways of delivering learning, 'Innovation is a kind of a broad church. While there is innovation in terms of the subject matter, there is also a huge amount of innovation in the way we deliver training today. We have made huge strides in that particular area – while a vast majority of the training would be delivered through the classroom earlier, 40 percent of training is delivered through electronic training today. We are also pushing out through mobile learning using smartphones and other collaborative electronic tools'.

3.5. Global sourcing evolution

World-class performers view their outsourcing contracts organically – as living, manageable opportunities for improving the overall business, and not just the outsourced function. This is a far cry from the 'throw it over the wall' mindset that marks many typical outsourcing relationships or the 'send it to India' mentality that marks so many 'poor', 'OK', and occasionally even 'good' relationships where the objective is to park the function with a service provider and work through them on a cost-service trade-off.

In practice, for world-class BPO, business process excellence and integration are necessary building blocks for leveraging provider impact beyond a single functional area; for example, F&A, human resources, procurement – into global operations. How this can be delivered is revealed in another FAO deal at a major hi-tech manufacturer. In one example, the provider focused on completely changing the structure of reporting. This was organized around countries or regions, each with its own complete team. Adding a region, for example northern Asia, or Western Africa, meant building a completely new team. According to a senior provider executive: 'We've completely restructured to having global standard procedures and global teams doing inter-company and a global team doing reconciliations and then a global team doing journals and doing it in a standard manner. It's gone from being a major issue to almost a non-event when we need to bring on some of these countries. One of the barriers to strategic flexibility and business growth is the cost of entry. We've reduced that'.

The trademark of world-class performance organizations is different – they evolve their contracts to reconstruct their own business operations and optimize outsourcing services globally. A global imaging products manufacturer wanted not only to save money but also to benefit from process standardization, process improvement and process centralization from its outsourcing initiatives. A provider executive said: 'They were doing things differently in each country and we helped to standardize and improve processes by making all processes consistent with best practices. Additionally, we brought more visibility on the processes by providing detailed metrics which allowed ourselves and the client to clearly see and understand the root cause of issues'. As the client executive said, 'They have provided us with a lot more reporting on what is going on in these areas than we ever had before. They can tell us things about our process that we never knew – how much time to post an invoice, the difference it makes whether it's covered by a purchase order or not, the average time banks are holding on to our money, the percentage of decline to direct debits per country. It all about the whole set of metrics that they bring along as standard. The other thing that they have done – again, with our agreement – is to move from a dedicated team per country to a front/back-office arrangement, without any impact on the business. That has proved to be quite efficient in getting the processing away from the language specialists'.

The FAO exercise helped a major ASEAN bank move up the finance value chain. A senior executive in-charge of finance operations commented, 'We want to become a world-class finance team and as part of that, there is obviously an emphasis on driving less complexity and delivering efficient, accurate, timely and relevant information to the Enterprise. So we have set ourselves some very clear metrics in terms of cost base, risk, what world class finance looks like and this is where the offshoring dynamics fit in as well. Over time, the scope of work has radically changed – we have certainly evolved from what was a very transactional and task-focused initial set up to very much starting to push up the high-value end of finance. We have more reporting and analysis built out of India, and a developing analytics capability as well. So we have certainly moved up that value chain within Finance, which has been part of the maturing of the FAO model'.

This trademark practice of global sourcing and evolution is well exemplified in three detailed cases of Microsoft, BP and EMC in Chapters 11–13. One strong lesson from these three cases, and indeed all world-class BPO performers, is that clients must invite providers into the strategic tent if they want business and strategic benefits beyond cost efficiencies.

3.6. Inviting providers into the strategic tent

One of the many myths of outsourcing is that outsourcing cannot achieve innovation, but strategic business outcomes. Our several studies have found plenty of examples to contradict this. Thus, in an accompanying study, 21 outsourcing arrangements were delivering IT and business process innovations, and 7 of these were also delivering strategic innovations, significantly enhancing the firm's product/service offerings for existing targets, or enabling entry into new markets. For instance, we found an Asia-Pacific leisure company using providers to introduce technology and processes (to automate and thus speed up) roulette to increase revenues from high rollers. Similarly, a car parts distribution company introduced remote computerized car monitor-ing to pre-empt mechanical breakdown and provide positive response in terms of spares and repair through its providers.[5]

Increasingly, client organizations are engaging BPO providers to help them with their strategic moves into new markets and new geographic areas, as well as to facilitate explosive growth through mergers and acquisitions (M&A). In short, world-class performers have a different mind set and ways of operating with their strategic providers.

On being allowed into the strategic tent, the provider account execu-tive for a high-tech manufacturer recalled a discussion with the client's senior vice president who said: 'I may yell at you for the quality of your service levels or cost, but the things I talk about with my boss are the things that really matter and that's our ability to support the compa-ny's growth in evolving markets'. These were, in fact, the only priorities talked about even at the contracting stage.

Another provider executive at a software tools manufacturer gave an example of client collaborative practices and leveraging provider capa-bilities in a procurement deal. 'We knew they were a bit of an acquirer of companies and they said they did not have the piece of M&A due diligence about understanding how procurement would be impacted – how prices would change, for instance. We (the supplier) became part of this kind of acquisition team and we evaluate contracts and we provided a preliminary report on the impact the acquisition would have on procurement. So, that was a recent innovation we implemented in the last 18 months', he said.

A further example is in a supply chain outsourcing relationship at a manufacturer. The provider said: 'What we are doing now is identifying three or four potential areas where they are having business challenges affecting their profitability and we're figuring out what kind of invest-ments/projects we need to drive improvements to their profitability and then gainshare on the value we bring'.

When one client chose to relocate its headquarters to a new city, they looked for a provider who could recreate back-offices in the new loca-tion. The client chose a provider with a global presence and a proven track record of recruiting professionals to enable the move. 'So the move meant that a lot of people needed to be fired in our previous location and we needed to recruit people here in our new location. So it is a challenging move. We selected [the provider] to manage this kind of huge project – [the provider] has the brand image, trust, confidence, and experience to manage this kind of project', said the client.

3.7. Conclusion

The key priority of world-class performance organizations is to focus on business and strategic benefits beyond cost efficiencies. We see top performers achieving this in numerous ways. Invariably, they set off with this initial goal, but they also anticipate the outsourcing experience as a living evolution for achieving improved business performance. This evolution is supported by adopting a cost plus innovation agenda. World-class performance businesses have global ambitions embedded in their evolutionary approach to outsourcing – not only to optimize outsourcing services on a global basis, but also to use outsourcing to reconstruct their own business operations to function globally. The client needs to invite the provider inside the strategic tent, to leverage its capabilities for competitive advantage. These actions ensure that strategic business outcomes are targeted at the outset, and that the parties evolve their abilities to unceasingly deliver on the dynamic targets presented by contemporary strategic arenas. Our research confirms that adoption of these practices has immense positive impact on client business performance.

---

[1] For more on outsourcing drivers, see Lacity and Willcocks, *Advanced Outsourcing Practice* and Lacity, M., Solomon, S., Yan, A. and Willcocks, L. (2011), 'Business Process Outsourcing Studies: A Critical Review and Research Directions', *Journal of Information Technology*, 26(4), 221–258.

[2] We also note that some client organizations outsource for reasons other than reducing costs, adding business value or enabling strategic objectives. These reasons are not common, but research has uncovered that some clients use outsourcing to promote personal agendas such as eliminating a burdensome function, enhancing their career or maximizing personal financial benefits. In the early days of ITO, some clients used outsourcing to generate cash through the sale of IT assets to the provider. See Lacity and Willcocks, *Advanced Outsourcing Practice*.

3   See Lacity and Willcocks, *Advanced Outsourcing Practice*. Also Willcocks, L. and Lacity, M. (2012), *The New IT Outsourcing Landscape: From Innovation to Cloud Services*, Palgrave, London.

4   In a parallel study, we define collaboration as a co-operative arrangement in which two or more parties work jointly in a common enterprise towards a shared goal. Collaboration signals close partnering behaviour developed over and for the long-term distinguished by high trust, flexibility, reciprocity, risk-sharing and investment of time and resources essential for high performance. See Willcocks and Lacity, *The New IT Outsourcing Landscape,* Chapter 3.

5   See Whitley, E. and Willcocks, L. (2011), 'Achieving Step-Change in Outsourcing Maturity: Towards Collaborative Innovation', *MISQ Executive*, 10(3), 95–107. We found strategic business innovations through outsourcing in seven cases – in the banking, distribution, leisure, global mail and telecommunications industries.

Chapter 4

⌐⎯⎯ Key 3: Drive strong transition, transformation and change management capabilities

> **What's Inside:** In this chapter, we explore the capabilities associated with two major planned change events: the transformation of services through consolidation, standardization, optimization, technology enablement and labour relocation, and the transition of services from clients to providers.

4.1. Introduction

> To improve is to change; to be perfect is to change often. – Winston Churchill

Effective sourcing is all about adapting to change. The gap between world-class BPO performance and typical performers is large – not just in terms of attitudes towards change management, but especially around executing a robust change management programme. Eighty-eight per cent of companies working within a high-performance BPO relationship regard change management as important. This compares with 62 per cent of typical performers – a significant difference. However, the execution gap was much wider – 77 per cent of high performers successfully executed their change management programmes, compared with just 34 per cent of typical performers.[1]

Some changes are planned for and desired, while other changes are unexpected and unwelcome. This chapter explores the former – the capabilities needed to plan for and to create a desired future state. (Chapter 7 explores how to deal with unwanted changes that cause service issues,

Table 4.1 Change capabilities

General change capability	Specific type of change capability	Definition	Key concepts
Change management	Transformation management	The ability to dramatically alter the clients' existing services to improve performance significantly	• Transformation levers
	Transition management	The ability to effectively transfer services from the client to the provider	• Leadership • Stakeholder management • Knowledge transfer

relational traumas and commercial conflicts.) Specifically, we explore how to implement massive changes to a client's back-offices through a *transformation management capability* and how to smoothly shift services from the client to the provider through a *transition management capability*. These two specific capabilities may be conceived of as instantiations of a more general *change management capability*, the ability of BPO partners to effectively manage change (see Table 4.1).

Some clients desire massive changes to their back-offices. Their sourcing decisions are prompted by a desire to completely transform a low-performing back-office into a world-class service organization characterized by service excellence, low costs, scalability, flexibility, compliance and high customer satisfaction. The transformation levers for achieving world-class services are centralization, standardization, optimization, automation/technology enablement and labour relocation. In some world-class BPO relationships, the client leaders transform the retained organization themselves and then engage a provider to help operate, expand and improve the transformed services organization. We call this sequence the 'transform–transition–improve' approach.

In other world-class BPO relationships, clients transition existing services to a provider and then the provider deploys some or nearly all of the transformation levers in a model we call 'transition–transform–improve'. These different approaches demonstrate the principle of equifinality because a given end-state (world-class service organization) can be reached by many potential means (client does everything themselves via shared service and captive centres, the provider does (nearly) everything via 'transition–transform–improve' or the many hybrid options between the two extremes like 'transform–transition–improve'). Regardless of the journey, the resulting operating model should be a world-class service organization.

World-class performance creates organizations that are 'change capable'. Change management is an internal and ever-present capability that enables the client to achieve more organizational and strategic agility. However, it is important to embed this capability in the provider as well in order to be able to successfully identify and drive the modifications needed to gain and sustain world-class performance. The need for a strong leadership pair (see Chapter 2) is also a strong finding from our world-class performing case studies: both parties need transformational leadership in place to pinpoint and drive the changes needed for gaining and sustaining top performance.

4.2. Transformation management capability

BPO relationships need strong transformation management capabilities when the client needs to radically clean up their back-offices. Low back-office performance is often a result of corporate growth through M&A. Front-offices are the first to get assimilated after an M&A, and too often back-offices remain fragmented. Different strategic business units within the company don't invest many resources in their ragtag back-offices. Such support services are wrought with redundancies, outdated and non-integrated technologies and non-standardized, bureaucratic and inefficient processes. We call these 'messy' back-offices.

Five transformation levers can transform a messy back-office into a world-class service organization: centralization, standardization,

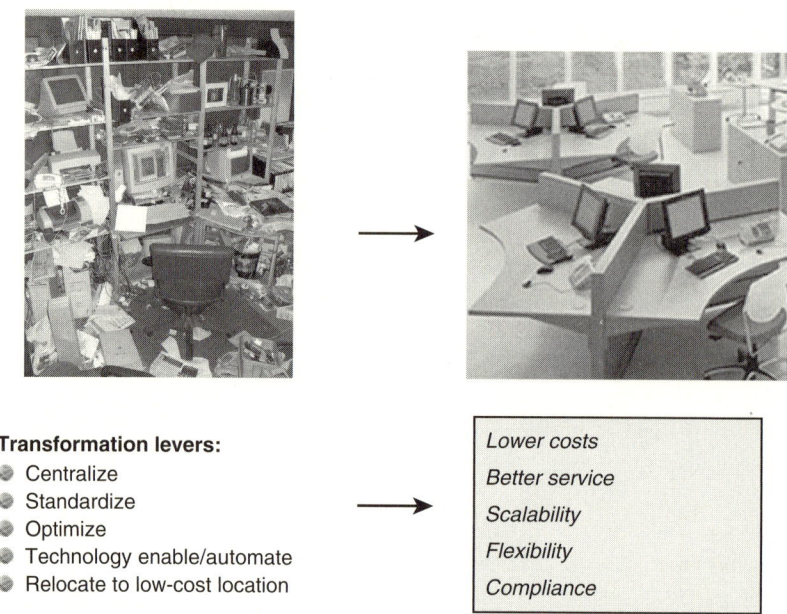

Transformation levers:
- Centralize
- Standardize
- Optimize
- Technology enable/automate
- Relocate to low-cost location

Lower costs

Better service

Scalability

Flexibility

Compliance

Figure 4.1 Levers for transforming a messy back-office to a world-class service organization

optimization, technology enablement and relocation to a low-cost destination (see Figure 4.1). The Everest Group survey had some particularly interesting findings about the first two levers. The Everest Group survey found that 62 per cent of high-performance BPO relationships affirm the importance of process consolidation and standardization in the BPO relationship compared with only 45 per cent of typical performers. Sixty-four per cent of high-performing relationships have successfully implemented more standardized processes compared to just 36 per cent of typical performers. In the client interviews, we also confirmed that consolidation (i.e. centralization) and standardization are among the five transformation levers that establish effective business services organizations:

Centralization: We found that centralization was most frequently performed by clients themselves. Client organizations centralized their business services by physically consolidating business service delivery centres into fewer facilities and/or by virtually consolidating the dispersed budget under central control. Physical consolidation reduces costs through economies of scale, whereas virtual consolidation centralizes decision-making authority, which quickens adaptation.

Stating how his client's budget consolidation helped service flexibility, a provider account manager for a telecommunications client said: 'Previously, the client's budgets were held in individual business units. The client moved it all into a budget that they held centrally. That meant that as we went through the planning and prioritization process the money was used where most required by the company and aligned to the company's strategic goals. If throughout the year there was a new need that came up, then we could easily move money from one place to another because it was held centrally. There are a lot of benefits to having a centrally held budget'.

After centralizing, many clients engaged BPO providers to help deploy some or all of the other transformation levers.

Standardization: Business process standardization provides another powerful lever that reduces costs and facilitates scalability and compliance. A number of clients relied on their BPO providers to help standardize the client's services. For example, a pharmaceutical company engaged a BPO service provider to help create global shared services for financial and accounting services. Prior to outsourcing, the client had over 100 checklists in the record-to-report process. The BPO provider reduced the number of checklists to three. 'You can imagine the savings from a headcount perspective that we were able to get when you are able to take steps like that in the operation', said the provider account manager.

Optimization: Optimization – the procedures used to make a service as effective and error-free as possible – reduces costs and improves service quality. In one case study, the provider found deficiencies in the client's forecasting tool and helped the client predict demand more accurately using new tools and techniques. In another case study, the provider discovered that the reason some invoices were not being paid was a high technical failure rate on faxed invoices. The problem was fixed through a technical upgrade.

Automation and technology enablement: Automation and technology enablement are so vital to performance that they are designated as one on the nine keys to world-class BPO performance (see Chapter 8). In this chapter, we focus on the *effects* of technology in transforming the client's retained organization. Chapter 8 focuses on specific *types* of technologies. Automation and technology enablement can reduce headcount, increase productivity, accelerate and improve service delivery, increase compliance, enhance controls and increase transparency.

On one HRO deal, the provider invested $25 million in new technology for its client, primarily to implement a web-based, self-service human resources portal. The provider delivered the first technology release within 6 months of the contract sign date and released further versions of the technology regularly. The impact was profound in the client organization:

> I think the PeoplePortal has been the first sign from within the business that something has changed, something has actually happened ... We had a lot of very good feedback, it was very good, the technology was great. – HR Director for client

Labour relocation: In contrast to the investment and issues in establishing an offshore captive centre, clients we interviewed relied substantially on BPO providers to relocate labour to lower-cost venues, which can remove up to 50 per cent of labour costs. Global BPO providers already have established delivery centres in low-cost areas like India, China, the Philippines, Eastern Europe and South America. As a transformation lever, relocation offered one-time cost reductions. As clients moved from establishing to operating shared services, they focused less on cost savings and more on the quality of remotely located teams. A director of global financial services for an energy company said of the BPO provider's staff in India: 'They have very high quality folks. We get together with them, we talk regularly, and they feel a part of our business. There is a tremendous amount of longevity in some of these employees and dedication to our work and the account that is just different, they tell us, from other areas. There are rewards that are above and beyond the norm'.

Thus, clients may choose to deploy transformation levers themselves, or may engage a BPO provider. The pro of doing it themselves is that clients keep all the savings. The con is that the client organization may lack the appetite to make a large upfront investment. Next we examine the transition management capability in more detail.

4.3. Transition management capability

A strong transition management capability, headed by a strong transition team, helps to transfer services from the client to the provider successfully. The transition team must manage all the stakeholders affected by outsourcing and transfer knowledge to the provider. Communication pervades all key transition activities, and our first transition management lesson is:

People need to hear key messages about outsourcing many times, from many people, and in different formats. Messages about outsourcing need to be repeated several times.[2] Most people care little about the organizational reasons for outsourcing. Instead, they want to know how outsourcing will affect them. Users of the service will need these questions answered: How will I request, track, receive and pay for services? What service levels should I expect? Who do I contact with questions? The retained client staff will want to understand what their new roles will be and what the future holds for their careers in the presence of outsourcing.

Provider staff will want to understand how they will work with their clients and how their performance will be assessed.

All the clients we interviewed stressed the importance of frequent communications between the client and provider. One client, for example, said, 'Good and frequent communications are certainly key'. Planned meetings may be scheduled daily or weekly depending on the type of work assigned to the provider. The transition of work, however, often entails other stakeholders besides the client and provider. At one client company, having all parties on weekly calls was one of the key lessons learned. When one legal services provider was given conflicting instructions from the client and external law firm, a tri-way call was the best way to resolve it, or a four-way call when the tool from the technology provider was also involved.

Since providers have been through hundreds, maybe thousands of transitions, their transition management capabilities tend to be quite robust. Providers know what they need to know before taking over a service. Several of the clients in world-class BPO relationships praised the provider's onboarding processes. For example, one client who reported an easy transition said he relied on the more experienced provider to drive the transition process. The Director explained: 'Our provider does a very good job of transition . . . [they] walked us through the whole process'. A global procurement process manager for a fragrance and flavours company made a similar point when he said, 'During implementation, the first element we have really benefited from is our service provider's methodology for doing the transfer. We have people from our provider participating here who had experience with this type of project before. They came with a solid methodology for managing the project and the planning, all these elements that we would not necessarily have done as well without them'. He also emphasized the importance of the provider's developing deep knowledge of the client's processes *before* kicking off the transition process, through the in-depth description of each process. This activity enabled both parties to understand clearly 'how the operations are running from the requisitions to the purchase to the purchase order and even after that on a step-by-step basis', he noted.

In contrast to the more experienced providers, many clients needed help to build a transition management capability. Transitions that affect the client's in-house staff require the most care. The client will need to develop human resource plans for nearly the entire staff, including the staff targeted to transfer to the provider, the retained staff members who will take on new roles, the retained staff members whose roles will not change, and most difficult of all, the staff members whose positions will be made redundant. In addition to the internal staff, all the internal users/customers of the service need to be educated about the outsourcing contract. Key transition management activities are listed in Table 4.2. Below we highlight activities that were particularly insightful.[3]

Assign powerful leaders and enough resources to make the transition team effective. These principles are confirmed and extended in the FAO deal at a

Table 4.2 Key activities of transition management

Key concept	Key actors	Key activities
Leadership	Transition team	• Assign powerful leaders and enough resources to make the transition team effective* • Visit with in-house customers before, during and after the transition* • Keep the transition team in place until the new model is stabilized*
Stakeholder management	Retained staff in new roles	• Envision the future for retained employees* • Train staff to assume new roles
	Redundant staff	• Make people whose work will be transferred accountable for successful migration* • Offer career counselling and outplacement services
	Retained staff in current roles	• Communicate outsourcing objectives and reassure them that their jobs are not effected
	Transferred staff	• Communicate the terms of the employment offer by provider
	Internal customers affected by the service	• Communicate outsourcing objectives • Educate about SLAs and client and provider responsibilities • Instruct customers on how to request services, accept services and provide feedback • Prove the concept*
Knowledge transfer	Provider staff who will perform the service	• Develop playbooks, process maps and other workflow documents* • Training (in class, online) • Work shadowing • Mentoring

* Key activity is explained in more detail.

global manufacturing company. According to the company's European corporate finance director, the credibility of the entire transition process depended on delivering to the pre-announced timelines. It required driving by senior, experienced managers who were actually involved in running the outsourcing, who could take rapid decisions and bulldoze obstacles out of the way when required. Also, because it was the company's first outsourcing exercise, it was being watched closely. Therefore, the client over-resourced the transition team and retained organization at the beginning, knowing that they could ramp it down later. The key success factors, he summarized, were: 'effective expectation management and communication across all levels, an over-resourced retained organization at the outset, sustained management focus, and having somebody with big boots accountable and responsible for the engagement'.

Visit with in-house customers before, during and after the transition. The importance of visiting in-house customers was corroborated across multiple top-performing deals. The global procurement manager of a fragrance and flavour manufacturer said, 'The provider won over a lot of people that were initially reluctant in our purchasing organization by showing what they were doing with other clients. Visiting the BPOs and showing how they were processing clients with similar processes or scope showing how they were doing it was a big plus'.

Large geographies also require continuous, on-the-ground information about the diverse business needs across regions. This acts as business input into the outsourced process and helps develop a better understanding of the dynamic business requirements. As described by an executive at a provider for a learning academy for a major telecoms company: 'We did a lot of joint visits to the area in the business throughout the course of the transition process and continued the visits after the contract went into effect. My counterpart and I would travel around the country every six months and visit key leaders in the business in those different regional areas. We operate in a vast country, so there are a lot of different needs in parts of that geography. That is a very important understanding to have in terms of different needs of the business. I have found that extremely useful to understand the business and then being able to provide feedback to the BPO team'.

Keep the transition team in place until the new service model is stable. One global financial services company learned this lesson the hard way. At this company, the CFO wanted to consolidate financial services from 25 locations worldwide to 6 regional shared services, supplemented by some outsourcing partnerships.[4] Part of the estimated cost savings for the new global shared services model came from lower management costs. The 'power players' on the transition team knew they were planning for their own redundancies. The Senior Vice President of the Americas Shared Services said: 'We actually did put our business case to management and said, "you don't need the same level management layer you have today. You need a strong management layer in India, and you need the solid customer center management layer onshore, but you don't need us"'. Senior management wanted the transition plan accelerated by 3 months to capture an additional $500,000 in savings. As a result, some members of the transition team were moved to other programmes or left the company before the new service model had stabilized.

Although this decision accelerated the cost savings, there was a price to pay in terms of a loss of focus. The transition team had always envisioned that India would be staffed with supervisors who acted as process experts and who would be responsible for the execution and quality of service delivery. However, the new manager hired to run the Indian centre had a different vision aligned more with Indian business culture. He organized the delivery centre so that supervisors were primarily responsible for managing employees and for allocating work to them. Initially, the Indian centre suffered from the resulting lack of SME. For example, when payments were missing, a significant amount of client knowledge is required to find and reconcile errors. Initially, the Indian staff couldn't perform these duties, so the six regional centres took them back.

Envision the future for retained employees. Several of our world-class case studies involve the creation of shared services and outsourcing. While the clients paid enough time and resources to training the provider staff, some neglected to pay enough attention to the retained employees. At the global financial services company mentioned earlier, many finance employees did not want to move from the 25 business units to the 6 regional services centres. Some simply did not want to relocate.

Others perceived the changed roles as deskilling them, switching them from client-facing services to transaction processing. In the end, about 60 per cent of the employees in the regional services centres were new hires. In hindsight, the transition team felt they could have prevented much of the resistance by proactively articulating the vision and career paths for the retained finance staff. In fact, the perceived deskilling did not occur. The resultant culture in these regional centres was strong and the finance staff relished their expanded role of servicing more clients across more business units.

Make people whose work will be transferred accountable for successful migration. Many organizations find it difficult to retain the cooperation of employees targeted for redundancy. Returning to the lessons of the global financial services company, it was very careful to treat fairly employees who would be made redundant and found a way to ensure they were accountable for the success of the migration. First, it gave employees plenty of notice – nearly a year and a half! It officially informed employees of the intention to downsize the regional centres in March 2004. Employees were told that the transition team did not know exactly who would be impacted, but that everyone would know by July 31, 2004. Some employees would be retained and some would be given severance packages. Some of those who would be let go were given 18 months advance notice that they would no longer have a job. Second, it built into the retention package a requirement that employees facilitate and sign off on the transfer of their work. Part of this responsibility was having the replacement workers shadow them in their daily jobs. To receive the full redundancy benefits, a person whose work was being transferred had to agree that his or her shadows were ready to take over the process. The Program Transformation Leader said: 'If you remember nothing else from the transition process, remember this: let the people that are giving away the work give it away. Make them responsible for it. They know the job the best and most will enjoy the process of teaching what they do every day'.

Prove the concept. In-house customers may legitimately question whether a BPO provider is capable of doing the work and may remain sceptical about BPO services until the concept is proved. One manager from a client company said that he tested the BPO provider with a low-risk, 3-month pilot project. He measured the quality of work for every work product coming out of India. He said: 'After three months, they saw that the quality was so high that they were convinced that these people were very good. That really impressed them'.

Develop playbooks, process maps and other workflow documents. Playbooks and other supporting documents like process maps and checklists provide instructions to the provider's team. Clients reported that BPO providers are quite good at developing and updating playbooks. A VP for one provider explained, 'We create a checklist, playbooks, guidelines, process maps and all the other things that go in making a much focused quality programme. Every work request is treated with the same quality of standards that we agree that they will follow'. The playbooks and other supporting documents help provider employees trained in one country (like India) to understand the nuances and requirements of serving clients from other countries (like the United States). Playbooks also standardize service and establish clear lines of responsibility. The Director for one client explained that playbooks 'provided us with understanding of how to better manage all of our document reviews. Things like the quality control checks, the communications, the standing meetings, those kinds of things. Having that template to kind of get things going really seems to help out a lot'.[5]

Playbooks, however, must be used wisely. One client warned that the provider executed exactly from the playbook and never proactively sought to improve it. The client said, 'What they didn't do is come back and say, 'This is unclear and this we have to change in order to make the process run more smoothly'. They just followed the process until we said, 'Guys, this is just wrong', and then we adapted the playbook'.

Transformation and transition management are two specific types of change capabilities, but in addition to these, world-class performers rely on an ongoing change management capability.

4.4. Ongoing change management

Change management is important for driving the outsourcing relationship towards greater levels of value. But this is not just change for the sake of change – it becomes an imperative for world-class BPO performance because it is a living relationship that is evolving to meet a client's ongoing business needs and opportunities in an ever-changing market environment.

World-class BPO arrangements are restless and progressive arenas – they constantly seek to align with the wider needs and aspirations of the client's business in its dynamic, global operating context. For world-class performance organizations, an outsourcing contract is often considered out-of-date not long after the ink dries. Their leaders have dynamic objectives for their outsourcing relationships, and find ways to leverage their management structures, processes and relationships, to deal with this dynamism.

The vice president of operations for a hi-tech manufacturer that has outsourced its procurement function described an emerging practice that adds value. The provider sends their category managers to interview the client's major stakeholders at the vice president level. The stakeholders talk about projects coming up for the year ahead and what commodities and services they are going to be spending money on. That 'heads-up' allows the provider's team to go back and develop long-term plans. The provider explained, 'Alright, we have a big project as they are going to be expanding their Bangalore facility. We need to have a facilities expert to go out and talk to the client VP of facilities and make sure exactly what we need to bid on, what sort of providers they like to use, and so on, to get in the heads of client leader initiatives. If we are going to buy a bunch of servers, they can discuss whether a reverse auction is the right way for it and they can get on board someone who actually understands that. We never had any of these planning meetings before (at the beginning of a fiscal year) and they are a huge value-add'.

4.5. Conclusion

World-class performance creates organizations that are 'change capable'. Leaders from world-class performing BPO relationships understand that enthusiasm at the top is key in shaping the engagement, but does not trickle down automatically to the operational ranks.

Therefore, partners from top-performing BPO relationships couple ambitious transformational projects with aggressive change management programmes. It is also important for the client's business users – who may be scattered worldwide – to understand and embrace the outsourcing objectives. World-class BPO partners communicate clearly and frequently to their business users and they deploy their best people for transition and project teams. High-performance BPOs not only place greater emphasis on change management, but are also vastly more successful in executing change management plans as compared to typical BPOs.

---

[1] Mindrum et al., 'Achieving High Performance in BPO'.

[2] As professors, we know all too well that important information needs to be communicated at least three ways to ensure 100 per cent of the class has understood. Each vital message must be (1) written down in a centrally located place like an online syllabus, (2) verbally communicated in class and (3) emailed several times as reminders.

[3] For more on transition management, see Cullen et al., *Outsourcing*.

[4] For an entire case on this company, see Lacity, M. and Fox, J. (2008), 'Creating Global Shared Services: Lessons from Reuters', *MIS Quarterly Executive*, 7(1), 17–32.

[5] See Lacity, M., Willcocks, P. and Burgess, A. (2014), *The Rise of Legal Services Outsourcing*, Bloomsbury Publishing, London.

Chapter 5

⌘ Key 4: Adopt a partnering approach to governance

What's Inside: This chapter explains how a partnering approach to governance begins with an attitude called the 'Partnership View' and how this attitude promotes partnering behaviours that lead to better BPO outcomes.

5.1. Introduction

> I think accepting the provider as part of our infrastructure and not treating them as a vendor but more of a partner has been very successful for us. – VP of Global Shared Services for a pharmaceutical company

Adopting a partnering approach to governance is a key practice associated with world-class BPO performance. A partnering approach to governance begins with an *attitude* we call the 'Partnership View' in which a client regards the provider as a strategic partner rather than as an opportunistic vendor. The partnership view manifests itself in partnering *behaviours*, such as openly communicating with each other and by including the provider in 'the whole picture' of the end-to-end business process, even when the provider is only directly accountable for discrete sub-processes defined by SLAs. Partnering behaviours produce better BPO results, which in turn reinforces partnership attitudes and behaviours, preparing the ground for the next crucial interaction (see Figure 5.1).

Initially, the partnership view helps a provider get its service levels to 'green' status, meaning that it is meeting contractual obligations. A client with a partnership view doesn't beat the provider up during transitions, but instead gives it the time and assistance it needs to get services on track. Once service levels are green and stable, this in turn allows the client to trust the provider more, leading to more partnering behaviours like letting providers help with the end-to-end process.

Figure 5.1 The virtuous cycle of the partnering approach to governance. The partnership view is an attitude that promotes partnering behaviours that lead to better BPO performance, which in turns reinforces the partnership view and leads to more partnering behaviours

The virtuous cycle is evident in the case of a retail client and its BPO provider. The client and provider leads are both dedicated to the partnership view of the relationship, which builds partnering behaviours. During the transition, the provider missed an SLA for various reasons, including some obstructionist acts by clients, some missed deliveries by third-party vendors, as well as some blunders by the provider. Rather than beat up the provider, the client lead supported the provider to get service back on target. The provider explained: 'If we're down on service level by five percent and up on inventory by five percent for a period of four months, that's business ground for termination. That's our contractual penalty. We've been in that situation before and we haven't been terminated because of the trust relationship that has been built with our stakeholder. He knows that our team cares tremendously about their business and we know they care tremendously about our team. That's what weathers us in bad times'. The relationship is now world-class, with the provider deeply involved in the client's end-to-end process to improve KPIs like inventory turnover and lower levels of stock outs. A key point from this story is that the leadership pair establishes and holds dominion over the partnering approach to governance.

Next, we examine the partnership view and partnering behaviours in more detail.

5.2. The partnership view

All research sources identified compellingly the importance of the partnership view as a distinguishing contributor to world-class BPO performance. From our comprehensive review of all academic research findings, the partnership view was one of the most important relationship governance factors that determined BPO outcomes.[1] From the Everest survey, 85 per cent of the client respondents from high-performing BPO relationships consider the service provider to be a strategic partner compared to 41 per cent of the client respondents from typical BPO relationships. Our interviews with client and provider leads revealed how the partnership view works in practice. The attitude must be held by the leadership pair and must be reinforced through the ranks in the client and provider organizations.

In world-class-performing BPO relationships, the client executives deeply hold and proselytize for the partnership view. Consider how client leads from five different top-performing BPO relationships spoke about their service providers – they used terms like 'strategic partners', 'spirit of a partnership' and 'we are in it together' (see Table 5.1 for the full quotations). In turn, provider leads from different top-performing BPO relationships all used the terms 'partner' and 'partnership' (see Table 5.1).

Client executives must actively diffuse and reinforce effectively the partnership attitude throughout the client organization. When client employees lapsed into complaining and blaming the provider, the client executives from world-class relationships buttressed the partnership view. Client executives committed to the partnership view will replace their own employees when they cannot or do not embrace the right attitude. This can be a sensitive issue since client executives are often not aware of the dissidents within their organizations, and because service providers do not want to complaint about obstructionist clients. In one case, the gentle provider approach: 'Can you tell me how to more effectively deal with so-and-so' was enough for one client executive committed to the partnership view to reassign the employee. Similarly, provider leads must also diffuse and reinforce the partnership view among their ranks.

The partnership view must manifest itself in partnering behaviours, else the term 'partner' becomes tumescent. In one struggling ITO relationship, the CIO said he wanted the provider to stop talking about the 'partnership' and to start performing. He said that around his

Table 5.1 Representative quotes on the partnership view from BPO leaders

Client lead	Provider lead	Quotation
√		I'm not interested in being a recipient of service. I want us to be *strategic partners*. It is a word that is tossed around in a clichéd way. But for me, strategic partner means: let's talk about my five most important objectives and how that overlaps with the things that the provider does. – Client Commercial Director from an energy company
	√	We operate in the *spirit of partnership*. I think that also means full transparency and being willing to give feedback real-time versus letting things swirl around. I think that's important. The other thing is making the BPO provider feel like they are a part of the team so they are not always surprised . . . when I know something is coming, then they know something is coming so they don't have to react at the eleventh hour. – Client account manager from a consumer products company
√		We have a very strong concept that we talk about in outsourcing and that is what we call 'TOGETHER'. *We are in it together.* There is nothing that the provider has to do or we have to do – we have to work issues together. – Senior Director for a technology company
√		It is so far from a traditional outsource arrangement . . . it's about how do we get that *partnership* going . . . If I look at [our provider], I certainly think flexibility is very high up there from a behavioural trait they have. They were willing to work with us. They were willing to do what we needed done. – General Manager for customer service

Client lead	Provider lead	Quotation
√		We felt that we could actually find a partnership in South Africa that would have no detrimental impact to our customers. WNS appeared to be a business that we could work with as a *partner*, not just as a supplier. – General Manager for British Gas Residential
	√	I really think it's a true *partnership*. It's not a question of you're the supplier, you sort it out, we're dumping everything on you, make it happen. It's a shared approach. – Managing Director
	√	As a company, [my client] very much treats everyone as *partners*. And that's an important concept I think in a good relationship is you're not just a vendor to be beaten up; you are actually a partner with the company. – Account Manager
	√	I think that what's developed the *partnership* is now we're in the meetings and we're really talking more than just about a BPO relationship. We're talking about how we can improve their business and help them. – Account Manager
	√	It truly is a *partnership*. They understand what our cost drivers are and they realise it's a zero sum game. And they know if they want more value someplace else, it isn't just going to magically appear. And so we have to work together and collaborate on what are the priorities we need to have going forward. And how do we best spend the dollars both of us are spending here to achieve that goal? And it's a very open and honest discussion around that. – Account Manager

office, the 'p' word had become as obscene as the 'f' word. His point: a partnership view must ultimately facilitate partnering behaviours that drive performance. Next we examine some examples of partnering behaviours.

5.3. Partnering behaviours

Clients who think of providers as opportunistic vendors behave differently than clients who think of their providers as partners. Clients who view their providers as vendors exhibit behaviours such as only communicating with providers on 'a need to know' basis, planning for the short-term, holding providers exclusively and strictly to the contractual SLAs and aggressively defending their own position when conflicts arise. In contrast, clients who view their providers as partners exhibit partnering behaviours such as openly communicating with providers, planning for the long term, including the provider in the end-to-end process and resolving issues collaboratively (see Table 5.2). How partners resolve conflicts is so crucial to performance, that it is one of the nine keys to world-class performance and discussed in great detail in Chapter 7. In the chapter, we provide illustrative examples of some other partnering behaviours.

Table 5.2 Examples of partnering behaviours

	Vendor behaviours	Partnering behaviours
Communication	Need to know basis, secretive	Transparent and open
Planning time horizon	Short term	Long term
Boundaries	Tight boundaries around SLAs	Open boundaries by including the provider in the end-to-end process
Conflict resolution	Aggressive defence of one's own interests	Collaborative approach (detailed in Chapter 7)

5.3.1. Transparent and open communication

In Chapter 2, we identified transparency as one of the attributes of a great leadership pair. Effective leaders, we noted, keep each other informed about all operational issues as well as strategic directions that may affect the BPO relationship. Clearly, transparency begins with this leadership pair. But a partnering approach to governance also means that this behaviour is encouraged among the rank and file. At first, this can be quite scary, as leaders often want to be the only conduit for communication. For example, one call centre provider lead became much more transparent by allowing his agents to directly speak with the client's sales and marketing teams. This was a big mindset change for the provider lead because normally he managed client expectations by buffering them from unchaperoned contact with frontline employees. Now, transparency and open communications are part of the drivers of excellent performance on this account. He said, 'I'm the account director, right? So my role is to manage the account but also to ensure that we are always being perceived in the best possible way. I asked myself, 'do we really want to put frontline people in front of senior clients?' They might be overly honest, they might be completely incorrect, all the rest of it. And actually, that's been the best part of the whole process – they are more than capable' (see Chapter 14 for the full case history).

5.3.2. Involve the provider in long-term plans

A global manufacturer and its service provider increasingly spend less time on short-term plans and more time on long-term projects. The supplier executive describes how this happens: 'When you go into a governance meeting, you need to clearly split the meeting into an operations focus and a continuous improvement/innovation focus. How much time you spend on the two areas is dependent on where you are on your operational maturity scale. When you initially go live, there are usually more operational issues and thus the client is very much focused on SLAs – i.e. how do we get them to go green and how can we hit consistent performance. After a period of time, when the SLAs go green, you then spend less time on the day-to-day operations focus but instead focus the majority of the meeting time on innovation and continuous improvement i.e. this becomes the main event. We cover continuous improvement and innovation very formally with the client i.e. we clearly cover how we are progressing process standardization activities and how we are improving processes. This all means we can report in the functional committee clear status on continuous improvement'.

5.3.3. Include the provider in the end-to-end process

We have a responsibility to deliver to our contractual obligations, and that includes meeting SLAs, which are targeted at being efficient. However, we also put emphasis on making sure we drive the right end-to-end results, making sure things are better for the client, meaning we target being effective. – Provider Account Manager

The Everest Group's BPO survey and our interviews found that the top BPO performers include the provider in 'the whole picture' of the end-to-end business process, even when the provider is only directly accountable for discrete sub-processes defined by SLAs. While SLAs are an important part of the contractual governance for any outsourcing relationship, one big drawback of SLAs is that they focus management attention on past performance instead of future performance. Another issue with SLAs is that when clients hold providers accountable *only* to their SLAs, then they are missing opportunities for extracting significant additional value from the outsourcing relationship.

Excellence in service delivery is a characteristic of world-class BPO performance, but partners in these relationships also look beyond that to innovations and better business performance. This translates into regularly re-examining SLA so that they help achieve business goals that the outsourced processes support. Beyond SLAs, clients from world-class BPO relationships focused providers on the client's KPIs (see Figure 5.2).

As an example, consider the end-to-end business process for accounts payable. Clients want to pay the correct amounts owed to the right entities at the right times. Clients may engage BPO providers to do some of the tasks associated with accounts payable, such as posting invoices. An SLA for that task would likely involve accuracy, timeliness

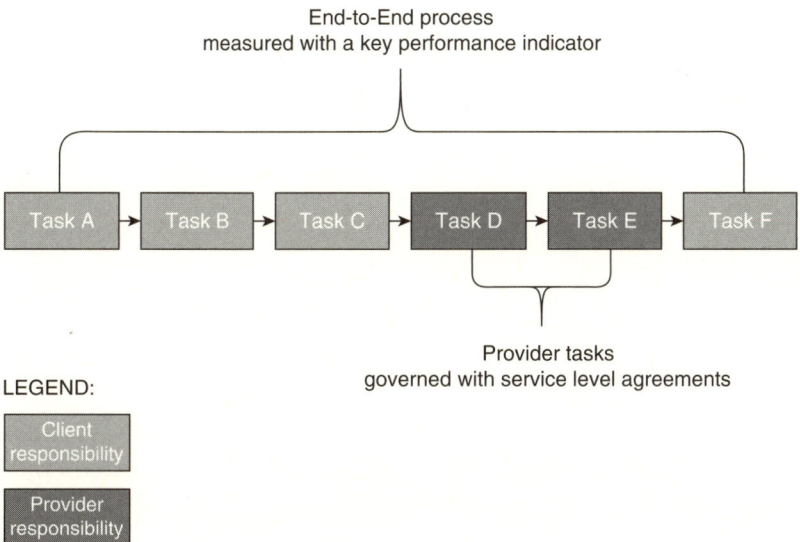

End-to-End process
measured with a key performance indicator

Task A → Task B → Task C → Task D → Task E → Task F

Provider tasks
governed with service level agreements

LEGEND:

Client responsibility

Provider responsibility

Figure 5.2 SLA versus end-to-end process management

and responsiveness. The BPO provider might get quite good at posting invoices, but so what? How does this task improve the client's bottom line? Once service levels are met, world-class BPO partners trust the provider to do more. They let them see the entire end-to-end process and work together to improve KPIs, often by relying on the provider's domain expertise and business analytics capabilities (see Chapter 9). In this example, a KPI might be percentage of invoices paid within terms. Clients want all of their invoices paid on time because they then get discounts and also it prevents vendors from calling clients about unpaid invoices. Anything that a provider can do to improve this KPI benefits the client's bottom line. As discussed in more detail in the Microsoft case in Chapter 11, this is exactly what their BPO partner did – Accenture helped Microsoft move from 70 per cent of invoices paid on time to 92 per cent! That's the power of a partnering approach to governance.

Similarly, the UK telecommunications company, TalkTalk, and its call centre provider, CCI also improved BPO performance when TalkTalk included CCI more closely in its end-to-end processes (see Chapter 14 for an entire case study on TalkTalk and CCI). At TalkTalk, the client initially only held CCI accountable to its SLAs, but the partners realized they were leaving a lot of value on the table. CCI spoke to TalkTalk's customers every day. The call centre agents took calls when customers first signed up for TalkTalk's service, when they wanted to add services and when they wanted to cancel services. CCI's Account Director said, 'We know why customers are taking products and why they're not taking products and what happened at point of sale that resulted in this complaint or up-sell. So there are really clever things that you can leverage from having all that activity in one site'. This 360 degree customer view provides deep insights into helping TalkTalk achieve its KPIs on conversion rates from marketing campaigns, retention rates, up-sells, cross-sells and customer satisfaction. CCI adopted this last KPI as one of its own major KPIs and even awards agents' bonuses based on their individual scores. That is deep alignment indeed!

5.4. Conclusion

Our findings on governance are very different from what most people might assume. Most people tend to think of BPO governance in terms of governance *structures*, such as joint operating, management and executives committees. While our research confirms that these governance structures are important, they are pervasive practices present in all substantially sized BPO relationships. Governance structures are thus a 'hygiene' factor, because the absence of such structures may result in poor performance, but the presence of governance structures does not in itself necessarily lead to high performance. In practice, if not designed correctly, they can inhibit, rather than enable, world-class performance.

The combined evidence from all our BPO research streams enriches the Everest survey findings about a partnering approach to governance. It points to three actions for stepping up to world-class performance:

Signal collaborative behaviour and practices early, and always. Collaboration is a cooperative arrangement in which two or more parties work jointly in a common enterprise towards a shared goal. In business relationships, the word 'collaboration' signals close partnering behaviours developed over and for the long term, distinguished by the high trust, flexibility, reciprocity and investment of time and resources essential if high performance on individual and shared goals is to be achieved.

Leadership is fundamental, starts in the boardroom, but must operate at every level in and across the collaborating organizations. Leadership is shaping and mobilizing adaptive work,[2] that is, engaging people to make progress not just on the technical but also on the adaptive problems they face. Senior leaders, initially on the client side, shape the strategy, context, resources, mind-set and incentives for world-class performance. Other leaders ensure that these are applied and sustained operationally over the long term. Leadership manages out risk and manages in opportunity. As one client manager put it: 'We created a place where people could innovate and that's the act of good leadership; making it safe for people to stick their necks out'.

World-class performance is built on cycles of trust and performance. Look to create a virtuous circle between trust-building, win–win incentives on strategic and operational criteria over the longer term and the reinforcement effects of superior delivery. Parties need to work at three kinds of trust. *Personal trust* reflects confidence in a person's ability to work for common aims with integrity. *Competence trust* reflects belief in the others' ability to deliver on their promises. *Motivational trust* arises from the right incentives and penalties being in place to drive win–win behaviours.[3] Trust is built over time through demonstrable performance. As one oil client executive put it: 'You build trust by spending time together. You need to have capacity within the organization to do that and to build competence and business understanding (in the supplier) . . . You have to invest in the relationship'.

---

[1] See Lacity, Solomon et al., *Journal of Information Technology*.

[2] An adaptive challenge is when people's hearts and minds have to change; when all technical fixes fail; when conflict persists despite all remedial action; when a crisis arises. See Heifetz, R. (1994), *Leadership Without Easy Answers*. Belknap Press, Cambridge, MA.

[3] Weeks, M. and Feeny, D. (2008), 'Outsourcing: From Cost Management to Innovation and Business Value', *California Management Review*, 50(4), 127–147.

Chapter 6

⚷ Key 5: Align the retained organization, outsourced processes and provider staff

What's Inside: This chapter explores how world-class BPO clients align their retained organizations, outsourced processes and provider staff by transforming back-offices from 'pyramid' shapes to 'diamond' shapes, by transforming employees from 'back-office' doers to 'front-office' service coordinators, by transforming internal clients from 'users' to 'customers' and by transforming provider relationships from an 'us versus them' to an 'it's all us' culture.

6.1. Introduction

> Our business users don't know they are talking to the provider. One of my things is that whoever answers that phone, no one needs to know that it is us or anybody else that we use. – Client Lead for a large HRO relationship

Aligning the retained organization, outsourced processes and provider staff is one of the keys to world-class performance. In Chapter 4, we discussed the transformation levers clients use to transform their back-offices, including centralization, standardization, optimization, automation/technology enablement and labour relocation. In this chapter, we focus on the resulting shape of a client's retained organization and three key stakeholders – internal business clients, employees in the business services organization and BPO providers.

Transitioning to a BPO relationship can be tough on workers in the retained organization if steps are not taken to help them succeed in the new environment. Their roles will often shift and they will find themselves charged with managing and coordinating the outsourcing service relationship rather than simply managing others' executing tasks. There may also be cultural differences between the retained and outsourced workforce, and such differences need to be dealt with carefully. Sometimes it's the provider employees, with their über-professionalism and intimidating pedigrees, who alienate some of the retained client employees. One client said of the provider: 'Some of my staff would say, "Hey, the provider needs to be less aggressive"'. Such cultural differences perpetuate the notion of provider as 'other'.

Clients with world-class business services organizations, that is, services characterized by service excellence, low costs, scalability, flexibility, compliance and high customer satisfaction, transformed their retained organizations in four ways (see Figure 6.1):

1. Structures transformed from 'pyramids' to 'diamonds'
2. Employees transformed from 'back-office' doers to 'front-office' service coordinators
3. Internal clients transformed from 'users' to 'customers'
4. Provider relationships transformed from 'them' to 'us'

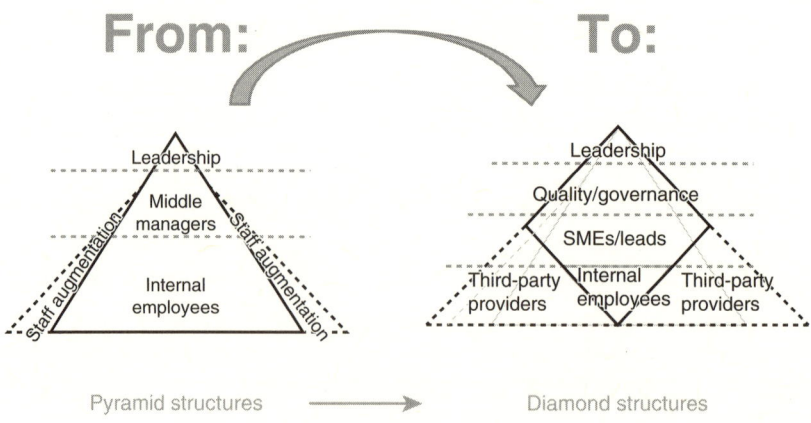

Figure 6.1 Transforming the client's retained organization[1]

6.2. Structures transformed from 'pyramids' to 'diamonds'

The Everest Group survey found that 50 per cent of best-in-class BPO relationships modified the broader organizational design to optimize the BPO operating model compared to 29 per cent of normal BPO relationships. We have identified the shape-shift of back-office functions from 'pyramids' to 'diamonds' as a major trend in IT, Finance, Accounting, Indirect Procurement and Human Resources functions (see Figure 6.1). We are predicting that a similar transformation will occur in other back-offices, such as enterprise legal functions.[2]

Pyramids are heavily populated with employees, most of whom are at the bottom of the pyramid. The benefit of this design is that employees continually build valuable, client-specific experience as they are promoted higher up the pyramid. The pyramid model is strong on retained knowledge, but it is also costly. Back-office managers trying to recruit college graduates must compete with providers who can court them with far richer career paths and many more peers. The model also tends to rely on staff augmentation with expensive domestic workers to fill in skills gaps, and to scale up resources. The pyramid model is also characterized by a significant class of middle managers who manage both employees and supplemental staff.

Diamond-shaped retained organizations replace the heavy bottom of the pyramid with providers. Many transactional activities that were once performed by employees are performed now by providers, typically in a lower cost location. There are fewer middle managers, but more SMEs and Project Leads. The diamond-shaped organization also needs more quality assurance and governance skills to coordinate services with providers. The benefits of the diamond-shaped retained organization are lower costs, access to providers with best-of-breed skills and greater flexibility because providers can more easily adapt to increases or decreases in service volumes.

6.3. Employees transformed from 'back-office' doers to 'front-office' service coordinators

Aligning the organization's corporate culture with new ways of working and integrating the culture of the outsourced workforce is not easy. Some retained employees will not be able to adapt to the newly designed retained organization. For example, one client said: 'I think this was a real fight where we were already seeing some of our no-fits between the new type of role that people would be asked to do and the profile of the people we had'. One provider told us a story about client-side middle managers having a hard-time shifting from service delivery to relationship management. She found people still crossing the line: 'They can't help themselves sometimes, especially if they did the job before'. We have called these client-side managers 'comfort seekers' – people who managed what was most familiar and what they liked to manage, whether or not that had any real relevance to the new work of managing the provider's performance. A provider executive described one case: 'She clearly loved delivering the service . . . encouraged people to ring up like they used to do, gave second opinions, even did tasks that were really not her responsibility. The only solution in the end was to hire her'.

Moving the business services organization to a diamond-shape requires a different type of workforce than the pyramid design. The Everest Group survey found that clients from best-in-breed BPO relationships transform the retained organization in terms of roles, responsibilities and requisite skills. Our current interviews and past research strongly support this finding. In the diamond-shaped business services organization, far fewer employees are doing transactional activities and many more are coordinating service delivery with BPO providers and internal clients. Middle managers need a different set of skills, although many clients and providers we interviewed said it was difficult to get the client's middle managers to shift from managing resources and processes to managing inputs and outputs to/from providers. For example, one client said: 'Where I think we've perhaps fell down a little is perhaps we didn't equip some of those people who were managing the relationship with the necessary tools and skills. What we did was find really good functional managers and we said, 'Hey, you're a really good functional manager, why don't you manage the relationship with the provider?' Rather than finding a really good contract manager who understood how to get the best out of the commercial relationship'.

One provider agreed that functional managers do not necessarily make good relationship managers: 'The reality is that relationship managers [in the client retained organization] need a vastly different skill set. Just taking your best accountant and putting them in the role of relationship manager doesn't work well; An accountant is a very analytic job and a retained organization needs to be a very relationship focused job: it doesn't necessarily always connect well'. On this account, the provider and client worked together to redesign the client's retained organization to great effect. The provider explains: 'Each of the client's business units had new roles and responsibilities related to how things were going to work in the future state. They actually gave people the title of Relationship Manager which was very helpful. I think that explains why our contract is more successful, with fewer incidents and higher satisfaction of the customer, than other relationships'. Another client learned from a previous BPO relationship how to best prepare middle managers for their new roles: 'We rewrote their job descriptions and we did coaching, but my best advice is get your people to the provider's centers early. The earlier you do this, the faster you open their eyes to the possibilities. Meeting the people and understanding what they do opens them up to their new roles'.

We have spent considerable time studying the roles of the retained organization. Initially, we identified nine roles of the retained Information Technology functions,[3] but soon realized that these roles are needed in any retained back-office.[4] (The roles are listed in Table 6.1; for further information, see suggested reference.[5]) The nine capabilities all demand high performers who can develop into a high-performance team. In contrast to the more traditional skills found in service functions, there needs to be a much greater emphasis on business skills and business orientation in nearly all roles. There is also a significantly increased requirement for 'soft' skills across all roles.

Table 6.1 The nine client retained capabilities

Capability	Reason the capability is required
1. Leadership	To integrate the effort with business purpose and activity
2. Informed buying	To manage the sourcing strategy to meet the needs of the business
3. Business systems thinking	To ensure that capabilities are envisioned in every business process
4. Relationship building	To get the business constructively engaged in operational issues
5. Contract facilitation	To ensure the success of contracts for external services
6. Architecture planning	To create the coherent blueprint for a technical platform that responds to present and future needs
7. Provider development	To identify the potential added value from the providers
8. Contract monitoring	To protect the business' contractual position now and in the future
9. Making IT and process work	To rapidly troubleshoot problems being disowned by others across the technical supply chain

6.4. Internal clients transformed from 'users' to 'customers'

The Everest Group survey found that in 60 per cent of the best-in-class BPO relationships, internal business users receiving services critically influence the direction of the BPO relationship compared to 30 per cent of normal BPOs. From the interviews, we learned that clients from high-performing BPO relationships transformed their internal business 'users' into educated 'customers'. Whereas 'users' consume resources with little thought to costs, educated 'customers' make informed choices about service levels, functionality and costs they incur. The identification and negotiation of service levels and reporting on end-to-end service performance are important practices to aid the transformation from users to customers. Once complete, the shift from users to customers considerably empowers the client executives in-charge of retained organizations to more meaningfully contribute to business objectives. Rather than responding to a user's request with, 'I am sorry, it is not in my budget', the client executive works with the customer to consider the business value versus costs of customer requests. We also found across the four streams of research that providers developed capabilities, and assisted clients, in creating that customer mentality. But in practice, however much 'leaning' the provider does, the client's retained organization has to be ready to shape the context for becoming a customer if meaningful change is to occur.[6]

An important concern for the executives in-charge of retained organizations is figuring out the organizational interfaces. If internal customers request services directly from providers, will contract service volumes be exceeded, triggering excess fees? The answer is to always provide the internal customers with the pricing and volume data they need to make informed decisions. For example, at one public institution, desktop printing is controlled through software. Every time an internal customer hits the print button of any software product (e.g. MS Office, Adobe Reader, Google browsers), a pop-up window displays the cost to print the current request and asks the customer to confirm the request. Customers are warned when volumes are close to exceeding the agreed upon thresholds. This is a simple example, but it saved the organization $1 million in printing within the first year of installation.

6.5. Provider relationships transformed from 'them' to 'us'

Philosophers from Hegel to Foucault have discussed the notion of 'other', that is, the human propensity to distinguish who belongs inside the group versus who is relegated outside the group. 'Others' are segregated, marginalized or even excluded. In the context of BPO, clients from world-class-performing BPO relationships view and treat the provider more as in-group compared to clients from troubled BPO relationships that view and treat the provider more as 'other'. A client said of her top-performing BPO relationship: 'We don't treat the provider like a vendor. They are extensions of our team. We know the names of their staff. We treat them like they are ours. I think that's been great. I feel like they belong to us and they feel like they belong to us. That goes all the way up and down the chain of command'. Another BPO client echoed a similar sentiment: 'We treat everyone as one team. Badge colour does not matter'.

Transforming the provider relationship from 'them' to 'us' requires clients to integrate the provider meaningfully into the client's organization. Clients from world-class BPO relationships more frequently invite providers to key meetings, include the provider in end-to-end process performance not just SLA management (see Chapter 5) and are more transparent about their business objectives (see Chapter 3). They also treat the provider's remotely located staff as part of the global delivery team by collaborating virtually and physically with them. Effective client leaders visit remotely located provider staff once or twice a year even after the relationship has stabilized.

One high-performing BPO relationship between an energy company and a global provider serves as an exemplar for integrating the provider into the client organization. The client leader tasked his own leadership to meaningfully include the provider's remotely located staff. The client and remotely located provider employees have monthly meetings to encourage and financially reward continuous improvement and innovation. This client leader has also transformed the behaviour of the remotely located provider employees by encouraging them to challenge the client more, 'We absolutely encourage – and I've done this face-to-face sitting there within India – to challenge us. We know we are complex, we know that we create some of our own problems; we are our own worst enemies in some areas. We absolutely want you to point some of those things out and point out some ideas. Not only is it not disrespectful but I will find it disrespectful from now on if you tell me nothing and I have to figure it out myself. We have tried to make that out positive. It's generated lots of good ideas that we've been able to put into practice'.

A key process advantage is the depth of the relationship with the provider. At a major hi-tech manufacturer, the client executive said: 'Ours is a fast operating company. The supplier always responds when we need new things and we trust them. For example, if they are managing credit calculation, they are absolutely free just to discuss with all our customers in our name, with all our sales people, with all our marketing people. So it gives them more empowerment and it gives us an added value'.

To get the provider better accepted into the client organization, one client asked that the provider's logo be removed from all the emails and the provider's name from voicemail boxes. The client said: 'One of the initial things was trying to remove roadblocks and get my organization to make sure they accept the provider as part of the operating model. That was difficult for our organization where there were functional groups that were not giving them information, not treating them with the same respect and giving them the time of day of giving other colleagues in the organization. By removing those provider logos and titles, whatever job you are doing, you are doing for the client. You might be receiving a paystub from the provider, but you are working for the client'.

6.6. Conclusion

Ultimately, successful clients obtain a 'one-team' mentality across all workforces and the alignment of all workforces into an integrated and unified organizational structure. Internal customers from world-class BPO relationships do not know or care which part of the end-to-end process is performed by the retained client staff or by provider employees. The ultimate result of aligning the retained organization, outsourced processes and provider staff is a seamless service experience for internal customers.

---

[1] The figure of the pyramid and diamond was adapted from Jim Lammers of Express Scripts and from Sandy Ogg of Unilver.

[2] Lacity et al., *The Rise of Legal Services Outsourcing.*

[3] Feeny and Willcocks, *Sloan Management Review.*

[4] Willcocks, L. and Feeny, D. (2006), 'The Core Capabilities Framework for Achieving High Performing Back Offices', *Global Sourcing of Business and IT Services*, Palgrave, London, pp. 97–113.

[5] Cullen et al., *Outsourcing*.

[6] This was a very common finding across the four research streams. In Feeny, D., Lacity, M. and Willcocks, L. (2005), 'Taking A Measure of Outsourcing Providers', *Sloan Management Review*, 46(3), 41–48 we found service providers harnessing a customer development capability with precisely this education aim. In interviews we found particularly compelling that this shift was noticeable in those that had moved furthest towards high performance.

Chapter 7

⚷ **Key 6: Resolve issues together and conflicts fairly**

What's Inside: Resolving issues together and conflicts fairly using a collaborative approach is a distinguishing characteristic of world-class BPO performers. We identify six principles of a collaborative approach to problem-solving based on an analysis of 15 storylines of common problems that arose in actual BPO relationships.

7.1. Introduction

I think all our conflicts tend to start off quite aggressive, where we're defending our position. And then in order to actually get any resolution, it has to become collaborative. – Provider Lead

This chapter closely examines problems that arise in BPO relationships, including service issues that harm performance, relationship traumas that hurt rapport and commercial conflicts that financially damage one or both parties. We found that problems occur in all types of BPO relationships, spanning the spectrum of poor to world-class performers. We share 15 storylines of actual problems and explain how parties aimed to resolve them. Our research found that a collaborative approach is the best means to solve all types of problems that arise in BPO relationships.

We identified six principles of collaborative problem-solving. The parties (1) behave appropriately (or are replaced), (2) never assign blame, (3) treat all problems as jointly owned, (4) are transparent about all relevant data, (5) seek solutions that both parties can live with and (6) protect each other's commercial interests. When these principles were followed, the parties ended up with solutions that reclaimed or even strengthened performance.

In contrast, partners who assumed an aggressive approach ended up with results that weakened the relationship and at worst, saw partnership dissolutions and lawsuits. Aggressive approaches are characterized by a party's staunch defence of their own position, with little concern for the other party's interests. The other party normally reacts with a similar aggressive foothold. Sometimes, only one person holds an aggressive stance, and if his/her superiors spot that the problem-solver has become the biggest problem, replacing that person can pave the way for a collaborative problem-solving approach. We will see this theme revealed in several storylines told in this chapter.

This chapter then proceeds by explaining the six principles of collaborative problem-solving in more detail. Next, the absence or presence of these six principles is examined in 15 storylines of real-life BPO problems. The storylines are organized into three classes of BPO problems: service issues, relationship traumas and commercial conflicts. For other partners facing these problems, the stories offer extensive guidance.

7.2. Principles of collaborative problem-solving

Collaborative problem-solving approaches are characterized by six principles. They are:

Principle 1: The people involved behave appropriately or are replaced. Chapter 2 discussed the importance of the right leadership pair, and that key to world-class performance certainly turns the door to resolving issues together and conflicts fairly. An effective leadership pair embraces the principles of collaborative problem-solving, listens to the operational, commercial and political implications of each side and presents a united front to solve the problem and sell the resolution to their respective organizations. In addition to an effective leadership pair, the operational teams also need to be cooperative and supportive of the other party. In several of the BPO problems that we share in this chapter, the problem sometimes could not be resolved until a leader was changed or an obstructionist team member (or members) were removed.

Principle 2: No one assigns blame. Partners who adopt a collaborative approach to problem-solving never waste time by blaming the other party. True collaborators know that assigning blame won't fix the problem. We found this principle at work in many world-class BPO relationships. This quote from a provider lead illustrates this principle well: 'Throughout the process, we don't look at who performed the step that failed but what can we improve in the end to end processes so we can avoid that kind of problem in the future?' One client lead described the principle this way: 'Do not point your finger at the provider because when you do, four fingers point back to yourself'.

Principle 3: All problems are 'our' problems. Collaborative problem-solvers always view every problem as a shared problem. The first response is always, 'How can I help?' Each side is willing to invest the time, energy and resources to swiftly swarm the problem. Everyone rolls up their sleeves and gets to work.

Principle 4: Everyone is transparent. Collaborative approaches to resolving problems require a high level of trust, honesty and transparency. Transparency was frequently one of the top things interviewees cited when asked about the secrets to great collaboration. One provider lead aptly captured this principle in this quote: 'I'm committed to transparency with my counterpart. We try to be very open about what the interests are on each side so that when we're negotiating, we can negotiate commercial relationships that are good for the interests of both parties'.

Principle 5: The solution works for both parties. Ideally, a resolution will improve the circumstances for both parties, the so-called win–win solution. In reality, many outcomes result from tough but fair negotiations and compromises. One provider lead of an HRO relationship captured the idea of tough but fair negotiations when he said: 'I'd like to say we follow a collaborative, win–win approach to conflict resolution. We do butt heads quite a lot on small things. We both want to win. So what I try and do, and what I counsel my managers to do, is to find a win–win and trade something off. We can get this and you can get that'.

Principle 6: Each party protects the other party's commercial interests. Collaborative partners care about the other party's commercial interests. If a solution to a problem financially disadvantages one of the parties, then they both work to find an equitable compensation. The focus is always on problem resolution first and commercial consequences are dealt with later. Caring about a partner's commercial well-being is not altruism; it is actually in the client's best interest to care about and protect the provider's commercial interests and vice versa because service performance is tied to financial performance. (The data for this claim is presented in Chapter 1.) The aim is to create a new commercial deal that benefits both parties. We will soon see this principle at work in the resolutions to the problems of poor pricing models and when clients drastically over-estimated service volumes. In all these stories, the partners renegotiated the contract that resulted in a better deal for both parties.

7.3. Problems that arise in BPO relationships

During our research, we asked each client and provider to describe a significant problem and explain how the parties resolved it (or failed to resolve it). From the rich collection of problems described, we classified them into three types: service issues, relationship traumas and commercial conflicts.

Service issues are problems that disrupt service performance. Service issues may be caused by many things and by many parties, even parties or factors external to the BPO relationship, like severe weather. All services – whether insourced or outsourced – will have issues which disrupt performance occasionally. In this chapter, we describe six stories of service issues that arose in actual BPO relationships and show how the parties resolved them.

Relationship traumas are situations in which the parties disagree about how people should behave. As we have noted many times, BPO is still primarily a people business, and people can get in the way of a good BPO relationship. We describe four relationship traumas associated with work cultures, inattentive providers and uncooperative clients. Some problems were resolved by changing a leader, further corroborating the value of leadership pairs in driving top performance (see Chapter 2).

Commercial conflicts are circumstances that adversely affect the commercial interests of one or both of the parties. During contract negotiations, both parties aim to ensure that all sides benefit commercially from the relationship. Parties include adaptive contractual clauses to reduce risks and to accommodate uncertainties. Clauses for volume fluctuations, force majeure clauses, change of character clauses and external benchmarking to reset prices or service levels are found in many contracts. Parties also include early termination options, recognizing that there may be some unforeseeable circumstance in which one or both parties wish to terminate the contract. Much like human partners signing prenuptial agreements, clients and providers hope to never enact early termination clauses.

While significant commercial conflicts may never happen, or may happen at most once or twice in a long-term relationship, *any* occurrence will threaten the BPO relationship. Many clients lack the experience to deal effectively with a commercial conflict if one was to arise. Furthermore, the subject of commercial conflict in BPO relationships is often viewed as highly sensitive, indecorous and secretive, so clients may not have access to deep insights. We discuss five stories of commercial conflicts – some of which resulted in not-so-fond farewells and others that resulted in stronger relationships.

In sharing the stories of service issues, relationship traumas and commercial conflicts, we aim to provide deeper insight into the emotionally charged topic of BPO problems. For each storyline, we provide one or more illustrative examples, then analyse the story by extracting lessons and highlighting whether or not the parties embraced the six principles of collaborate problem-solving.

7.4. Stories of service issues

> If the work we're getting back is not what we expect, that's as much our fault as the service provider's because we're not being clear in telling them what we want, and tooling them up to deliver it. – Client Lead

This section highlights service issues that disrupted service performance (see Table 7.1). The examples cover several contexts including LSO, FAO and HRO.

Table 7.1 Principles illustrated in service issue storylines

Storyline	Context	Principles of collaborative problem-solving					
		People act appropriately	No one assigns blame	Problem is co-owned	Partners are transparent	Solution is a win–win (or at least acceptable to both parties)	Commercial interests of both parties are protected
1. A provider over-promises and under-delivers	LSO				O		
2. A client bypasses an onboarding process and receives poor quality	LSO	O–X					
3. A call centre service has a rocky transition	FAO	X	X	X			

4. Third-party software causes service performance to plummet	FAO	X	X	
5. A client under-estimates demand	LSO	X	X	X
6. A client wants a slicker tool	HRO	X	X	X

Legend: O = parties did not exhibit the principle
X = parties did exhibit the principle
O–X = parties did not initially exhibit the principle, but finally did

7.4.1. A provider over-promises and under-delivers

The story: On one LSO account, the client asked the provider if it could support foreign languages. The provider indicated that it could support foreign languages from its Indian delivery centre. After a trial period, it became apparent that the provider had never supported foreign languages from this location before, and the result – according to the client – was '*quite disastrous*'. The client lead was more annoyed that the provider was not forthright about its capabilities than he was about the provider's lack of capabilities. From the provider lead's perspective, he thought that he could quickly build the capabilities in India to delight his prestigious client. The partners agreed that the provider would stop providing foreign language support.

The analysis: A lack of transparency caused the problem in this story. Providers are quite reticent to expose their inabilities to clients, but the clients will eventually discover them. This storyline is most common in offshore outsourcing, particularly when the provider is in a culture characterized by greater power distance and lower individualism compared to the client.[1] A best practice for avoiding this service issue is to implement a rigorous onboarding process that includes training, documentation, shadowing and quality review. But as the next storyline attests, not all clients are willing to make that onboarding investment.

7.4.2. A client bypasses an onboarding process

The story: Like the previous story, the client is also located in the West and the provider is located in India on this account. The contract stipulates that the parties would develop playbooks before work was assigned to the provider. One person in the client organization tried to assign new work to the provider without developing the playbook first. The client instructed the provider to '*make their best attempt*', but the client was not happy with the result. The provider lead reiterated that his company relies on processes, playbooks and technologies to deliver quality service. The person in the client organization learned his lesson and never bypassed the onboarding process again.

The analysis: In this story, a person is not acting appropriately. The client is the root cause of the service issue by asking the provider to sidestep its quality assurance process. If clients wish to bypass the onboarding process, then they need to view all new work as experimental. Radiant. law, a UK-based law firm, routinely tested its provider's capabilities without a detailed training and onboarding process. Radiant.law deliberately sent over-challenging work to its South African-based provider just to see if it could do it. One co-founder of radiant.law said, 'If we send something to South Africa and it doesn't come back right, I will pull an all-nighter, if necessary, to fix the document myself. Experimentation is the only way to know how far we can take the people or how far we can take technology'. In this case, the client did not blame the provider when it did not perform well.

7.4.3. A call centre service has a rocky transition

The story: One client transitioned the help line for its accounts payable function to a provider. Soon after, the volume of calls surged. The provider suspected that the increase in volume was due to repeat callers, which would mean that the provider was not resolving the callers' issues the first time. Rather than just beat up the provider, the client took the calls back in-house to give the provider time to analyse the calls and to develop a plan on improving the service. The provider discovered that some of the 'repeat callers' were the same people calling up with a completely different question, but the provider employee ticketed the new call as a repeat call. Thus, some of the repeat volumes were caused by insufficient training on how to tag calls. Some of the issues were caused by the fact that it was year-end and people were scrambling to pay their invoices and complete expense reports. The client and provider agreed to an immediate plan and then developed a long-term plan to get service back on track. The provider praised the client's behaviour, 'They absolutely pitched in to help . . . They stepped in when they didn't have to do. They could have just said, "Tough luck, you just missed your SLA"'. The client explained his collaborative approach: 'Other clients might have said [to the provider]: 'This is your problem, don't bother me. It's your issue'. What I try and do is say: 'We are in this together'.

The analysis: The story provides strong evidence of three principles of collaborative problem-solving: the leaders acted appropriately, nobody assigned blame and the problem was jointly owned. Even when one of the parties is the primary cause of a service issue, both parties must take co-responsibility for fixing it. The story follows the advice of a popular psychologist, Dr. Phil McGraw, who tells couples in troubled relationships: Somebody has to step up and be the hero. In this story, the client was that hero. In the next story, the provider stepped up to be the hero.

7.4.4. Third-party software causes service performance to plummet

The story: On one large account, the client implemented a new ERP system and the provider was put in-charge of ERP operational support. About a month and half after the go live day, user complaints skyrocketed. The users immediately blamed the service provider, not the ERP vendor. The provider lead recalled, 'So there was a lot of emails and a lot of yelling and screaming about, "What the hell is going on?"' The client and provider leaders worked together to investigate the problem. They each assigned senior-level governance to oversee the resolution. The provider lead recalled, 'We absolutely threw resources at it from consulting, from operations, from analytics to figure out what it is and lower the backlog and fix the root causes while, at the same time, putting Band-Aids on all the places that it was bleeding'. It took 4 months to get service issues completely resolved. The root cause was primarily a lousy implementation on the parts of the ERP vendor and client. The service provider contributed to the problem by not having measures in place to detect issues sooner.

The analysis: Like the previous story, the leaders in this story acted appropriately, did not assign blame and co-owned the problem. During the ERP problem-resolution process, the provider lead described the approach, 'We did a pretty good job of putting the right structure and the right resources in place to simultaneously mitigate the pain and fix the root cause. Both parties were pretty good at not blaming each other'. More impressive was the time, energy and resources the provider allocated to a problem for which they were not the primary cause.

7.4.5. A client under-estimates demand

The story: On one LSO account, the client severely under-estimated the number of lawyers the provider would need to staff for document review. Although the client lead recognized that it was the client's fault for under-estimating the volume of work, he praised the provider for working with them to address the problem. First, the provider more than doubled the size of the staff within 4 weeks of the engagement. But as the project neared its completion deadline, both parties realized they still did not have enough resources. The client and provider decided that working overtime was the best way to meet the deadline. The client also paid for the employees' transportation, security personnel and facilities management costs for weekend shifts. Eighty per cent of the provider's employees volunteered to work extra hours and the project was completed on time. The client said: 'We have jointly identified that if something is not working that well, if it is clunky, we'll pretty much come up with a solution'.

The analysis: The leaders acted accordingly, did not assign blame, co-owned the problem, developed an acceptable solution and fairly compensated the provider. The client and provider in this example were sensitive about demoralizing and burning out the provider's staff, so they made the overtime work voluntary. They offered significant financial incentives and did not punish employees who could not or would not work overtime. The provider did not blame the client for under-estimating demand, but rather took joint responsibility for solving it. The client responded in kind and recompensed the provider justly.

7.4.6. A client wants a slicker tool

The story: A client from a consumer products company is very marketing-focused and values slick user interfaces on all of its software products. One of the provider's tools did not have a glitzy interface. The provider was willing to customize the interface for an additional fee. The client did not think it should pay to improve the provider's tool. This debate went back and forth for quite a while. Finally, the provider agreed to find a cloud-based alternative that could replace its proprietary system. The provider lead said: 'We are looking at how we can make a swap out in a manner that commercially will work for each party with minimal to no investment on the part of [the client] and that isn't a huge margin eroding thing on our end. We are working very collaboratively on that'.

The analysis: This story demonstrates the value of thinking outside the box to find a solution that works for both parties. Rather than focus on the tool at hand, the partners stepped back and focused on the features the client wanted. Furthermore, the partners were committed to finding a solution that did not harm the commercial interests of either party.

7.5. Stories of relationship traumas

> The provider appointed a delivery account manager and through the initial period, the relationship did not work. I don't know whether it was chemistry or what; He may have been a very good person but I couldn't work with him. – Client Lead

This section presents four storylines about relationship traumas (see Table 7.2). The examples cover multiple contexts including HRO, call centres, ITO and supply chain management outsourcing. Most of the storylines find that the clients are primarily at fault. This finding might be an artefact of our sample or it might accurately reflect the population of BPO relationships. In general, BPO providers have considerably more experience working with clients than clients have working with providers. The following stories offer a number of lessons that can help fix or avoid relationship traumas.

7.5.1. Clients and providers clash over the providers' work habits

Following are three stories that all deal with the same relationship trauma: the client wants to tell the provider how to manage the provider's employees.

The first story: On this HRO deal, some of the provider's staff was located at the client site. Although the client was paying the provider based on outcomes, it still wanted to dictate how the provider's employees

Table 7.2 Principles illustrated in relationship traumas

Storyline	Context	Principles of collaborative problem-solving					
		People act appropriately	No one assigns blame	Problem is co-owned	Partners are transparent	Solution is a win–win (or at least acceptable to both parties)	Commercial interests of both parties are protected
7. Clients and providers clash over the providers' work habits	Multiple examples	O		X		X	
8. An SME client wants more of the provider's attention	ITO	O–X					
9. A client lead makes much ado about nothing	Supply chain	O–X	O–X	O–X			
10. An uncooperative client team hinders the relationship	Supply chain	O–X					

Legend: O = parties did not exhibit the principle

X = parties did exhibit the principle

O–X = parties did not initially exhibit the principle, but finally did

should behave. The client lead expected the provider's staff to maintain the same work hours as the client's staff. He constantly questioned how the provider's staff was spending its time. The client lead did not want the provider's staff in training or in meetings during 'the client's time'. The provider lead countered that his company was meeting its service levels, so the client lead should not be micromanaging the provider's staff. In the end, the provider acquiesced, although he called it a compromise. He said, 'We sort of came to a compromise. We set up some guidelines that we wouldn't do team building activities until 4:00 in the afternoon. There would only be so many training days per year, per person. We sort of set up some guidelines we could both live with and move forward from there'.

The second story: In a nearly identical storyline as earlier, on an account halfway around the world, a client lead wanted a refund because the client claimed that the provider employees only worked 6 hours per day instead of 8. The provider lead felt that the client should not be meddling with his staff. He said: 'I said it was my own responsibility to organize my team. If I'm able to perform the SLAs by having half of the staff that was expected, it's my decision. The same as if I have a problem and I have to duplicate the number of people, it's my problem'. The provider lead concluded the story, 'We are now billing the client the proper price for the service, not related to the time the people are spending on the contract'.

The third story: In this third example, a client and provider disagree on the role of middle managers. The context is an offshore customer-care deal where the South African-based provider answers calls from the client's UK-based customers. The client felt that the provider's middle managers were too 'hands off'. The client is accustomed to middle managers who listen to calls daily and who coach call centre agents. Conversely, in South Africa, middle managers are accustomed to delegating work to the teams. The issue was resolved by the provider doing what the client asked.

The analysis: We attest that the clients in these stories did not act appropriately. Clients need to learn to manage the inputs and outputs to and from service providers rather than try to micromanage the provider's resources. This lesson has come out very strongly from prior research.[2] If clients want complete control over the human resources that deliver a service, then they should retain the service in-house. In short, clients need to stay on their own side. We understand the client's reasoning, particularly if the contract is based on FTE-pricing. Client's think: 'I am paying for the provider's dedicated staff so I better be sure they are productive'. However, even with FTE pricing, a better way to ensure that provider employees are productive is to require yearly mandatory productivity improvement clauses, which are discussed further in Chapter 10. Turning to the providers' behaviours in the stories earlier, they were diplomatic; they worked with their clients to develop compromises that both sides could accept.

7.5.2. An SME client wants more of the provider's attention

The story: This small- to medium-sized enterprise (SME) engaged a cloud provider for its infrastructure and software services. At the beginning of the outsourcing relationship, the client lead felt he was not getting the same priority as the provider's larger customers. He said: 'We were getting a memo at 3:00 telling us that we had an outage at 1:00 and now it is fixed. I wanted something at 1:02 that said, 'We've got an issue, we're looking at it'. After expressing his concern to the provider, the provider changed its notification process to include contact lists for all its clients, not just the large ones. The CIO concluded: 'I was very happy that they took that into consideration and implemented this not only for us but their other accounts so that we could understand what was going on within the environment. I would say that was handled really well'.

The analysis: In this story, the provider was initially neglectful, but quickly acted to change its behaviour. This story is interesting because most of the clients in our research are quite large. We only studied four outsourcing engagements in which the client employed fewer than 250 people.[3] Small-sized clients often do not warrant the provider's full attention, but SMEs can build social capital with providers outside of the formal BPO relationship. Among our other cases, one SME client works on open source projects with its major provider which builds valuable social capital and credibility when suggesting enhancements to the provider's service. A CEO from another SME serves on the Board of its main provider – there may be no better way to guarantee service excellence! Staying close to the provider's other SME customers is also a great way to keep a provider's attention.

7.5.3. A client lead makes much ado about nothing

The story: On one supply chain outsourcing account, the client lead escalated every small issue to the client's CFO. The provider lead tried working with the client lead, telling her: 'Let's work together to get this resolved'. She continued to escalate every small issue and made it a big problem at the client end. The client CFO finally intervened. He sent a scout to the provider's delivery centre to investigate. When the scout returned with a good report, the CFO replaced the original client lead. The new client lead reported that since the replacement, there had not been any major conflict. He said: 'Both parties work hard at it to ensure there are no conflicts. We have had a few bumps on the road but those are normal in marriages as well'.

The analysis: This case offers a great moral: Beware of the problem-solver who becomes the problem. As Chapter 2 attests, an effective leadership pair is essential to world-class BPO performance, in part, because the pair works together to swiftly solve problems. In this story, the client lead was not acting appropriately, she blamed the provider for everything and she would not resolve problems with the provider; she became a bigger problem than the operational ones that needed to be solved. The CFO was correct to investigate the situation and then replace her.

7.5.4. An uncooperative client team hinders the relationship

The story: On this supply chain deal, the initial client lead was not effective at working with the provider. His poor behaviour, in turn, sanctioned obstructionist behaviour from the entire client side team. Eventually, the client lead left the company, and the new client lead worked very well with his provider counterpart. However, the client's operational team was still uncooperative. The new client lead said: 'They would do everything possible to slow down, not provide, not cooperate with [the provider], and not allow them to be able to provide the best service possible'. The new client lead essentially mandated cooperation. He said, 'This is not optional'. When he replaced a few obstructionist people, the remaining team received the message that he was serious. The relationship went on to improve some KPIs for the client.

The analysis: This story is similar to the previous story in that the initial client lead was ineffective and needed to be replaced. The situation was worse in this story because most of the client team – not just its leader – was uncooperative. Resolving relational traumas often require tough decisions, including personnel termination.

7.6. Stories of commercial conflicts

The world fell apart [after the Global Financial crisis in 2008] and the foundation wasn't strong enough to withstand that because we did not have a lot of sophistication in our commercial arrangement . . . It's taken us awhile to come to terms with the fact that volume baselines were wrong, wildly wrong because the forecast in growth on [the client's] part just wasn't, wouldn't happen. –Provider Lead

This section presents five storylines about commercial conflicts (see Table 7.3). The examples cover multiple contexts. Two storylines have appeared before in the service issues section: a client's forecast for service demand is way off target and a provider over-promises and under-delivers. They reappear here because the financial consequences were severe enough to damage one or both parties. Of all the problem types, commercial conflicts are the most serious because BPO relationships are first commercial transactions – a provider MUST earn a profit and a client MUST meet its business case. Commercial conflict resolutions require that parties embrace all six principles. In two storylines, partners adopted NONE of the principles of collaborative problem-solving and the relationships resulted in good riddance in one case and a multimillion pound lawsuit in another.

Table 7.3 Principles illustrated in commercial conflicts

Storyline	Context	Principles of collaborative problem-solving					
		People act appropriately	No one assigns blame	Problem is co-owned	Partners are transparent	Solution is a win–win (or at least acceptable to both parties)	Commercial interests of both parties are protected
11. A poor pricing model leads to a disadvantaged partner	Multiple examples	X	X	Ẋ	X	X	X
12. A client pays for bloated provider staffing	FAO	O-X		O-X	O-X	O-X	
13. A client over-estimates demand	Procurement	X	X	X	X	X	X
14. Partners fight over gain-share	Procurement	O	O	O	O	O	O
15. A provider over-promises and under-delivers	ITO	O	O	O	O	O	O

Legend: O = parties did not exhibit the principle
X = parties did exhibit the principle
O–X = parties did not initially exhibit the principle, but finally did

7.6.1. A poor pricing model leads to a disadvantaged party

Poor pricing models are one of the most common causes of commercial conflicts. We share two stories – one in which the pricing model caused provider losses and the another in which the client was not meeting its business case.

The first story: This story discusses the rocky launch of one FAO deal. Part of the problem was a faulty pricing mechanism that prevented the provider from recovering its costs. Initially, the contract used transaction-based pricing. The provider calculated the price per transaction by modelling the number of provider employees, capital assets and overhead needed to perform the service for the expected volume of transactions. After about 2 years, the service character changed so much that – according to the provider – 'Our unit pricing started to not look right anymore'. The provider was losing money. From the client side, the relationship was not working for them either. The client lead said: 'Every time we had an idea, it was stopped in its tracks. We got to a point where we really weren't getting anywhere. They weren't bringing practical ideas to the table. The relationship was getting very, very strained between the two operational management groups'. Both parties agreed to renegotiate the contract. The client wanted a new provider team in place, which it received. Both parties agreed to move to FTE pricing. The leadership pair now operates effectively. The provider lead recounted: 'We actually operate extremely collaboratively underneath the guiding principles which we call our joint ways of working. Under those guiding principles, we look at what are the right tenets of a successful partnership? It's not always going to be about one person's interest or the other's interest, we need to understand how each other define success'. The client lead described the new relationship approach this way: 'Once we went through a lot of pain two years into the relationship in terms of partnering, it created a far more collaborative environment and a far healthier environment for the account where we're happy to be straightforward and honest with each other'. Now, when the provider performs well, the client recognizes them for that. If performance slips, the partners work together. The client continued: 'It's dealt with in a very transparent and professional manner. It takes a lot of the politics and unnecessary tension out of the relationship'.

The second story: On one account, the initial contract was priced using different rate cards for different types of work. After the transition, the client came to the provider and explained that the client's business case was not being met because the client under-estimated the complexity of the pricing mechanism and the amount of skills needed. The client asked to renegotiate the pricing mechanism. The provider agreed to a flat rate card in exchange for a longer contract and an increased scope of work. Both parties negotiated a better deal and the relationship is a high-performance one. Said the client: 'Our BPO partner has performed very well. Put simply – they execute. We have found that if we set the bar high, they do all that they can to jump over it. In addition to providing transactional services that exceed SLAs, they help us to think strategically about running our business'.

The analysis: Pricing conflicts are what have been called quite 'wicked' problems[4]; fixing them requires all six principles of collaborative problem-solving. As the BPO market develops, partners are trying to move away from resource-based pricing to transaction-based and outcome-based pricing. These types of pricing mechanisms require considerable assumptions about the costs, character and volume of services to be delivered. After deals go live, one of the parties may be severely disadvantaged. For clients, sticker shock over a large, unexpected invoice will give way to the grim reality that its initial business case is severely jeopardized. When clients are not meeting their business case, they often become aggressive scrutinizers of every invoice and argue that additional services or volumes are in scope. For providers, pricing based on unfounded assumptions can result in puny margins, or worse, financial losses. When a provider cannot earn a profit margin because prices do not recover costs, the client's service is bound to erode and both parties suffer. On one world-class BPO account, the partners do not think the contractual pricing model produces a 'fact' about who owes who what, but instead produces a starting point for a conversation. This is a good lesson to learn.

7.6.2. A client pays for bloated provider staff

The story: On one FAO relationship, a new client lead came on the account and repeatedly questioned why he was paying for provider employees in a high cost area when most of the other work was located in a low cost area. The client lead wanted to move these resources to a low cost area. After taking 7 months to respond, the provider lead said the client could not request staff relocation until next year and the client would have to pay for the severance packages, as the contract specified. The client lead was very annoyed at this answer because at the same time, the provider was trying to sell the client additional consulting services. The client said: 'I told them that they are not getting the message of strategic relationship and this is not the way to start things off. I had one of them calling me to meet with me about consulting work and I said, "Why would I give you more business in consulting if you're basically giving us a hard time about correcting our account elsewhere?"' Eventually, the provider assigned a new provider lead. She immediately investigated the work the onshore team was providing for her client. She determined that there was not enough work to occupy all the onshore resources. She retained just half the staff to perform the client's work and she moved those roles offshore. This paved the way for a revitalization of the relationship that eventually became world-class. This story, which was first mentioned in Chapter 2, highlights the value of an effective leadership pair.

The analysis: The first provider lead was non-responsive, did not co-own the problem and was not transparent about the work the onshore staff was doing. Why wasn't the first provider lead more responsive? This FAO deal is quite large, with a couple of hundred FTEs devoted to this client. From the first provider lead's perspective, the client was complaining about a very small percentage of the provider's dedicated staff. Although a fraction of the deal, the client was irritated because he was paying over a million dollars a year for the onshore staff. The provider's replacement cued in early to her client's irritation, and she certainly was willing to act right, be transparent, co-own the problem and find a solution that was acceptable to both sides. She moved the resources offshore, gained her client's trust and went on to gain world-class performance.

7.6.3. A clients over-estimates demand

The story: On one procurement deal, the provider was initially paid just an administrative fee. The provider's real profits would happen after the client transferred an estimated £80 million worth of spend across seven categories. Six months into the deal, only £30 million in spend had been transferred to the provider. The partners initially thought that £25 million worth of learning and development spend was going to be transferred, but the actual number was only about 30 per cent of the estimate. This under-estimation threatened the provider's ability to meet its projected profitability targets. Rather than simply say 'too bad' to the provider, the client recognized the threat to the provider's financial position and the effect that would ultimately have on the BPO relationship. The partners held many strategic planning sessions to address the shortfall. The partners agreed that it was in both of their interests to transfer over the intended critical mass of spend to the provider. This would be achieved by adding eight more categories of spend, bringing the provider's controlled spend to nearly £100 million by year end. The client would save money on the eight new categories it shifted to the provider, so it was content. The provider got a larger deal, yet a more challenging one because procuring 15 smaller categories rather than 7 large ones increased its transaction and administration costs. The second effect is that the provider had less negotiating leverage with suppliers since the value of each deal was smaller. But overall, both parties consider the solution a win–win.

The analysis: In storyline 5, we discussed a situation in which the client *under-estimated* service volumes, causing a service issue but not a commercial conflict. From the provider's perspective, unexpected increases in service volumes usually means more revenue, so it usually welcomes this surprise. From the client's perspective, it doesn't welcome volume surges, but it typically understands that it has to pay more money when it exceeds volume ceilings; it would have to pay more even if the service was insourced.

When clients drastically *over-estimate* demand, it can threaten the commercial interests of one or both parties. If a client has to remunerate the provider a minimum fee when volumes fall below the negotiated floor, the client's commercial interests are harmed because it pays for services it is not using. As evident in the procurement story, a provider's commercial interests are often severely affected when the size of the deal is much smaller than anticipated. This situation clearly calls for a collaborative approach that embraces all six principles to re-establish both parties' financial health. Often times, the best solution is to renegotiate. Clients should find new business to give the provider to compensate for the lost volume and in return, providers should not make the client continue to pay for services it is not using.

7.6.4. Partners fight over gain-share

The story: In one engagement, the client and provider escalated the fight over gain-share allocations to a formal dispute. The context was a procurement deal in which the provider was responsible for the procurement software and procurement services. The contract stipulated that the provider would get a percentage of any discount above a vendor's list price for any new products the provider bought for the client. The provider renewed a hardware vendor contract on behalf of the client that was 55 per cent lower than the hardware vendor's list price. The provider calculated a multi-million dollar gain-share, claiming that the contract was for new products as evidenced by new material codes. The client refused to pay. The client claimed that the previous contract with the hardware vendor already had a 50 per cent discount and the client was purchasing the same material, it was just that the vendor's newer models used different codes. The client allocated about 150 hours of in-house legal counsel to the dispute and brought back the advisory firm that helped negotiate the original contract into the deliberations. The client put so much energy, time and resources to the dispute that, in the end, the client reported that 'the provider gave up'. Although the partners resolved the conflict, the partnership was weakened according to the client. He said: 'It went all the way to the dispute process, and it left an incredibly bitter taste with our executive team'. Eventually the provider's procurement services division was bought by another provider. The client thought, 'Good riddance!' The client lead is very pleased with the new services provider: 'The [new provider] is incredibly customer-focused first, provider-focused second. It's an incredible reversal compared to the previous provider'.

The analysis: This story is the epitome of an aggressive approach to problem-solving. None of the six principles are evident. What went wrong? Any reasonable person would agree that the spirit of the agreement is that the provider was to earn a gain-share on new products, not on existing products for which the client had already negotiated steep discounts with vendors. In this situation, the provider held too firmly to the letter of the contract and in the end, the client was thrilled to be rid of them. In world-class BPO relationships, the parties understand that the spirit of the agreement is more important than the letter of the law. This story also has another lesson to offer about incentivizing providers. We revisit the best and worst ways to implement gain-sharing in Chapter 10.

7.6.5. A provider over-promises and under-delivers

We saved this storyline for last because we wanted to show that lawsuits can happen when parties fail to resolve conflicts collaboratively.

The story: One example at the extreme end of performance failure was the circumstance in which one major provider over-promised on delivering a £50 million customer relationship management system. After nearly 2 years of little progress, the client terminated the contract. The client built the system itself for £265 million and subsequently sued the provider. The client argued that the provider's claims during the tendering process were fraudulent and constituted negligent misrepresentation. The client contended that it would have contracted with one of the other bidders if it had known about the provider's erroneous claims. The client also sued for breach of contract. The court found in favour of all of the client's claims of misrepresentation, deceit, negligence and breach of contract and awarded damages in excess of £200 million.[5]

The analysis: Are some broken promises too big to forgive? This client thought so, but no client or provider wants to end up in court. Although this story places fault only on the provider, one can imagine that the client is not blameless. Developing complex systems requires a tremendous amount of interorganizational collaboration. One wonders if the client did all that it could to integrate the provider into the organization. When the project was delayed and costs escalated, did both parties stick to the letter of the contract instead of the spirit of the contract? Did both parties look to renegotiate a win–win? It seems that both parties assumed an aggressive approach to conflict resolution, resulting in commercial losses for the provider and an extreme seepage of resources to recover losses for the client.

We hope that this story and the stories shared in this chapter inspire people at all levels to resolve problems collaboratively.

7.7. Conclusion

> When we are negotiating a contract change or a change order, we are really, really collaborative on how we work on solutions and commercial frameworks that are going to meet the needs of both parties. It's not a win–lose; it's very much a win–win. – Provider Lead

This chapter found that a collaborative approach is the best way to resolve service issues, relationship traumas and commercial conflicts. Among the three types of problems, commercial conflicts are the most serious because they severely and adversely affect the financial interests of one or both parties. We have noted that true commercial conflicts are not common. Most BPO relationships in our case study research have never experienced a significant commercial conflict. The most common response to questions about significant commercial conflicts resulted in mirrored responses such as these:

> The provider lead: 'We don't really have significant conflicts. In the last five years, we haven't had to escalate any dispute to the executive committee. We do a good job of sorting things out at the operational level'.

> His client counterpart: 'I can find lots of examples of relatively small issues but nothing that I would say is significant. We have a good process for dealing with issues that arise operationally. There haven't been any real major issues that have required any more formality. It's just worked'.

However, BPO is still an emerging set of practices. As the BPO market evolves into more sophisticated pricing models and to broader scopes of services, some miscalculations and unfounded assumptions are expected. Preparing for a potential conflict by learning more about it is like buying flood insurance – one hopes one never needs it, but it is comforting to know one is covered. Reading about the stories in this chapter is time well-spent if one can learn their lessons of resolving issues together and conflicts fairly.

---

[1] For more information on cultural differences in offshore outsourcing, see Lacity, M. and Rottman, J. (2008), *Offshore Outsourcing of IT Work*, Palgrave, London.

2 Lacity and Willcocks, *Advanced Outsourcing Practice*.

3 See Lacity, M. and Reynolds, P. (2014), 'Cloud Services Practices for Small and Medium-sized Enterprises', *MIS Quarterly Executive*, 13(1), 31–44.

4 'Wicked' problems are difficult to solve because of incomplete, contradictory and/or changing requirements.

5 See the entire court ruling at http://www.scribd.com/doc/32707026/EDS-v-BskyB-court-decisions

Chapter 8

⊶ Key 7: Use technology as enabler and accelerator of performance

What's Inside: This chapter examinés BPO technologies that improve clients' costs, services and controls. Self-service portals, automation, business analytics and forecasting tools, workflow tools, governance tools and cloud services can deliver great benefits to clients, provided they understand important caveats.

8.1. Introduction

> Robotic Process Automation is the next wave of innovation and will dramatically change the way business and BPO service providers deal with their customers. –Martin Conboy[1]

Technology enablement is of the most important practices associated with world-class BPO performance. The Everest survey found that 40 per cent of clients from high-performance BPO relationships consider technology provided by the service provider to be an important component, compared to only 27 per cent of typical performers. Even greater numbers of clients from top-performance BPO relationships – 56 per cent – believe that it is important to gain access to technology in a BPO relationship, while only 34 per cent of typical performers agree. In a 2014 survey of 189 buy-side executives by HfS, buyers with technology-enabled transformational BPO deals reaped much better results in terms of costs and business outcomes compared to buyers who describe their BPO models as 'lift and shift'.[2]

In our innovation survey, clients, providers and advisors identified new tools or technologies as the most frequent type of innovation delivered in an outsourcing relationship. In our academic review, the provider's technical/methodological capability was the second most important capability after the provider's human resource management capability. Technical/ methodological capability is an operational capability important to both client and provider firms. Academic research finds strongly that clients experienced better outsourcing outcomes when both clients and providers were technically mature.

From our case study research, we identified many clients commending their BPO provider's deployment of technology to enable lower costs, better service and tighter controls. In this report, we focus on six common technologies and what they enable:

- reduced headcount and accelerated service delivery through self-service portals,
- reduced costs and standardization through automation,
- optimized services by capturing and reporting on errors and waste using business analytical tools and improved product delivery rates using forecasting tools,
- enhanced controls and compliance using workflow tools,
- increased business value and collaboration between the client and provider organizations using governance tools and
- reduced infrastructure costs and speedier enhancements through cloud-computing.

Although we discuss the benefits of these technologies, we note that technologies are never silver bullets; the data that feeds these technologies must be standard, accurate and timely. Technologies that are broadly disseminated – like self-service portals – require large numbers of users to be trained, and not all users welcome the change. 'The portal is great, but we've also had people who just can't get the hang of using the technology', said one client at a major aerospace defence company. Moreover, effectively deploying technology for analytics, forecasting, workflow and governance requires clients and providers to commit to a high level of transparency and collaboration.

8.2. Self-service portals

Since the advent of personal computers, ever more tasks are performed by knowledge workers instead of support staff. First, we had fewer secretaries as more knowledge workers began to type their own memos, emails and reports. Now, user-friendly, web-enabled, self-service portals allow end-users to perform tasks that require more business process expertise – like travel and expense reimbursement, or supply orders. Self-service portals reduce direct costs by reducing staff support, and speed service access and delivery. In our case studies, we have several examples of how self-service portals in human resource functions reduced costs and improved service. On one HRO account, the provider implemented eHR, a portal that enabled client users to manage their own benefits, training, travel and expenses. It is also used for recruiting. 'We had a lot of very good feedback. The technology is great', said the client.

Self-service portals in procurement are also common. These tools allow clients to request resources directly from their portable devices. In some BPO deals, the self-service portals are accessible by third-party vendors, which reduce the number of calls to the help desk. 'We implemented a vendor portal for the accounts payable vendors which is driving a lot of basic questions to be answered there, as opposed calls coming into the Helpdesk', one provider explained. 'We are in the early implementation phase, but we have a lot of good responses from their vendors about how much easier it is. They can get the information they need more timely, when they want it as opposed to someone calling in and having someone call them back. That I think has been a benefit'. The client corroborated the value of the vendor portal '[The provider] set up a vendor portal which allows the supplier to see a picture of his account with us. So, instead of ringing us and saying, 'where's my invoice?', he can see what the progress is. 'When are you going to pay me?' It's on there, on the schedule. So that's helpful'.

8.3. Automation

The year 2014 might be dubbed 'BPO robotics' based on the buzz from analysts. Consider these reports:

- 'I am Robot: will Robotic Process Automation (RPA) revolutionise the BPO industry?'[3]
- 'Robotic Automation – What next for BPO's?'[4]

- 'Robotistan – A Place for Everyone in Business Processing Outsourcing to Move to in 2014'[5]
- 'Robotic Process Automation for Utilities'[6]

Although the term 'BPO Robotics' connotes visions of physical robots wandering around offices performing human tasks, the term really means automation of BPO tasks that were previously performed by a human. It almost always means a software solution, such as voice recognition software (software that understands speech) and 'chatbots' (software that produces speech). We prefer the simpler term, automation, because it is less hyperbolic.

We have many examples from our research that show that automation reduces costs and increases standardization, and invoice automation is one example from the case studies. On one BPO account for FAO services, the provider had already reached 100 per cent service levels for processing invoices and had reduced costs through labour arbitrage and process standardization. With focus on further reducing the cost per invoice, the provider identified electronic invoicing as a prime candidate for doing so. 'We proposed to implement an optical character recognition (OCR) system and an electronic invoicing solution to make AP invoicing automated and paperless. This change was driven through because we agreed to focus on the business outcome of reducing cost per invoice', said the provider. While electronic invoicing is likely to reduce the provider's headcount, thereby impacting their revenue, a gain-sharing arrangement provides an incentive for the provider to propose further process and technology automation initiatives, which not only bring long-term rewards for the client, but also benefit the provider through project scope expansion and contract extensions. This example may be more pedestrian than a 'robot' but the business benefits are nonetheless impressive.

8.4. Business analytics and forecasting tools

The Everest Group survey found that 'domain understanding and analytics' is one of the eight best practices of high-performing BPO relationships (see Chapter 9). Technology is one of the prime enablers of business analytics – the ability to continuously analyse past business performance to gain insight and to identify ways to improve performance. Clients are highly desirous of business analytic capabilities. However, doing it on their own can cost an organization a million dollars or more. Increasingly, clients are turning to their service providers to help deploy business analytics. Service providers are increasingly using business analytic tools to report on KPIs that are standard within an industry. '[The provider] provides us with a lot more reporting on what's going on in these areas than we ever had before. They can tell us things about our process that we never knew before, like how much time to post an invoice, the average time banks are holding onto our money, the percentage of decline to direct debits per country, and so on and so on and so on. They have a whole set of metrics that they sort of bring along as standard', said a client. Another powerful benefit of KPI standardization is the provider's ability to aggregate and disseminate learning across clients. Today, an increasing number of clients are expecting providers to infuse new ideas and innovations based on business analytics of standard KPIs across clients and industries.

In world-class performing accounts, business analytics is increasingly the most critical driver of innovation – once other transformation levers such as labour relocation, centralization and process standardization have been deployed. While business analytics examines past business performance, predictive analytics forecasts the probabilities of possible future outcomes and plans accordingly. Clients in top-performing BPO relationships increasingly rely on the provider's technology-enabled predictive capabilities. In the next chapter, we will explore several cases in detail.

8.5. Workflow tools

World-class performing BPO relationships rely increasingly on technologies that enable better controls and compliance. These operational tools, used by both clients and providers, facilitate complete transparency in the day-to-day operations of the relationship. One of the best examples is the Controller Workspace, a centralized tool used to manage the FAO relationship between Microsoft and Accenture. The tool is a central repository for all data about close and compliance processes that may be accessed by employees located around the globe to get accurate, timely and reliable data. In the record-to-report function, for example, all the tasks needed for daily close are listed, including the person responsible and the current status of each task. Microsoft's finance controllers and staff as well as Accenture's service delivery personnel all have one shared window into the daily operation. In 2011, the tools used in this relationship won the Global Excellence in Outsourcing Award (GEO) for Innovation, sponsored by the IAOP.[7]

One LSO provider developed a proprietary project management tool with a super easy interface for busy lawyers. Lawyers think in terms of legal matters, so generic tools like Microsoft's Project are often ill-suited for legal work. The LSO provider's tool is based on easy-to-use templates that treat legal matters as projects that have milestones, deadlines, roles, responsibilities and results. The tool's dashboard identifies activities that are on track, at risk or running over budget or deadline. The LSO provider also helped create the new project management culture within the law firm, including half-day workshops to teach lawyers how the tool will help them better serve clients.[8]

On another BPO account, the client describes how the provider's workflow tool enabled military precision in the financial close process: 'Closing down at the month-end is a military operation. We have a very, very, very fast financial close process and we need final figures transmitted electronically by the afternoon of the second working day. What they (the provider) brought to the party was a progress-chasing tool that allowed everybody to track the progress of every process on a minute-by-minute basis. So planning our military operation has become so much easier'.

8.6. Governance tools

Governance is the set of activities that are necessary to manage a BPO relationship, including the management of SLAs, performance reporting and billing. Like workflow tools, good governance tools provide a shared view of timely and accurate information. Governance tools also facilitate complete transparency among the senior levels managing the BPO relationship, such as C-suite executives, global, regional and divisional functional leaders, commercial directors and contract managers. Again, one of the best examples is the Governance Workspace – a centralized tool used to manage the FAO relationship between Microsoft and Accenture at the strategic level. In addition to SLAs and performance reporting, the Governance Workspace also incorporates a planning and control tool which helps eliminate unnecessary and unwanted surprises by showing, in real time, the status of service and by providing an efficient reporting tool for SLAs, measurements, transactions and deadlines.

An integrated business intelligence/governance suite helps to escalate the provider's role from operational managers to business advisors. As noted by our colleague Craig Mindrum in the high-performance BPO report[9], the Accenture BPO Navigator – an integration of business intelligence and governance – developed by Accenture, is a central portal that provides real-time visibility into a client's business performance, including operational and contractual metrics and analytics. The tool incorporates performance benchmarking data from multiple BPO relationships, enabling a rich source of information with which to 'navigate' towards higher levels of value. A provider executive describes how the Accenture BPO Navigator operates for his consumer goods client: 'We can look at our retention dashboard by business group, by demographics, by geography and look at where there are retention challenges or how one area of the business differs from another. What does that enable us to do? It enables us to look collectively at company policies that might impact retention. It allows us to detect trends that we can address. But more importantly, it allows us to collectively refine the forecast coming into the recruiting process'.

8.7. Cloud delivery

Cloud-computing will help drive innovations in future generations of BPO. Providers are increasingly working on offering software as a service (SaaS), platform as a service (PaaS), infrastructure as a service (IaaS) and hosted services. Integrating some of these can achieve business process as a service (BPaaS), reflecting the focus on business-specific services.[10] Clients, however, will need to assess the cost–risk–benefit profile of private, public and hybrid options and the capabilities of competing suppliers. Our research also points to client concerns around security and legal risks, contact and relationship challenges, lock-in and management issues.[11] However, it is already clear that cloud-computing can – if managed carefully – be harnessed to business purpose. As one executive told us: 'Cloud computing in its best form lowers the barrier to actually getting the business what they want'.

Updates can be made to the software, and new configurations and capabilities can be implemented through the cloud configuration. On one procurement deal for an electronic design automation client, the provider moved the client's procurement platform to the cloud to lower the client's costs and to speed-up their access to upgrades. The provider explains: 'One of the biggest innovations was moving the client to this on-demand platform. And as a result, they now see regular innovation because, given that it's in the Cloud, updates are made to that software and new configurations and capabilities are implemented through that Cloud configuration. The client would have had to pay a consultant to come in and hardwire their CD version. So that's certainly helping them innovate from a technology standpoint'.

As one example among many of this trend, Australia-based Qantas has moved its massive frequent flyer programme to a cloud-based computing platform in order to keep up with growing demand. Its 22-year-old Fortran-based system has been replaced by an Oracle on Demand service, incorporating a scalable architecture designed to cope with changes in demand. Using Oracle's Siebel Loyalty and On Demand offerings, the system can provide consistent service to more than 7 million members, while also dealing with rapidly growing member activities. Qantas also sees the new platform as providing the opportunity to target loyalty promotions and extend its loyalty programme by introducing new partners – something that would have been difficult with the older system.[12]

8.8. Conclusion

World-class BPO relationships rely on technology enablement. However, based on our research, there are important caveats, insights and guidelines for action.

Beware the cloud-washing, robot-washing and other trend-washing. Many technology charlatans woo customers with promises that their business problems will evaporate with the next generation of technology. We've seen some providers claim that they are 'green', 'cloud' and 'robotic', only to discover that they replaced their light bulbs with LED lighting, virtualized a few servers and installed some advanced features of Microsoft Office. For many clients, the initial unbridled glee for the next-technology magic carpet ride almost always ends with a less than enthusiastic journey. As information technology professors, we understand that technology can greatly improve business performance, but technologies are implemented in organizational contexts that require leadership, change management and complex data migration and integration.

Technology diffusion often takes longer than anticipated. There are reasons for seeing the impacts of cloud, robotics and other new technologies as emerging more slowly and over a much longer-time horizon than many commentators suggest. One is that a technical innovation, or set of technical innovations, typically goes through three phases – invention, commercialization and diffusion. By 2013, cloud, for example, was still dominantly in the commercialization phase, though diffusion of parts of cloud business services, as with many internet-related services such as eBay and Facebook, could be very rapid. A second reason is that diffusion of an innovation rarely takes place at a steady linear rate. Rather research shows that it tends to follow an S-curve, starting quite slowly, needing to demonstrate many attributes and passing through several phases before being widely adopted.[13] Clearly, new technologies will be on a far from frictionless journey towards having substantive impacts on individuals, organizations, sectors and economies.

Additionally, new technology users face a significant learning curve which takes considerable time to climb before the sizable impacts anticipated actually materialize. In our view, there are near-term developments involving a relatively fast take-up of new services, together with supportive technical and contractual advances. Here the cost imperative will dominate, but organizations and providers will mature ·in their ability to manage services and learn better. This will enable them to move to more innovative uses of BPO technologies at the organizational level. We see this learning strand as accelerating over the next 10 years.[14]

Understand the maxim: garbage in, garbage out. The technologies described in this report contain powerful algorithms and striking dashboards, but their value is highly reliant upon the quality of the data they process or express. Data structures, data collection procedures and data reporting procedures must be defined to ensure consistency, accuracy and timeliness – which can be a challenge. 'After transition, the teams were performing well but couldn't report on it yet. We had to get the data reporting protocols locked down, get the reporting structures in place, and have our reports posted consistently on a regular schedule in a format that made sense and was visible and consumable', said a provider delivery manager.

Business Intelligence technologies, in particular, can require complicated extracting, transforming and loading of data from disparate systems. One provider eases the client's data burden by collecting data in a simple spreadsheet that requires about ten key fields to be entered. Clients with standard IT platforms get the most from BPO technologies. For example, Microsoft has a single-instance global ERP system that facilitates process standardization, rollouts and onboarding for new subsidiaries (see Chapter 11 for the detailed Microsoft case study). While it has been identified as a key enabler of shared services, few global firms have achieved this milestone.

Clients must decide upon the customization–standardization trade-off. The provider's proprietary tools are built for deployment across clients. The benefits to the clients are faster access and lower costs compared to building custom tools. The interface to most tools can be customized, but building custom capabilities can be costly. There is clearly a customization–standardization trade-off here.

For instance, one client interviewed was not pleased with the interface tool to the learning system software, although they were pleased with the robust functionality. They wanted the provider to invest in overhauling the interface, which the provider did not find feasible for a single client. Eventually, the parties agreed not to use the proprietary tool but collaborated to find a hosted solution.

The value is in the integrated toolkit, not any individual tool. Many providers have a suite of technologies to manage BPO relationships. While an individual tool may not be an optimal fit for the customer, the entire suite can add real value. One client explained: 'The provider brought in a group of small but effective proprietary tools that they had, but we would never develop, which is the advantage of outsourcing. For example, they had a piece of de-duping software that now resides on our systems and checks for duplications. They also offered us a service in going back before the outsourcing implementation and checking for duplications of vendor invoices – have we paid the same invoice twice? They have another tool that set up a vendor portal, which allowed the supplier to see a picture of his account with us. None of these are fantastically huge systems but there's a whole set of little pragmatic tools that they bring to bear, which has been very useful for us in our aim of going back to the beginning and improving the process'.

It is not so much the tools' capabilities per se that enable world-class BPO performance, but rather the partnership capabilities that precede effective technology deployment and the collaboration that results. Clients and providers have to be willing to share details about who is doing what and to what level of performance. In short, partners must build a collaborative, trusting and transparent relationship in order to apply technologies, industry specific knowledge, business process expertise and client-specific context to drive world-class performance.

---

[1] Conboy, M. (2014), 'I am Robot: Will RPA Revolutionise the BPO Industry?' http://outsourcemagazine. co.uk/i-am-robot-will-rpa-revolutionise-the-bpo-industry/

[2] Fersht and Sutherland, HfS Research White Paper.

[3] http://outsourcemagazine.co.uk/i-am-robot-will-rpa-revolutionise-the-bpo-industry/

[4] http://virtualoperations-us.com/wordpress/wp-content/uploads/2013/02/robotic_automation_-_ what_next_for_bpos.pdf

[5] http://www.globalservicesmedia.com/global-services/analysis/205566/robotistan-a-place-everyone-business-processing-outsourcing-move-2014#sthash.fcB7IMaF.dpuf

[6] http://outsourcemagazine.co.uk/robotic-process-automation-for-utilities/

[7] See IAOP's Global Excellence in Outsourcing 2011 Award Winners: https://www.iaop.org/ Content/19/165/3131

[8] For a detailed case study on use of this tool, see Brown, L. (2012), *Just Enough Project Management for Lawyers*, Elevate Services white paper, http://elevateservices.com/cael/

[9] Mindrum et al., 'Achieving High Performance in BPO'.

[10] A detailed account of these options is provided in Willcocks, L., Venters, W. and Whitley, E. (2011), *Cloud and The Future Of Business 1 – The Promise*, LSE/Accenture, London, see www.outsourcing unit.org

[11] See Willcocks, L., Venters, W. and Whitley, E. (2011), *Cloud and The Future Of Business 2 – The Challenges*, LSE/Accenture, London, see www.outsourcing unit.org

[12] For details of the research, see Willcocks, L., Venters, W. and Whitley, E. (2014), *Moving to the Cloud Corporation: How to Face the Challenges and Harness the Potential of Cloud Computing*, Palgrave Macmillan, Basingstoke, UK.

[13] Rogers, E. M. (2006), *Diffusion of Innovations*, Free Press, New York.

[14] From Willcocks, L., Leslie P. and Venters, W. and Whitley, E. (2013), 'Cloud Sourcing and Innovation: Slow Train Coming?: A Composite Research Study', *Strategic Outsourcing: An International Journal*, 6(2), 184–202. ISSN 1753–8297.

Chapter 9

☞ Key 8: Deploy domain expertise and business analytics

What's Inside: World-class BPO relationships leverage the service provider's domain expertise and business analytics capabilities. The partners deploy algorithms, models and sophisticated statistics on big data to identify weaknesses and opportunities and then redesign processes to deliver measurable business outcomes.

9.1. Introduction

World-class BPO relationships deploy domain expertise and business analytics to improve the client's business performance. We define 'Domain Expertise' as the extent to which a provider has experience with and understanding of the client's business, industry and technical contexts, processes, practices and requirements. From a comprehensive review of all academic research findings, domain expertise was identified as one of the top three provider capabilities along with human resource management and technical/methodological capabilities.[1] However, we have long found – based on our vast case study research – that domain expertise is table stakes. Clients expect any competent provider to have strong domain expertise.[2] This finding is also confirmed in the BPO survey conducted for this research project: domain expertise only weakly distinguished high-performing from normal-performing BPO relationships. But our research uncovers a hidden key to world-class performance: domain expertise is the contextual catalyst for analytics – the real value generator. Without the tacit experiential knowledge feed from domain expertise, analytics correspondingly underperforms.

All research sources identified compellingly that analytics is a powerful discriminator between normal-performing and top-performing BPO relationships. The Everest survey found that 42 per cent of the top BPO performers considered analytics provided by the service provider as an important component of the BPO relationship compared to 28 per cent of the normal-performing BPOs. In high-performing relationships we studied, the provider applied their domain expertise to deploy a rigorous analytics process that measured the right KPIs, deployed tools and techniques to measure and report on KPIs and deployed algorithms, models and sophisticated statistics to identify weaknesses and opportunities and then redesigned processes to deliver measurable business outcomes (see Figure 9.1). As more data was collected and analysed, domain expertise increased.

The iterative domain expertise and analytics processes produced high-performance results in the clients we interviewed, as demonstrated in three case histories (see Table 9.1). The first case is about a national grocery retailer. It collaborated successfully with its BPO provider to implement new forecasting tools, techniques and methods that improved the client's stock fill rate from 80 per cent to 95 per cent, reduced inventory by 27 per cent and reduced error rates by 50 per cent. In the second case, an aerospace manufacturer worked with its BPO provider to add new KPIs and processes to manage third-party vendors. This allowed the client to improve customer-order fill rates

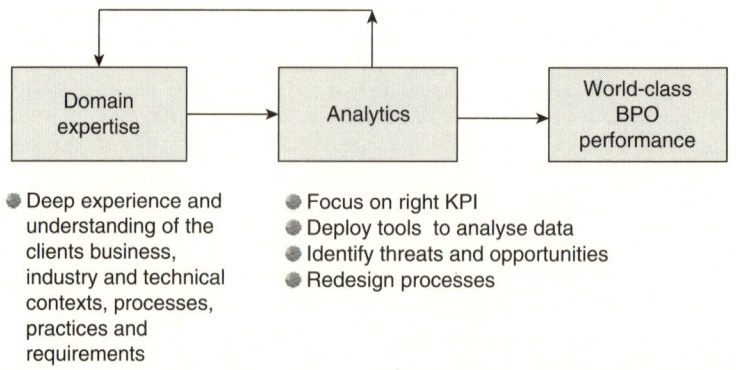

Figure 9.1 Domain expertise, analytics and world-class performance

Table 9.1 BPO case studies of domain expertise and business analytics

Client	Domain expertise	Analytics project	Business outcomes
National grocery retailer	Forecasting product demand	Developed new forecasting tools	Improved the client's stock fill rate from 80% to 95%, reduced inventory by 27% and reduced error rates by 50%
An aerospace manufacturer	Third-party vendor management	Created new KPI	Improve customer order fill rates for new parts from 60% to 85%
Healthcare insurance companies	Claims processing	Created a Rework Prevention Tool	Saving the client $25 to $50 in administrative costs per overpaid claim and $6 to $12 per underpaid claim

for new parts from 60 per cent to 85 per cent and turnaround times for delivering parts to grounded vehicles from 21 hours to 17 hours. The third case discusses how a BPO provider helped several healthcare insurance companies improve the claims adjudication process by using analytics to predict claims likely to result in rework. The predictive tool now intercepts more than 50 per cent of claims that would have been reworked, saving the client from $25 to $50 in administrative costs per overpaid claim and from $6 to $12 per underpaid claim.

9.2. The case of a grocery retailer

A large, national grocery retailer was concerned about replenishment in its retail stores. It wanted to engage a service provider who would focus on continuously improving supply chain performance. While cost was an important consideration in provider selection, the ability to improve performance was the client's main criterion. The client's vice president of replenishment explained: 'Outsourcing was more about service to our customers than about cost reduction. The outsourcing model is obviously woven potentially to save us money, but it wasn't our prime motivation'. The grocery retailer outsourced the replenishment for over $1 billion worth of general merchandise to a provider with proven supply chain expertise and a willingness to expand that expertise to learn about the peculiarities of the client's business model. The vice president of replenishment explained: 'Not every retailer is the same. We're not all cut from the same bolt of cloth. Each one has a specific operating model, we have different strategies, each one is unique for each retailer'.

The provider applied their domain expertise and analytics capabilities to deliver world-class performance. The client and provider first selected the right KPIs that mattered most to the client: stock fill rate and inventory levels. The stock fill rate – defined as the percentage of requested stock filled at the retail store – required focus. The inventory level – the amount of inventory in warehouses and distribution centres – was deemed as too high and tying up precious capital. The provider realized that the client's legacy forecasting tools required improvement as well, being over a year away from a leading practice tool implementation. The provider also built a custom-forecasting tool that used logic to forecast better year-round and seasonal products. The provider also built analytic tools for improved product management. The client and provider used the data to redesign business processes. The vice president of replenishment summarizes the analytics process: 'On the planning side, we work collectively and implemented a new tool that enables planning and allocation of products to stores. They've also extended that into allowing them to do category management and financial planning as well, in terms of forecasting. They have also, in the last 18 months, they have a number of resources on the ground spending time re-engineering and designing new or the right processes to drive the business functions all the way from the initial category strategy to getting the product moving through the supply chain which includes the vendor community through our network and eventually getting to those stores to support the sales plan'.

The provider helped the client increase the distribution centre stock fill rate significantly (beyond industry norms) and improved inventory currency. Processes were also improved, which led to less rework, improved efficiency and adherence to timelines. Client leads outside of general merchandise replenishment are impressed with provider's analytic tools and capabilities, and frequently seek the provider's advice on their replenishment issues. The client also plans to use the provider's analytic tools in other parts of their business. According to the account executive, 'The business clients recognize that we're pretty good at logistics and supply chain in general and because of that trusting relationship, my client has other leads that come to me and need help. They ask 'How are you getting data? How are you dealing with this type of issue? I'm stuck'. Of course, we help them whenever we can'.

9.3. The case of an aircraft engine manufacturer

An aircraft engine manufacturer with spares distribution centres located on four continents was experiencing poor customer-order fill rates. On-time accurate fulfilment is vital because any missing part can result in an aircraft being grounded. The manager of Global Workshare said: 'We could be missing one bolt and not be able to ship an engine out on time'. Lacking sufficient analytic tools and capabilities in-house, the company sought to expand the scope of work with their existing service provider. The provider's strong credentials in inventory planning and replenishment coupled with a credible track record on existing transactional processes gave the client confidence to ask the provider to deploy analytics and manage inventory in their distribution centres to improve customer order fill rates. Because of the existing relationship, the provider already has deep domain expertise about the client's business.

The provider deployed their proprietary scientific service parts management tool to improve inventory modelling and to calculate optimum inventory targets. The provider then standardized processes for measuring and reporting on KPIs and automated some parts ordering processes.

Armed with better data, the provider was able to perform root cause analysis on non-fulfilment of customer orders. As a result of the analytics, the provider discovered that delays were caused by multiple process issues including missing parts and incorrect fulfilment by distribution centres. They analysed parts availability versus order fill rates and provided insight into the gaps. The service provider measured, reported and acted on the new KPI. The provider account executive explains: 'These data points did not exist before. It gave us tremendous insight into root causes associated with low performance. We are now using data and analysis to drive discussions with multiple teams within their organization. Our discussions are extremely constructive and focused on process improvement opportunities. The common objective is to improve end customer experience by fulfilling their demands faster. The client is pleasantly surprised to see the performance improve'.

Performance did indeed improve: The provider helped the client improve the customer order fill rates for new parts from 60 per cent to 85 per cent and the turnaround time for delivering parts to grounded aircraft from 21 hours to 17 hours. According to the manager of Global Workshare, the provider achieved this performance within 8 months. The momentum continues as the partners plan to continuously push the optimization curve to manage the trade-off between fill rates and inventory levels. They are working with buyers to generate supply alerts, using data from sales, forecasting and engineering to better forecast sporadic demand and tweaking replenishment algorithms and rules to adapt to the changing environment.

9.4. The case of reducing healthcare claim errors

The proper payment of healthcare claims is an irascible problem for healthcare insurance companies. In the public sector, the US federal government's Medicare programme provides health insurance to 48 million Americans. Due to its vast size, the overpayment of claims to healthcare providers (doctors, hospitals, clinics) has been nothing short of scandalous. In 2009, for example, the Federal Office of Inspector General found that Medicare was massively overpaying providers, such as paying $17,000 for wound pumps that the healthcare providers bought for $3,600.[3] In the private sector, the cost of claims errors is also quite high. According to one study, a healthcare insurance company with 6 million members spent an estimated $400 million in overpayments per year.[4]

Healthcare insurance companies hire teams of auditors to randomly audit claims, but less than 5 per cent of audits spot an erroneous claim, thus auditors spend 95 per cent of their time examining perfectly valid claims. According to Accenture, nearly one-third of administrative costs in healthcare claims is spent on auditing and fixing errors. What can be done to help reduce overpayments without spending a fortune on more audits?

Mohit Kumar and Rayid Ghani from Accenture Technology Labs used predictive analytics to help solve this problem. They developed a tool called the Rework Prevention Tool.[5] Before explaining the tool, let us first examine the old process (see Figure 9.2). Healthcare service providers send claims into an insurance company's submission system. The claim is automatically validated and priced based on factors such as patient eligibility, authorized services rendered, insurance coverage and contracts with healthcare providers. The payment is finalized and sent to healthcare providers. The claims process, however, is not necessarily over because erroneous payments result in rework. Erroneous claims might be spotted by random audits or by disputes from healthcare providers or patients. According to Kumar and Ghani, 'In our discussions with major insurance companies, we have found that these errors result in loss of revenue of up to $1 billion each year'.

Kumar and Ghani inserted a rework prediction tool in the process to identify claims with high risk factors associated with errors. The researchers had access to millions of claims and first had to tag which claims resulted in rework based on data from auditor quality control, provider dispute and financial recovery systems. Each claim has a vast

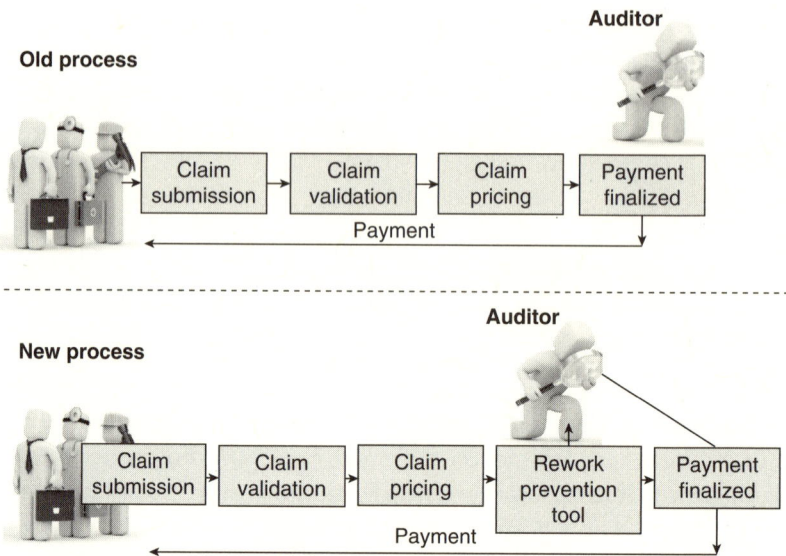

Figure 9.2 Inserting predictive analytics into the healthcare claims process (Source: Adapted from Kumar et al. 2010)

amount of data about the patient, healthcare provider, diagnosis codes, procedure codes, resulting in over 15,000 categorical and numerical features the researchers used to build their models. They developed a metric that predicts the likelihood a claim will result in rework. The rework prediction tool kicks out claims that have a high likelihood of errors and puts them in a work queue for review by human auditors. Furthermore, the tool generates an explanation for auditors so they have some idea why the claim is at risk for errors. The human auditors fix any errors, approve the final payment and provide feedback to the tool for continual machine learning.

The researchers deployed their tool at two US healthcare insurance companies. The predictive tool intercepted over 50 per cent of claims that would have been reworked, saving the clients $25 to $50 in administrative costs per overpaid claim and $6 to $12 per underpaid claim. This aggregates between $15 and $25 million in savings each year for a typical healthcare insurer. That is the power of predictive analytics!

9.5. Conclusion

Our own studies in financial services, resources and hi-tech sectors[6] found that several key actions were needed by the client to harness the provider's domain expertise and analytics: establish standardized metrics and dimensions early; build high-quality technology and data infrastructure, secure senior management support and focus on what one respondent called 'relentless business alignment' through change management and governance. The combined evidence from our BPO research streams enriches this study and the BPO survey findings. The evidence points to three actions for stepping up to world-class performance:

Invite the provider inside the tent. Powerful business analytics reflects the high level of collaboration and teaming between the parties. Service providers need to understand early their client's strategic initiatives. For example, one provider Account Executive said: 'The biggest one is understanding the client's business. Using their business outcomes to create the right delivery model for them. That's the first one. It is absolutely critical to know what their objectives are, advancing objectives I'm talking about. [So the issue is getting access to their]. . . executive level people and using those objectives to create the right delivery model and set performance levels for our team supporting them'.

Build the internal team for transition and evolution. It is vital to have the internal SMEs on board during transition. For example, one bank successfully transferred knowledge and experience to its provider who codified and standardized practices for re-use. The bank incented the SMEs with job redeployment guarantees.[7] However, top-performing BPO clients retain and build expertise and capability, *even when outsourcing.* In one resources company, people within the global reporting and analytics team and the seven core business process teams had extensive technical knowledge about the data warehouse environment and also software tools used for reporting purposes, together with a deep knowledge of the business context. This mix of technical and business knowledge is important when implementing business analytics systems. The balance between business and technical skills was well recognized, and stretches across client and provider. A Process Architect said: 'You need a leadership group for analyzing and viewing the world, and a group of people to translate those business needs into design layout and technical requirements'.

Leverage the provider's proficiency in analytics. Increasingly the market contains providers with the depth and expertise to offer functional, industry specific, enterprise-wide and platform services in analytics. Our combined studies across sectors show that world-class BPO clients are distinguished by their ability to identify and leverage providers' distinctive capabilities. In the effective BPO arrangements we have reviewed, providers help clients move from descriptive analytics – standard and ad hoc reports, drill down, alerts – to predictive analytics – for example, statistical analysis, predictive modelling, forecasting, optimization. These latter direct performance towards competitive advantage, and deliver measurable business outcomes.

---

[1] Lacity, Solomon et al., *Journal of Information Technology*.

[2] Feeny et al., *Sloan Management Review*.

[3] See 'Fleecing Medicare: A Case Study', by Patti Neighmond, at http://www.npr.org/templates/story/story.php?storyId=102128252

[4] Anand, A. and Khots, D. (2008), 'A data mining framework for identifying claim overpayments for the health insurance industry', INFORMS Workshop on Data Mining and Health Informatics, 2008.

[5] This case study is based on material from Kumar, M. and Ghani, R. (2010), 'Online Cost-Sensitive Learning for Efficient Interactive Classification', *Proceedings of the 27th International Conference on Machine Learning*, Haifa Israel Kumar, M., Ghani, R. and Mai, Z. (2010), 'Data Mining to Predict and Prevent Errors in Health Insurance Claims Processing', *KDD'10*, 25–28 July 2010, Washington, DC.

[6] See for example Shanks, G., Bekmamedova, N. and Willcocks, L. (2012), 'Strategic Business Analytics: Enabling Alignment and Organizational Transformation', *Proceedings of the European Conference in IS*, June, Barcelona.

[7] See Oshri, I., Kotlarsky, J. and Willcocks, L. (eds) (2008), *Outsourcing Global Services*, Palgrave, London, Chapter 11 on managing dispersed expertise in offshore outsourcing.

🔑 Key 9: Prioritize and incent innovation

What's Inside: We describe the process world-class BPO relationships use to prioritize, incentivize and deliver innovations to clients. Many examples of innovations that improved the client's operational efficiency, process effectiveness and strategic performance are highlighted. This chapter also covers what innovation practices *don't* work well.

10.1. Introduction

Clients and providers from doing-OK and good-performing BPO relationships frequently have an argument about innovation. At the beginning of a deal, the usual sticking point is how innovation will be funded. Sometimes clients volunteer an innovation fund against which approved client/provider proposals can draw. However, if incarcerated inside a traditional cost-focused contract, such an initiative rarely had the size or priority to divert attention from urgent operational issues. Two or three years into a deal, we found many clients asking their providers, 'Well, the service levels are green, but where's all the innovation you promised?' The truth is that providers are reluctant to spend time and expert resources on an ancillary part of the contract, especially when clients do not work with the provider to achieve the more business impactful innovations beyond minor operational changes. Juxtaposed against these scenarios are the world-class BPO performers that report consistent delivery of innovations to clients. Recall these innovations presented in Chapter 9:

- The supermarket chain that collaborated successfully with its BPO provider to implement new forecasting tools, techniques and methods that improved the client's stock fill rate from 80 per cent to 95 per cent, reduced inventory by 27 per cent and reduced error rates by 50 per cent.

- The BPO provider that helped two healthcare companies improve the claims adjudication process by using analytics to predict claims likely to result in rework. The predictive tool now intercepts more than 50 per cent of claims that would have been reworked, saving the clients $25 to $50 in administrative costs per overpaid claim and $6 to $12 per underpaid claim.
- The aerospace manufacturer that worked with its BPO provider to add new key performance indicators and processes to manage third party vendors. This allowed the client to improve customer order fill rates for new parts from 60 per cent to 85 per cent and turnaround times for delivering parts to grounded vehicles from 21 hours to 17 hours.

How do world-class BPO relationships deliver such impactful innovations? Such results are not automatic outcomes from outsourcing. Specifically, clients must motivate BPO providers with incentives and both parties must nurture a collaborative culture that inspires, funds and injects cycles of innovations in the client organization. The entire process can be termed 'dynamic innovation'. *Dynamic innovation is characterized by continuous, energetic and sustained efforts that improve the client's operational efficiency, process effectiveness and/or strategic performance.* An overview of the dynamic innovation process is given in Figure 10.1. The process describes how world-class BPO relationships incentivize innovation, how they deliver cycles of innovations in the client organization and the effects of these innovations on client performance. We found that innovation is rarely a one-time, big-bang project, rather than multiple innovation projects deliver substantial improvements to the client's performance over time. In one case study, for example, the client and provider have completed 53 continuous improvement projects that delivered bottom line results including cost savings, faster product delivery times and higher fulfilment rates. The effects of innovations accumulate overtime to improve the client's performance in terms of operational efficiency, process effectiveness and/or strategic impact. The entire process is spearheaded by an effective leadership pair (see Chapter 2 for in-depth coverage of leadership pairs).

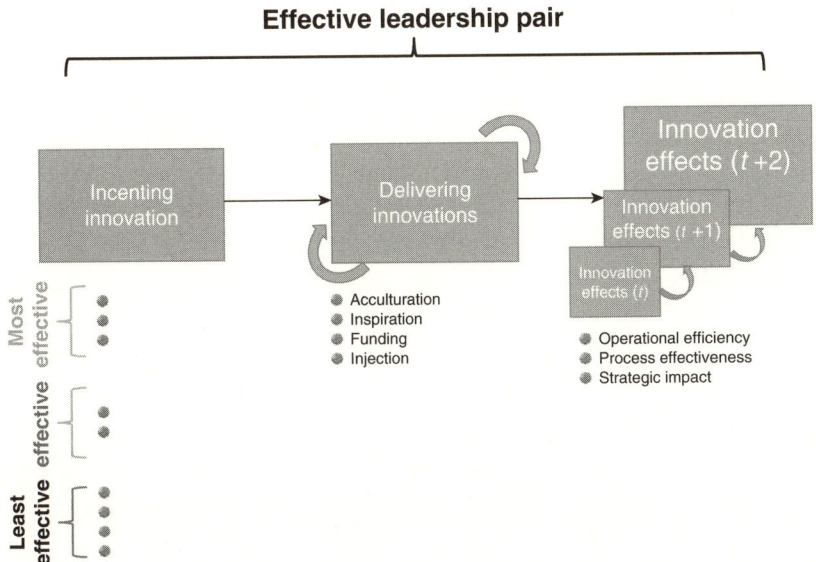

Figure 10.1 The dynamic innovation process: Clients incent providers to deliver many innovations each year that improve the client's performance in terms of operational efficiency, process effectiveness and/or strategic impact. The effects of any one innovation may be small at time t, but the effects of multiple innovations accumulate significantly over time ($t + 1$, $t + 2$, etc.). The entire dynamic innovation process is jump-started and led by an effective leadership pair, representing both client and provider interests

In this chapter, we explain how clients and BPO service providers work together to foster dynamic innovation. We look at sample innovations, incenting and contracting for innovation and how innovations are delivered. We also assess the management implications of our findings.

10.2. Definitions and examples on innovations

Academics often define innovation as an idea, practice or object that is *perceived* as new by an individual or organization.[2] But what do practitioners mean by the term 'innovation' in the context of BPO relationships? In earlier research, we found clients defining innovation as 'doing things differently for the better', and 'realizing there is a different and better way of doing something, and combining this with the ability to deliver'.[3] Based on our recent in-depth interviews with BPO client–provider executive pairs, clients and providers define innovation by their own test: an innovation is any activity that improves the client's performance. Our survey of 202 outsourcing professionals found the same result.[4] The top-ranked definition of innovation by clients, providers and advisors was 'something that improves the customer's services or costs, regardless of its novelty'.

What do innovations comprise? Throughout our interviews and survey, we asked practitioners to provide specific examples of innovations and how those innovations improved client performance. Although dynamic innovation is a sustained process over time, it is still interesting to learn about specific innovations, even in isolation from a more integrative innovation agenda.

In the innovation survey, we asked respondents to briefly describe a successfully implemented innovation. We coded the 85 innovation examples into eight categories (see Figure 10.2). The most common type of innovation was a new tool or technology (35%), such as a new customer tracking tool, asset management tool, e-invoicing tool, optical character recognition tool and migration to the cloud. New or improved processes (16%) were the second most common types of innovation. Respondents described new or improved processes to evaluate salesforce effectiveness, to assess asset value and to train new workers, for example. Thirteen per cent of the innovations were unique, so we categorized these as 'other'. Examples included establishing a centre of excellence and restructuring a back-office. Automation was the fourth largest category, describing 12 per cent of the innovations.

Respondents also pointed to the significant consequences of innovations to the client's improved performance. One respondent described a report delivery innovation that reduced turnaround time from 20 hours to 20 minutes. Another respondent described a workflow automation system that reduced the client's costs by 50 per cent. Another respondent wrote about a paper clearing-house solution the provider

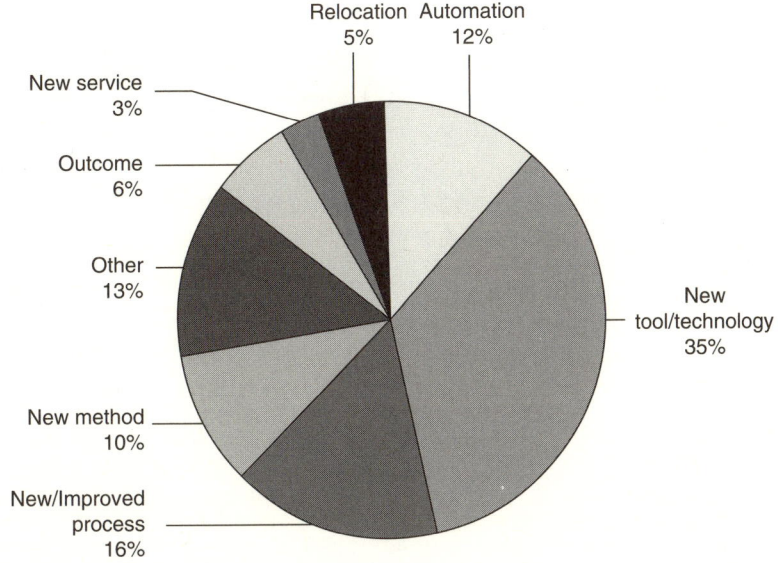

Figure 10.2 Categories of innovations (*n* = 85 innovations)

developed to allow electronic claims that previously could only be submitted via paper submission. The automation reduced costs and improved timeliness of claims submissions.

From the interviews, we collected multiple examples of innovations from each BPO relationship. Unlike the survey, it was difficult to categorize the case study innovations as strictly as technology, process, method or automated innovation. In reality, most innovations are more complex and include a mix of technologies, processes *and* methods as demonstrated in the next example.

One hi-tech manufacturer outsourced the posting of purchase orders to a BPO provider. The provider's tasks included taking and booking customer orders that were then handed over to the client's accountants for processing. It was taking the manufacturer, on average, 20 days to deliver product to their customers. Their competitors delivered within 10 days, a significant competitive advantage. The provider analysed the end-to-end process and determined what each partner needed to improve to reduce delivery time. The provider said: 'I'm only contractually obligated to create the order when I receive it. But we looked at the end-to-end order cycle time, and we crunched that data down. We drove that through. The client's customer satisfaction and the satisfaction from his sales guys were great because revenues increased because the sales guys could walk around and say, "Buy from [names competitor] but it takes ten days and we're at eight"'. This innovation used data analytics and new processes.

In Chapter 8, we described how one procurement provider for an electronic design automation client moved the client's procurement platform to the cloud. Cloud delivery lowered the client's costs and sped their access to upgrades. While one might conclude that this is strictly a *technical* innovation, in reality the *method* for upgrades changed and the *service* changed because the client had to sacrifice customization to realize benefits from the one-to-many cloud-computing platform.

How do these innovations come about? The next section introduces the dynamic innovation process and examines the best and worst ways to incentivize innovation.

10.3. Incenting innovation

As stated previously, innovation is defined by its consequences on the *client's* performance. Clearly, providers need incentives to focus on innovations that improve the client's performance (e.g. client efficiency, effectiveness, strategic impact) rather than to focus on innovations that solely benefit the provider (e.g. increased provider revenue or margin). Incentives can positively reward or negatively punish behaviour. Gain-sharing is a positive incentive that rewards good behaviour with financial compensation. Pain-sharing is a disincentive that punishes bad behaviour with a financial penalty. Both clients and providers in our study identified mandatory productivity targets, innovation days and gain-sharing at the project level as the most effective incentives for innovation. The threat of competition (according to providers) and special governance for innovation (according to clients) were reported to incent innovation effectively. The least effective incentives were innovation funds, benchmarking and gain-sharing/pain-sharing at the relationship level. Let us look at these in more detail.

10.3.1. Yearly productivity improvements

Many BPO relationships are still priced based on resource inputs, such as pricing per full time equivalent (FTE). Clients like the simplicity and predictability of FTE pricing, and they also realize that input-based pricing discourages the provider from implementing innovations that would reduce the number of FTEs because the provider's revenues would decrease. To overcome this disincentive, many BPO clients necessitate innovation by mandating productivity improvement requirements in the contract that require the BPO provider to improve the client's productivity, most typically by 4 to 5 per cent per year. Both clients and providers reported positive results from mandatory productivity targets.

For example, the provider for one consumer goods client implemented a number of innovations, including new dashboards for better reporting and transparency and a new employee referral recruitment programme to attract high-skilled talents like engineers. Pertaining to the new dashboards, which are powered by the provider's analytics, the client said: 'I'd say one of the recent innovations that we began to push for and the provider responded to beautifully was more fact-based analysis, the ability to look at analytics. So, bringing in a lot more analytical rigor. It was not part of the original relationship. They really brought that to the table'. The provider for this client confirmed that the innovation was prompted by the productivity requirement: 'The dashboard is an innovation that we have implemented in the last year at no additional cost to the client. It is a part of our ongoing continuous improvement and stepping up our game in the BPO space'.

10.3.2. Dedicated time to drive the innovation agenda

Innovation objectives can quickly slide down the list of priorities if everyone's attention is focused on operations. In world-class BPO relationships, the partners allocate dedicated time each year to drive the innovation agenda. These clauses are called a number of things, including innovation days, invest days or innovation forums. They work slightly differently on each account, but the essential commonality is collaboratively defining the innovation agenda for the coming year. On some accounts, invest days are essentially free consulting days by the provider's top-gun consultants. In these deals, the only stipulation is that the client and provider have to agree each year how the days will be used for possible mutual benefit.

Innovation forums are typically scheduled quarterly. Clients use the forums to learn more about the provider's latest tools, technologies and capabilities. One provider explains how she works with her consumer products client during the quarterly innovation forum: 'So we have in every major service line what is called an innovation forum at least once a quarter. We bring what we see in the marketplace and the client brings what they are seeing in their marketplace. So we bring, for example, what we see in consumer goods and services space that relates to talent management. The client will bring what their business challenges are and what their internal HR strategy is. We'll look at this, combine it together, and figure what our continuous improvement agenda needs to be collectively over the next quarter'.

10.3.3. Gain-sharing at the project level

In the innovation survey, we asked respondents about the best options for designing innovation into outsourcing contracts. Respondents could tick multiple options from a choice of innovation funds, invest days, special governance for innovation or gain-sharing on innovation benefits. By far, across all three communities (clients, providers and advisors), gain-sharing was identified as the best way to design innovation into the deal. Specifically, 79 per cent of customers, 77 per cent of providers and 78 per cent of advisors indicated that gain-sharing on innovation benefits was the best way to contract for innovation. Among all the ways to incent innovation, gain-sharing packs the most punch because it promises to increase the provider's revenue as well as the client's performance.

Despite the fact that gain-sharing was the top-ranked response in the innovation survey, clients indicated in a follow-up question that only 40 per cent of innovations delivered used gain-sharing. On the one hand, our case study research also found fewer than half the clients contracting for gain-sharing clauses, or even when gain-sharing was included in the contract, only half of these clients availed the gain-sharing option. On the other hand, some clients reported that gain-sharing was prompting powerful innovations on their accounts. These mixed results are best explained by looking at the unit of analysis. Gain-sharing was most effective at the project level and least effective at the relationship level.

At the project level, the client and provider negotiate the gain-share for one project at a time. The levels of uncertainty are much lower at the project level than at the relationship level. Thus, partners can better estimate savings to be shared for innovation projects. One of the best examples of gain-sharing comes from the Microsoft case study (see Chapter 11). Microsoft has a global BPO contract for financial and accounting services with Accenture. The partners avoid the battles gain-sharing usually triggers by agreeing to the gain-share in advance, project by project. Specifically, the partners agree upfront how much Microsoft's bill will be reduced. Accenture is guaranteed a share of that savings, and if Accenture can outperform, it pockets the difference. If Accenture underperforms, it absorbs the loss.

10.3.4. The threat of competition

In the absence of contractual incentives, several providers in our study still felt highly pressured to deliver innovations to clients because of the ubiquitous threat of competition. For example, one provider said: 'There is nothing in our contract that says we have to innovate at all. In my mind, if we don't innovate, at the time of contract renewal, the client will take this business somewhere else if we can't prove that we are delivering value beyond transactions'.

On another BPO account, the provider sees innovations as a way to differentiate their services in a highly competitive market: 'I think it is part of the valued added that we bring. We are constantly challenging ourselves to step up our game to improve all the time and adding value to the client's business. In doing so, we are also creating some offerings within our BPO space that are very different than conventional BPO'.

10.3.5. Special governance for innovation

Large BPO relationships are governed typically by operating committees focused on day-to-day operations, management committees focused on monthly invoices and service-level reports and steering committees comprised of the senior most executives, but who only meet annually (unless there is an escalated dispute). Sixty per cent of the clients responding to our innovation survey indicated that innovation needs special governance outside the jurisdiction of these existing committees. However, only 42 per cent of providers agreed. From our interviews, we found that the people selected to lead are more important than the structures erected to govern (see Chapter 2).

10.3.6. Innovation fund

An innovation fund is a separate account set aside to fund future innovation projects. On our survey, innovation funds were recommended by 38 per cent of clients, 30 per cent of providers and 33 per cent of advisors. Research suggests that these lower percentages may be due to the fact that such funds are often too small to excite and motivate parties.[5]

10.3.7. Benchmarking

Some respondents on the innovation survey suggested that benchmarks incent innovation. Third-party benchmarking of best-in-breed prices and service levels are intended to incent providers to increase performance in step with competitors. While many interviewees said their companies do external benchmarking to gather market data, none supported the idea that benchmarking is an effective mechanism to incent innovation. In reality, we learned, external benchmarks often triggered more disputes than innovations. For example, when an external benchmark found that the provider's unit price was well above best-in-breed price, the client wanted the price reduced. The provider claimed the comparison was unfair because the provider was maintaining the client's old technology; newer technology – the provider argued – would be more efficient and thus have a lower price.

10.3.8. Gain-sharing/pain-sharing at the relationship level

Gain-sharing at the relationship level establishes targets for the overall performance of the relationship, usually assessed yearly. Clients and providers reported many problems with this gain-sharing mechanism. Some clients think gain-share targets are too low. One energy client provides an example. His contract provides a gain-share if the provider exceeds targets and a pain-share if he misses targets. Every year, the provider exceeds the targets and earns a gain. On the one hand, this energy client is delighted with the provider's performance. On the other hand, he suspects the initial targets were too low. He said: 'The standards were a bit one-sided and not difficult to meet. It ensured that each year there was a good bit of gain, and the gain went to the provider. We lose the notion of pain/gain. You should be truly delivering something fairly extraordinary to benefit from gain-sharing. That wasn't necessarily the case'.

Some clients and providers could not agree on a baseline performance measure, resulting in the parties abandoning the notion of gain-sharing even though it was designed into the deal. For example, one tele-communications client and BPO provider hoped to use gain-sharing to prompt innovations in new hire training, but they had no good way to measure the baseline. The provider explained: 'In one of our contracts, we actually agreed to put incentive based mechanism in place, and we contracted for that. However, once we got into the contract we found that the baseline was not really measurable so that was never imple-mented. But certainly, the intent was there. So we could never agree to what baseline was so we could never demonstrate that we moved away from that baseline. It was quite disappointing for everybody'.

10.4. Delivering innovation

Partners may negotiate innovation clauses into the contract, but inno-vation typically does not occur at first. In fact, the most typical pattern we found – even in ultimately world-class relationships – is that client performance got worse during the transition phase, then performance stabilized, then performance significantly improved as the effects of the provider's first transformation levers – labour arbitrage, centrali-zation and standardization – took effect. The challenge – and what differentiated world-class performance from normal-performing rela-tionships – was sustaining the innovation agenda over time. From the survey and interviews, we sought to better understand how cultures nurture innovation, which parties come up with the ideas for innovation, how are innovations funded and how are they delivered.

While partners may incent innovation by including productivity targets, allocating innovation days and agreeing to gain-share on innovation projects, innovation still won't happen unless both clients and providers implement a process which we have described as AIFI:

- **A**cculturating (across parties at all levels),
- **I**nspiring (joint, provider and client-generated ideas),
- **F**unding (in general proposers fund innovations) and
- **I**njecting (strong change management to transition individuals, teams and organizational units from the present to future state).

10.4.1. Acculturation

Academic research on BPO relationships has generally found that cultural distance, defined as the extent to which the members of two distinct groups (such as client and provider organizations) differ on one or more cultural dimensions, negatively affected outsourcing outcomes.[6] This was particularly relevant in the cases of offshore outsourcing. In general, research found that clients find it easier to work with providers that share a similar culture. However, cultural distance can be overcome with a capability called Cultural Distance Management, the ability of client and provider organizations to understand, to accept and to adapt to cultural differences.

Acculturation explains the process by which two or more cultures merge to form a cohesive culture. Merged cultures often end up borrowing aspects of both the client's and provider's cultures. In several BPO relationships we studied, the partners went so far as to brand the provider's delivery centres with the client's company colours, logos and office layouts. For their part, clients recognized the special holidays and festivals in the provider's culture.

In the context of dynamic innovation, a culture that encourages and welcomes innovation ideas is crucial. In world-class BPO relationships, client executives actively encourage all levels in the provider organization to challenge the status quo, to question assumptions, in short, to find innovations that will improve the client's performance. One top-performing BPO relationship between an energy company and a global provider serves as an example. The client and the remotely located provider employees have monthly meetings to encourage and financially reward continuous improvement and innovation. This client leader has also transformed the behaviour of the remotely located provider employees by encouraging them to challenge the client more: 'We absolutely encourage – and I've done this face-to-face sitting there in India – to challenge us. We know we are complex, we know that we create some of our own problems; we are our own worst enemies in some areas. We absolutely want you to point some of those things out and point out some ideas'.

Cultural issues are not restricted to just two organizations (the client's and provider's). Within companies, subcultures exist. The client's centralized business services organization that 'owns' the BPO relationship and the client's decentralized business units that receive BPO services may have different cultures. Typically, the client's centralized business services organization values tight cost controls, high productivity and process standardization. The client's decentralized user communities are bothered by controls, procedures and standards; instead they often value responsive, flexible and custom services. The provider's centralized organization that sells BPO services and allocates resources to accounts and the provider's globally dispersed service delivery centres in places like India, China, the Philippines and Brazil likely have different cultures. The provider's centralized culture will likely value aggressive growth and profitability. The provider's globally dispersed delivery teams want to please both their supervisors and customers, which can leave them caught between conflicting cultures.

The BPO leadership pair is tasked with acculturation, the process by which two or more cultures merge to form a cohesive culture. In the context of dynamic innovation, the resulting culture must be transparent so that even remotely located provider employees understand how their work contributes to the client's performance. One provider explained: 'When someone is sitting in a place miles away, it is really important for that person to understand the impact of what he or she is doing to the client organization. As soon as you are able, get that culture in offshore delivery locations, or even onshore delivery locations, so they can relate to what kind of impact they are bringing to the client. I think it makes a huge difference in performance'.

The culture must also encourage, welcome and reward innovation ideas.

10.4.2. Inspiration: Generating innovation ideas

One question we sought to answer is: 'Which stakeholder is the primary source for innovation ideas?' Anecdotally, clients seemed to claim clients generated most of the innovation ideas and providers seemed to claim providers generated most of the innovation ideas. Consider what this pharmaceutical client said: 'Although the SLAs are green, we feel the providers haven't brought enough innovation to the table for us. I don't think any of the continuous improvement ideas have necessarily been driven by the providers, most of them have been client driven'. Another client from an aircraft engine manufacturer allocated the credit for innovation ideas as follows: 'I'd say it's probably 70 percent from our side and 20 percent from the provider side and remainder 10 percent is jointly'.

To get a more representative answer, we asked respondents of the innovation survey to identify which stakeholders were the primary sources for innovation ideas (see Figure 10.3). Overall, 189 clients, providers and advisors responded to this question. They agreed that the majority of innovation ideas either jointly were created between clients and providers (37%) or providers created innovation ideas on their own (35%).

Jointly developed innovation ideas. As the survey indicates, many innovations are collaboratively identified, most frequently during the execution of innovation days, invest days or innovation forums. For example, at one bank the partners create a jointly developed innovation plan every year. The provider explained: 'Between ourselves and the client, we ask: 'What additional value in innovation can we bring in any given year?' We have our basic operational plan for any given year. What sits on top of that is that is an innovation plan that we try to focus on at least four to six key value innovations in any given year'. The provider delivered training more efficiently and effectively to the client by moving 40 per cent of the training courses online, including mobile learning

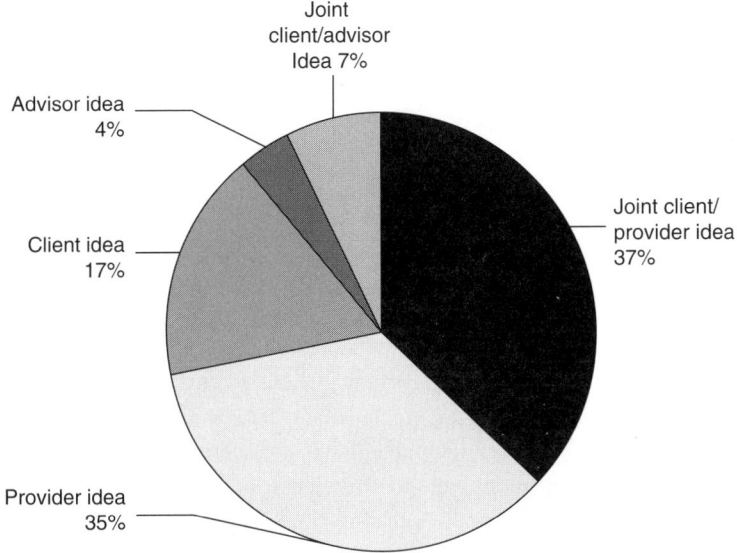

Figure 10.3 The primary source of innovation ideas (*n* = 189 respondents)

capabilities through smartphones. The innovations are not separately funded but rather part of the overall base contract.

Provider-driven innovation ideas. In the innovation survey, providers were credited as the primary source of innovation by 35 per cent of respondents. Providers are well poised to propose innovations – if incented to do so – because of their breadth and depth of expertise. Concerning breath of BPO expertise, providers are able to generate innovation ideas because BPO is core to the provider's business but non-core to their client's business. In contrast to clients, providers focus intensely on BPO, execute services frequently, cross-fertilize ideas across a global client network and spot BPO trends quickly. Providers also have deep insight into the client's data and processes, which afford them a vantage for identifying innovations that can really impact the client's business value.

The evidence for the provider-driven innovation is most convincing when presented by BPO clients. For example, one electronic design automation client was quite pleased with his procurement provider's ability to innovate based on their expertise. Of the provider account delivery manager, he said: 'He's constantly thinking about procurement savings, category expertise, supply chain management and so on. That's what you get by having someone focus on one area specifically'. This client also said that providers can attract and retain top talent better than a client's in-house function.

10.4.3. Funding innovation

On the innovation survey, respondents were asked to indicate who funded the innovation project. In alignment with the primary source for innovation ideas, 45 per cent of innovations were jointly funded, 34 per cent were provider funded and 20 per cent were client funded. We mapped funding responses to the source of the idea responses (see Table 10.1) and found that, in general, the stakeholder(s) who propose innovations help fund innovations. People may be only incented to pitch innovation ideas if they themselves would benefit and thus would are willing to finance the innovation project in whole or in part.

10.4.4. Injection – Change management

Clients from world-class BPO relationships understand that they cannot be passive recipients of innovations, but clients must aggressively manage the changes the innovations bring to their organizations. In other words, provider incentives lay the foundation for dynamic

Table 10.1 Source of innovation ideas and funding

	Provider's idea	Client's idea	Joint provider/ client idea	Total
Provider-funded	35	4	16	55 (36%)
Client-funded	13	12	5	30 (20%)
Jointly funded	14	14	39	67 (44%)
Total	62 (41%)	30 (20%)	60 (39%)	152 (100%)

innovation, but the execution of dynamic innovation requires strong change management to transition individuals, teams and organizational units from the current state to the desired future state. Change management is so important that it was identified as part of the nine key practices for delivering world-class BPO (see Chapter 4).

Innovations have to be accepted by two groups of clients – the client leads responsible for the BPO relationship and the cadre of globally dispersed end-users. Sometimes, it's the client leads that kill an innovation idea because they lack the energy or resources to lead the change management effort an innovation idea requires. For example, one hi-tech client relayed this story: 'For some of the provider's ideas they've made aware to us and we've gone, 'yeah, thanks for telling us but actually we don't care to do it'. They say, 'We can make you more efficient in this area if you do so and so and so and so'. And we said, 'yeah, but we're not prepared to do so and so and so and so, so we'll have to stay inefficient'.

Similarly, another telecommunications client leader has not been very proactive on innovation. According to the provider on this account: 'Over the years, we run an annual innovation day where we bring people in from overseas and we showcase the latest products and things like that that we have. Over the last five years, the take-up of the innovation has been a little bit underwhelming'.

The risk, of course, is that the providers will stop investing their time and resources in identifying innovations if clients continually reject ideas. If the client leaders are excited about an innovation and if those leaders are respected within their own organizations, then they are usually successful in their change management efforts. One hi-tech provider on a top-performing BPO relationship said of his client lead: 'He knows the business very well. He knows how relationships work and he's very politically savvy. So I think it's very important your relationship person is respected within the client organization, has weight with them and is a very strong political operator'. This client lead said that effective change management needs to be driven from the board, but that a powerful leader has to be in-charge of operations. He recounted: 'You need quite senior and experienced managers driving it who could make rapid decisions when needed and who could bulldoze obstacles out of the way when required. So I think it really does need board level, that's clear, but you need somebody with a bit of clout actually actively involved in running the thing to make it happen'.

10.5. Conclusion

World-class BPO relationships are good at sustaining innovation, but many other BPO relationships still need to work on incenting, contracting for and delivering dynamic innovation. Here are some management guidelines for action based on our research:

It is never too late to innovate. We found several top performers – for example, Microsoft – introducing gain-sharing mechanisms after the BPO relationships stabilized. One aircraft engine manufacturer client on the road to high performance, just recently adding gain-sharing to incent innovation beyond the productivity improvement requirement: 'The provider is bound to demonstrate productivity gains year over year under the contract terms. But there is no incentive for the provider to go beyond that. So what we did was incent through gain-sharing model anything that went beyond the required percent of productivity gained. It's not only the provider, we made it a joint productivity gain initiative so there is also reward and recognition for our own people when we go beyond the threshold'.

On another account, the contractual clauses stayed dormant for several years until a new client executive took over the account. Before his arrival, the client never used the hundred plus days devoted to innovation in the contract. Under the new leadership, the partners used 50 per cent of the invest days his first year in-charge and 100 per cent of the invest days the second year. The client reported positive benefits.

Innovations escalate along a novelty curve. We have already discussed that dynamic innovation entails continuous, energetic and sustained efforts that improve the client's performance over time. We also found that on many accounts, the novelty of individual innovation increases over time. At the beginning of a BPO relationship, the more experienced providers frequently brought best-in-bred innovations in technology, tools, processes and methods to their less-experienced clients. But as BPO relationships matured, the client had already absorbed the best-in-class innovations available from the provider. The next round of innovations, therefore, required more novelty. The provider for an electronic design automation client explained: 'Early on, what we brought to the client was, "Well, here's best-in-class, here's where you are, let's close that gap". That's really what drove a lot of the innovation. I think we've exhausted a lot of those opportunities. Now, given that they've reached best-in-class, for them to be innovative, they've got to do something that's maybe a little bit out there. And so we're in the middle of working on some exciting things there'. As with anything more novel, the partners have to address risk-sharing and intellectual property ownership.

Time for an innovation mind-set. Effective innovators incentivize innovation and recognize that creating incentives can only take you so far. Delivering innovations requires a process we call AIFI. It has been frequently remarked that 'If you always do what you always did, you will always get what you always got'. To achieve step-change improvements, organizations need to break the strong forces of habit and administration in their outsourcing arrangements, and mandate innovation. The outsourcing industry increasingly cannot ignore the innovation potential and value buried in and passed up by its more traditional modes of operation. The practices we document in this chapter add up to no less than a mind-set and behaviour change for all parties determined to meet the dynamic innovation challenge.

---

[1]   An academic version of this paper was published in Lacity, M. and Willcocks, L. (2014), 'Business Process Outsourcing and Dynamic Innovation', *Strategic Outsourcing: An International Journal*, 7(1), 66–92. Sections reprinted with permission from Emerald Publishing. A shorter executive version of this paper was first published in Lacity and Willcocks, *Sloan Management Review*.

[2]   Rogers, *Diffusion of Innovations*.

[3]   See: Willcocks, L., Cullen, S. and Craig, A. (2011), *The Outsourcing Enterprise*, Palgrave, London.

[4]   Lacity, M. and Rottman, J. (2012), 'Delivering Innovation in Outsourcing: Findings from the 2012 Outsourcing World Summit', *Globalization Today*, March, 26–31.

[5]   Source: Weeks, M. and Feeny, D. (2008), 'Outsourcing from Cost Management to Innovation and Business Value', *California Management Review*, 50(4), 127–146.

[6]   Lacity, Solomon et al., *Journal of Information Technology*.

Chapter 11

⌕ Microsoft case study: Engaging a BPO provider to help create OneFinance

What's Inside: The Microsoft–Accenture BPO relationship for financial, accounting and procurement services stands out as a world-class BPO performer. This chapter presents clear evidence that the BPO partners use all nine of the practices associated with world-class performance. As of 2014, the relationship's exceptional leadership pair has been in place since the deal was first launched in 2007.

11.1. Introduction

> What makes this relationship work so well? We're in this together. We've been able to build that trust together. We enjoy doing things together. – Microsoft Senior Director

Microsoft was co-founded by Bill Gates and Paul Allen in 1975 when they developed a BASIC interpreter for Altair's microcomputer. Today, Microsoft is a US-based multinational corporation that develops, manufactures, licenses, supports and sells computer software, consumer electronics and personal computers and services. With 2013 revenues of nearly $78 billion and with over 100,000 employees, it is the world's largest software company.

In 2006, Microsoft was achieving extraordinary growth by allowing a high degree of autonomy for its subsidiaries. But autonomy also resulted in high fragmentation of the company's finance, accounting and procurement functions. Microsoft sought to standardize these processes globally with aims to reduce costs, improve service and compliance and

Table 11.1 Microsoft's BPO relationship

BPO type	Financial, accounting and procurement services
Initial contract date	2007
Outsourcing driver	Used outsourcing relationship to help create global shared services
Provider	Accenture
Number of provider FTEs on this account	450
Outsourcing outcomes	Significant cost savings, better use of in-house staff, yearly productivity improvements and delivery of new innovations

focus internal roles on more strategic activities. Microsoft launched its global shared services initiative called 'OneFinance'. It looked for a global BPO provider that was large enough to help create and run OneFinance.

Microsoft partnered with Accenture in 2007. The initial 7-year agreement spanned 90 countries and 450 individual roles (see Table 11.1). Within 18 months, the partnership designed and implemented a global set of standardized processes across 92 countries, improved internal controls and compliance, improved scalability and reduced costs by 35 per cent. In 2009, the partnership was extended to include more accounts payable and buy centre processes. The contract was worth $330 million in 2012 and was extended until 2018. Five years into the BPO relationship, the partners continue to innovate Microsoft's financial, accounting and procurement processes. In 2010–2011, for example, the partners moved 25 international subsidiaries from manual invoicing to electronic invoicing. The partners implemented new tools that increased transparency by allowing Microsoft's business users to see every dollar spent and timely measures on performance. New transformation projects are planned and delivered each year. During all this time, there has been a steady set of leaders managing the Microsoft–

Accenture relationship, which is key for sustaining high performance in this relationship.

The Microsoft–Accenture relationship is clearly a world-class BPO performer. The Microsoft executives in-charge of the Accenture relationship rated Accenture's performance 9 on a 10-point scale, with 1 indicating 'pitiful performance', 5 indicating 'meets expectations' and 10 indicating 'exceeds expectations'. In addition to the initial cost savings of 35 per cent, a number of other business benefits have been achieved, including better use of in-house staff, yearly productivity improvements and delivery of new innovations. Prior to the partnership, 75 per cent of the controllers' time and resources were spent on transactional activities and compliance, which dropped to 23 per cent after outsourcing. The partnership has delivered an additional 20 per cent in cost savings by streamlining, simplifying and/or automating key procurement and accounts payable processes.[1]

The Microsoft–Accenture BPO partnership has not just created, but it is also achieving that rare thing *sustained* world-class performance. Nine keys founded this success. However, we believe that the transformational leadership pair is the most potent among the nine key practices.

11.2. Key 1: Assign a great leadership pair

The leaders from Microsoft and Accenture created the vision of a world-class finance organization, aligned incentives between client and provider organizations, motivated and inspired and empowered the people in their chains of command and delivered more impressively – *continue to deliver*– world-class performance. The leadership pair displays all the characteristics of effectiveness. Each leader focuses on where the outsourcing relationship should go, not where the relationship was in the past or is in the present. For example, the Accenture lead said: '[the client lead] and I are both forward thinking in the way we do things'.

Each leader is transparent by being open and honest about all operational issues with his counterpart. The Accenture lead said: 'We're very transparent about what my client's objectives are or what he wants to do for the year. His success is based on my ability to execute them'. The leaders did not speak poorly about the other party. They admitted that they frequently disagreed, but they resolved these issues behind closed doors and presented a united front to their respective organizations. Each leader has high levels of credibility, clout and power within his own organization. It was clear that each leader enjoys working with his counterpart. The Microsoft lead said: 'We've been able to build that trust together. We enjoy doing things together. I enjoy doing things with my counterpart at Accenture'.

The individual leaders at both Microsoft and Accenture have been devoted to this partnership since the beginning. The stability in the senior leadership for Microsoft and Accenture has clearly contributed to sustaining world-class performance. This is not what we usually find in long-term agreements where client and provider account managers turn over every few years.

⌒⟓ 11.3. Key 2: Focus on business and strategic benefits beyond cost efficiencies

At Microsoft, the main objective of the outsourcing decision was to create a world-class financial organization. If processes were redesigned, standardized globally and technology-enabled, services would improve, compliance would increase and employees could focus on more strategic activities. Of course, cost savings were expected and included in the business case, but the main objective was a best-in-class, global financial organization.

Given these business objectives, Microsoft knew that they needed to find an outsourcing partner – not a vendor – to help transform financial, accounting and procurement services. Microsoft's Senior Director of Financial Operations described how clients who focus only on price are buying commodities, not differentiated services. He explains: 'A lot of companies buy outsourcing services like they are buying consumables. If you treat your vendor like that, I mean a vendor that you don't have a long-term relationship with, you can basically switch the vendor every day if you choose to in your purchasing. Price is probably the only real thing that you think about'.

In contrast to buying a commodity service based solely on price, Microsoft looked for a partner that could transform processes on a global scale. Microsoft selected Accenture because they had the best domain expertise, the most secure transition method and the global scale to service 90 or more counties.

⌕⤳ 11.4. Key 3: Drive strong transition, transformational and change management capabilities

Microsoft and Accenture created a dedicated transition and change management programme to ensure that their 230 'go live' events were successful. A combined team from Microsoft and Accenture created global, functional and subsidiary-specific communication plans to engage with the various impacted audiences. Each transition event had five major milestones, starting with a country-level launch event and ending with a formal hands-off to operations. Communication was critical. Microsoft held two-day, face-to-face meetings with subsidiary controllers to educate key stakeholders:[2]

> At the two-day Controller Connection session, we introduced the Microsoft financial controllers to the new operating model for finance. We collectively made sure people bought into the change. That made a big difference – Anoop Sagoo, senior executive, Accenture.[3]

Local leaders were assigned the responsibility for client readiness, signalling to the subsidiary that change was 'close to home'.[4] Assigning subsidiary leaders to the transition team gave subsidiaries confidence that 'one of their own' from the region was providing input and direction to the solution, rather than someone from corporate. Sagoo added: 'Microsoft committed their best people to make the outsourcing program a success. They put in as many hours as we did to get this right'.[5]

⚿ 11.5. Key 4: Adopt a partnering approach to governance

Microsoft and Accenture approach BPO governance with partnering attitudes, mirrored governance structures and end-to-end governance of Microsoft's KPIs.

Partnering Attitudes. The Microsoft executives in-charge of the BPO relationship indeed view Accenture as their strategic partner. The top Microsoft executives use a marriage metaphor to describe their relationship with Accenture: 'We are married' says Microsoft's Senior Director of Financial Operations. This metaphor is behind their mantra about working 'TOGETHER':

> TOGETHER is capitalized, and its meaning is exactly what you would find in the English dictionary. It's not different. The reason why it is capitalized is that you want to enforce the theme or the basic principle that we have to work TOGETHER. – Srini Krishna, Director of Global Vendor Management, Microsoft Finance Operations

Mirrored Governance Structure. Microsoft and Accenture set up a mirrored governance structure, meaning that everyone has a counterpart in the other organization. The mirrored structure facilitates effective communication and conflict resolution at the lowest possible levels. Microsoft's Senior Director of Financial Operations said: 'At the start of this contract, we built a mirrored governance organization. I am mirrored by the Outsourcing Account Delivery Manager within Accenture. Each of my global process owners, I have one for each of the three streams [Accounts Payable, Buy Center and Record] has a counterpart in Accenture. They all feel that they have a counterpart inside the other organization and together they own the delivery'. Because governance was so critical to success, Microsoft pays Accenture a fee to cover governance costs.

In world-class relationships we studied, client executives actively diffuse and reinforce effectively the partnership attitude throughout the client organization. When client employees lapse into complaining and blaming the provider, the client executives from world-class relationships buttressed the partnership view. This practice was certainly evident at Microsoft:

> I get frustrated when we don't think about the concept of working TOGETHER with Accenture. 'There is a saying that if you point your index finger at someone, then the rest of your fingers actually point at yourself'. That's why I think the concept of TOGETHER is so important. It drives a lot of the success that we have. – Senior Director of Financial Operations, Microsoft

From SLAs to End-to-End Governance. In our case study research, we found that excellence in service-level delivery is a characteristic of world-class BPO relationships. But partners in relationships that *sustain* world-class performance over the long term do not stop there; 'Green' indicators on service-level performance reports are not the end-game. In world-class BPO relationships like Microsoft, the provider doesn't just care that its services levels are 'green', but that it is driving the right behaviours that matter most to business clients.

At Microsoft, Accenture has done an exceptional job at meeting SLAs. There are about 25,000 SLA points annually and Accenture's pass rate is about 98.5 per cent:

> Are they meeting our SLAs? Well, they do. They are meeting them by a fantastic margin. When you start to look at the size and scale and so on of the operation then the SLA performance is truly exemplary. – Director of Global Vendor Management, Microsoft Finance Operations

The Microsoft–Accenture team is not content with merely meeting SLAs but instead continues to re-examine the SLAs. Microsoft cares more about Accenture *resolving* their service requests and issues than meeting an SLA to answer phones or respond to emails in a given time period. The partners are refining that SLA:

> Accenture has a responsibility to deliver to its contractual obligations, that is meeting SLAs (being efficient). However we also put emphasis on making sure we drive the right end-to-end results,

making things better for the client being effective. – Outsourcing Account Delivery Manager, Accenture

As the Microsoft–Accenture relationship matures, the partners increasingly focus on the end-to-end service metrics rather than just spotlighting that Accenture's SLAs within the end-to-end process are 'green' or not. For example, the partners aim to hit an end-to-end metric of 95 per cent of the journal entries on Microsoft's balance sheet being less than 3 months old. They now report the end-to-end metric to the Financial Controllers, not just the embedded SLA. Microsoft's Senior Director of Financial Operations explains: 'You could go to a Financial Controller in a country and show them a sea of green in SLAs while the process was actually pretty poorly performing. Now combining those SLAs and end-to-end metrics we can show that the end-to-end is working fine or not working fine, and the Accenture piece inside of that is performing well or not performing well. We put the spotlight on Microsoft also to make sure we drive the best outcomes for the company. Of course Accenture works TOGETHER with us to do this'.

11.6. Key 5: Align the retained organization, outsourced processes and provider staff

Global BPO deals are serviced by the provider's remote delivery teams located all over the world. Our research has found that providers need clients to acknowledge and reward the provider's staff so they feel connected to their clients. In world-class BPO relationships like Microsoft, the client's leaders personally visit remote provider employees at least once a year and frequently acknowledge and reward good work. The bottom line results are reduced turnover in offshore locations and provider employees who feel empowered to positively challenge the status quo. Accenture certainly values the way Microsoft acknowledges their staff:

The client recognizes that I fundamentally need to be successful in terms of creating an environment where my people can drive performance of my team. We collaborate to foster a positive working environment i.e., where Microsoft and Accenture focus on affirming and rewarding desire behaviours. A very simple example: whenever my client writes one email to one of my operators in Chennai to say he's done a fantastic job and sends it to the whole operation, it makes him feel better, makes him feel proud of himself. The people motivation dimension is important but other companies seem to forget about it just because it's an outsourced environment. But to me, we are still a people business and motivating people is still key. Microsoft actively supports us in our people recognition. – Outsourcing Account Delivery Manager, Accenture

11.7. Key 6: Resolve issues together and conflicts fairly

At Microsoft, the Senior Director for Financial Operations actually claimed that Microsoft and Accenture have never had a significant conflict. He said: 'I'm not sure that we've had a significant conflict. We've always kind of sat down and found a common ground or common financial outcome. Obviously, there are times when I said, "Enough is enough. This is as far as I go". I explained why I think it is fair why I won't go any further. I never had Accenture coming back and saying, "No way" on that. So, I don't think we've had a major conflict!'

Do the partners argue? Of course, particularly when a change has significant commercial implications. When record processes were added to the scope, the transaction-based pricing did not fit the record context well. After back-and-forth debates, the partners agreed that they had to find a common sense solution rather than rely on the letter of the contract. The parties split a settlement. What they learned going forward was that the contract model does not produce a 'fact' but instead produces a starting point for a conversation. They agreed that the top two leaders from each side would meet quarterly for 2 days away from the office. The idea is to vet issues before they escalate to the formal 20-person governance meetings. One of those executives said: 'So every quarter, the three or four of us go spend two days together, work through all these things and ensure that nothing ever comes to the boil'.

⚷ 11.8. Key 7: Use technology as enabler and accelerator of performance

Technology is clearly an important factor enabling the success of the Microsoft–Accenture relationship as evidenced by our interviews and by their 2011 GEO for Innovation. That award specifically mentions two technology innovations: The Controller Workspace and The Governance Workspace. Given that Microsoft is one of the world's leading technology companies, it is not surprising that they exploit technology to great effect in their BPO relationship with Accenture.

Four technology practices enable world-class performance:

1. Microsoft has a single-instance global ERP system, which facilitates process standardization, rollouts and onboarding for new subsidiaries. It has been identified as a key enabler of shared services,[6] yet few global firms have achieved this milestone.
2. Microsoft and Accenture reduced the number of systems used in financial, accounting and procurement operations from 140 to 40 worldwide.[7] Reducing the number of systems takes out costs and facilitates the standardization of processes.
3. Microsoft developed the Controller Workspace, a new, global, centralized tool that provides Microsoft's Financial Controllers oversight and management of such things as the daily close processes and the ability to delegate transactional activities to Accenture's Assistant Financial Controllers. The tool is a central repository for all data about close and compliance processes that may be accessed by employees located around the globe to get accurate, timely and reliable data.
4. The Governance Workspace is a tool designed for transparency and fact-based management of the BPO relationship.[8] The Governance Workspace supports the collaborative BPO governance structure discussed in Practice Key 4.

11.9. Key 8: Deploy domain expertise and business analytics

In world-class relationships we studied, the provider applies their domain expertise to launch rigorous analytics processes that measure the right key process indicators, deploys tools and techniques to measure and report on KPIs and applies algorithms, models and sophisticated statistics to identify weaknesses and opportunities. Then, the partners redesign processes to deliver measurable business outcomes.

Nearly all of the transformation projects at Microsoft are enabled by the provider's domain expertise and strong analytics. One example is the project to increase the number of invoices paid within terms. Prior to the transformation project, 70 per cent of invoices were paid within terms. Applying analytics, the data showed that decentralized Microsoft employees were not approving invoices until late in the cycle because they simply were not aware that discounts were at risk. After the transformation project, 88 per cent were paid within terms and the target is to reach 92 per cent in the coming year. Besides realizing the monetary discounts of paying on term, the service improved:

Paid within terms (PWT) is such an important concept because if you pay your invoices on time then, in general, you don't get questions from your vendors. The worst thing that you want to get is questions from your vendors because then you need someone who answers those questions. And, you get questions from the business because they get questions from the vendors. You want this to be a slick machine that performs in the background. That's a very good measurement that we've had. PWT is not a SLA, yet Accenture uses its insights to support us to deliver this business outcome. We've driven PWT over the last four years and improved a lot on that one. – Senior Director of Financial Operations, Microsoft

Another example is better cash forecasting. Global companies like Microsoft must allocate enough cash to each country to pay their employees and vendors. Because overfunding has less dire consequences than underfunding, companies tend to overfund, resulting in lost interest. By applying better analytics to forecast cash needs, the partners were able to decrease the overfunding rate from 10 per cent down to 2 per cent.

⚷ 11.10. Key 9: Prioritize and incent innovation

Most outsourcing deals we have studied are not designed for innovation, even though the parties may devote a lot of rhetoric to innovation. The three biggest innovation obstacles we've encountered are lack of governance, lack of proper funding and lack of aligned incentives. In the Microsoft–Accenture relationship, the partners overcame these three obstacles. The partners created a transformation programme with an associated governance structure devoted to innovation to embed innovations and transformation projects into the relationship from the start. The partners answered effectively the question, 'Who will pay the upfront investments for innovations?' Innovations are delivered via transformation projects and are funded by the client from the savings generated by outsourcing. Funding for innovation is driven by a programme that is outside of the economics of the original contract. This implies that Microsoft compensates Accenture for any impact the innovation would have on their original contract economics. They aligned incentives through gain-sharing, but avoid the battles gain-sharing usually triggers by agreeing to the gain-share in advance.

For transformation projects, the partners agree upfront how much Microsoft's bill will be reduced. Accenture is guaranteed a share of that savings, and if Accenture can outperform, they pocket the difference. If Accenture underperforms, it absorbs the loss. For example, if Accenture is charging $100 for service performed by person X and earning $10 in profit, a transformation project that would eliminate person X would normally mean a loss of $10 profit for Accenture. Microsoft incents Accenture by agreeing to pay, say, $20 after the transformation. Under this hypothetical scenario, Accenture doubles its profit and Microsoft is guaranteed a reduced bill by $80. If the transformation project exceeds or falls short of expected gains, Accenture pockets the additional gains or absorbs the losses. This mechanism was designed to properly incent Accenture. Microsoft's Senior Director of Financial Operations explains: 'If I run a project together with Accenture that takes that person away, then Accenture loses the revenue of 100 and a profit of 10. That would be stupid of Accenture to do. So what we then did was looked at those projects to make sure we have a split of the gain-share to make it attractive for both of us to do this'.

The overall affect is the creation of strong incentives for Accenture:

My client recognizes that I need to meet my financial commitments as the service provider. That may sound strange but there is a realization that, fundamentally, I have to be incentivized to do some of the things I need to do. The key message is a spirit of partnership that I don't think exists in the other engagements that I've come across. – Outsourcing Account Delivery Manager, Accenture

11.11. Conclusion

The Microsoft–Accenture BPO relationship is an exemplar of world-class BPO performance. We have noted that the stability of the leadership pair on this account is a key to sustaining world-class performance for nearly 7 years as of this writing. The leadership pair turns all the other eight keys to top performance. But its strength may also be its weakness. One of the interviewees said of its strong leadership: 'It is not a good or bad thing either way because you are fragile if you lose those people and things go sour. Right now, we have good people that are interested in doing these things together'. Hopefully, the leadership pair has institutionalized many of the keys to world-class performance and success will outlast any turnover.

---

[1] Additional evidence of world-class performance comes from a number of industry awards. In 2008, the Microsoft-Accenture OneFinance relationship won the Outsourcing Excellence Award for Most Strategic Relationship sponsored by the Everest Group and Forbes. In 2010, the relationship won the Best Mature Outsourced Service Delivery Operation by the Shared Services Outsourcing Network. In 2011, the relationship won the GEO for Innovation sponsored by the IAOP. In 2011, its Asia-Pacific operations were awarded for Best Customer Service by the Shared Services Outsourcing Network.

[2] Hawes, T (2009)., 'Strategic Outsourcing: One Finance: Microsoft and Accenture SLIDE DECK'.

[3] Rosenthal, B. (2008), 'Growing the Business to Drive Value', http://www.outsourcing-center.com/2008-08-growing-the-business-to-drive-value-article-37343.html.

[4] Hawes, 'Strategic Outsourcing'.

5 Rosenthal, B. (2008), 'Growing the Business to Drive Value', http://www.outsourcing-center.com/2008–08-growing-the-business-to-drive-value-article-37343.html.

6 Lacity and Fox, *MIS Quarterly Executive*.

7 Vitasek, K., Manrodt, K. and Krishna, S. (2012), 'Changing the Game of Outsourcing – The Microsoft OneFinance Case', *Journal of Information Technology Teaching Cases*, 2, 46–56.

8 See IAOP's Global Excellence in Outsourcing 2011 Award Winners: https://www.iaop.org/Content/19/165/3131.

Chapter 12

⚙ BP case study: Reclaiming world-class performance

> **What's Inside:** BP and Accenture's relationship is the longest standing among our cases, dating back to 1991. The focus of this study is on the financial and accounting services provided for BP's North American refining and marketing operations. This BPO relationship is fascinating because performance went from world-class, to humming along at good/okay performance, to a complete reclaiming of world-class performance after 2009. BP reclaimed top performance by enacting seven of the nine best practices.

12.1. Introduction

> My team had to awaken and say we need to push ourselves to improve our processes and drive value. We had a cultural shift from 'Accenture does some stuff' to a culture that we all own the end-to-end processes and Accenture delivery is an integral part of those processes. – BP Head of Shared Services

BP, formerly known as British Petroleum, is a global energy company with business activities in more than 100 countries in five major areas: Exploration and Production; Integrated Supply and Training; Refining and Marketing; Alternative Energy and Shipping and Operations. It had 83,900 employees worldwide and annual revenues of US $396 billion in 2013.

BP has been a pioneer in the outsourcing of business services. As early as 1991, BP consolidated all of its accounting centres throughout the United Kingdom in a single accounting system and at a single site managed by Accenture. The context for the current case is BP's financial and accounting services that support its North American refining

Table 12.1 BP's BPO relationship

BPO type	FAO
Initial contract date	1991
Outsourcing driver	Initial focus on core competency strategy; now uses outsourcing relationship to help deliver shared services
Provider	Accenture
Geographic scope of BPO	Global: Accenture services client from delivery centres in Aberdeen, Bangalore, Houston, Stavanger, Krakow, Istanbul, Athens and Buenos Aires
Number of provider FTEs on this account	330
Number of provider FTEs for all of BP	760
Outsourcing outcomes	Over their long history together, the relationship went from world-class performance to good performance and then back to world-class performance

and marketing operations (see Table 12.1). BP's North American refining and marketing operations wanted to create shared services for financial and accounting services in 2009. At that time, Accenture had long been performing a number of services within BP's procure-to-pay processes (e.g. entering invoices, updating accounts payable, matching invoices with receipts and helping with payments), record-to-report processes (e.g. fixed asset accounting, close processes and reconciliations) and order-to-cash processes (e.g. maintaining master data for franchisees and BP gas stations). In 2009, this part of the longstanding relationship with Accenture was still performing well, but a new BP executive in-charge of creating shared services through the BP–Accenture relationship could be significantly revived. He relocated the Accenture leads from Texas to Illinois to be closer to BP's financial operations. He requested a new Accenture lead to further infuse the relationship with new ideas and enthusiasm. The new BP and Accenture leaders reopened the books and 'kicked away the cobwebs to look at what we actually had'. They discovered some inefficiencies in the existing contract, such as BP not taking advantage of free consulting days.

After 2010, the relationship was reinvigorated to reclaim high performance. Clients filled in the Everest survey on high performance and rated the relationship in the top 20 per cent. During our interviews, the BP executives in-charge of the Accenture relationship confirmed world-class performance by rating Accenture's performance between 8 and 9 on the 10-point scale.[1] One BP executive went on to say: 'They are almost a 9, but that's a significant leap forward from where I thought we were two years ago'.

To understand BP's journey to reclaim world-class performance, we first describe the historical context of BP's sourcing strategy and decisions and then describe how these leaders reinvigorated or launched for the first time seven of the nine keys to world-class performance.

12.2. BP's history of outsourcing

Until 1987, BP had been partly government-owned, and by 1990 was still too bureaucratic and costly to succeed in a rapidly changing industry. The next 15 years saw BP transformed into a world leader in the oil and energy industry, not least through mergers with Amoco (2000) and ARCO (2001). An important component in its rise to world class has been outsourcing its business and IT services. Then CEO, John Browne, set the tone in the early 1990s, stating: 'failure to outsource our commodity IT will permanently impair the future competitiveness of our business'.[2] Subsequently, this philosophy was applied to all BP back-office functions.

As early as 1991, the CEO of the BP Exploration business unit took an important first step in what would be a thorough transformation of the company by outsourcing all of the division's accounting operations for Europe. The 1991 agreement consolidated all of BP's accounting centres throughout the United Kingdom into a single accounting system and at a single site managed by Accenture. In 1996, BP outsourced the accounting functions and IT support for its US upstream, downstream and chemicals businesses. In 1999, following its merger with Amoco, BP outsourced, on 5-year deals, its US upstream business to PWC and its US downstream businesses and upstream European business to Accenture.

BP was also an early, effective proponent of multi-sourcing. Against the fashion for single-provider, long-term deals, from 1993 to 1998, BP Exploration outsourced its IT to three providers – SAIC, Sema and Syncordia on a best-in-class basis.[3] In 2000, the then BP Amoco pioneered and experimented with a £400 million, 5-year outsourcing deal for US-based start-up Exult to manage the whole of the merged company's Human Resource operations.[4] Throughout the 2000s BP continued with its dynamic multi-sourcing ITO and BPO strategy, while looking for offshore advantages and drawing increasingly on Indian-based providers. In 2009, BP reined in its multi-sourcing strategy to pursue more bundled sourcing by consolidating its IT providers from 40 down to 6, on contracts worth $1.5 billion over 5 years. From 1991, then, BP's successes – and learnings – have shaped outsourcing by many other companies looking to learn how to improve the efficiency and effectiveness of their business processes.

Within the BP outsourcing portfolio, its long-standing, several times renewed and much-expanded F&A outsourcing relationship with Accenture continues to be an acknowledged BPO success story. Indeed the arrangement has won multiple industry awards.[5] In 1991 Accenture set up a shared service centre in Aberdeen, Scotland for F&A and SAP support. In 1996, in a pioneering development, Sun, Conoco and other oil companies came into the arrangement, leading to economies of scale and reducing BP's unit fixed costs. In 2002 Accenture also standardized all customers on SAP, providing them with synergies on cost and performance. By this date, financial operating costs had been reduced by 35 per cent by leveraging technology and scale, and despite a doubling of work volumes, F&A costs had been halved. In 2002, the BP CFO commented: 'Ironically, the deal we did with Accenture 10 years ago may be the single most successful deal that BP has ever done – in any function, anywhere. And that's deeply laden with irony, because your first one out of the box is the one you'd expect to be where you'd make all your mistakes. But we got it right, and it has been a tremendous success'.[6]

The relationship has been expanded and has maintained success ever since its inception. By 2007, the F&A outsourcing relationship consisted of 760 plus FTEs across four delivery centres at Aberdeen, Houston, Bangalore and Shanghai.[7] Throughout the 2000s, to further enhance cost and effectiveness, positions were increasingly moved to Bangalore. In addition to continuous improvements in the cost base and service effectiveness, one notable achievement to this date had been the transition of BP Castrol's F&A. This was managed through a collaborative approach, robust governance mechanisms, clear hand-offs between multiple stakeholders and the fact that improvements were customized to business requirements. The relationship also achieved world-class close performance by reducing close from 11 to 6 working days through consolidation and reporting using a new, web-based remote control tool. However, by the mid-2000s, the relationship had become routine. In an increasingly difficult business environment, the relationship needed to be recharged.

The next challenge BP set for itself and its ITO/BPO providers was to develop best-in-class capability for its global shared business service centres (BSCs). By 2010, BP had five captive centres and multiple service providers for F&A, HR, Procurement and IT & Systems. F&A outsourcing, led by Accenture, was based primarily at Bangalore, but also operated out of Aberdeen, Stavanger, Krakow, Istanbul, Athens and Buenos Aires. The challenge was to secure centralization, standardization and integration by migrating additional scope of work from all the BP businesses, not just Refining and Marketing, to the captive BSCs or outsourcing service providers (OSPs).

Once again, BP is operating as a pioneer in its global sourcing, and after 20 years, Accenture remains a key strategic partner in BP's commitment to best-in-class capability in F&A. In what follows, we detail the seven key practices the parties adopted in the process of re-learning to be world-class.

⌇ 12.3. Key 1: Assign a great leadership pair

As we found in other world-class BPO relationships, an effective leadership pair is a key success factor and often involves personnel changes in both client and provider organizations from senior level to more operational levels. We found instances where new leaders improved BPO performance from bad to good or from good to great.

The BP–Accenture relationship was unproblematic, productive (as indicated by green SLAs) and routine. What prompted a change in the BPO relationship was BP's desire to create the Americas shared services centre in 2009. To lead the effort, BP recruited from outside the company and hired a proven transformational leader who had previously created a world-class, global financial services organization for another company. BP took the initiative on providing transformational leadership, but it was also looking for new leadership from its service provider. The new BP Head of Shared Services immediately relocated the Accenture lead position from Texas to BP headquarters in Chicago. A new Accenture person was brought in to fill the role. The BP Head of Shared Services described the new service provider lead in this way: 'She's fantastic. She's very action-oriented. She pushes back and can challenge us in the right way. That's the difference I think in terms of making it a more strategic approach rather than sitting back and accepting business as usual'. A Commercial Director for BP described the effects of change in leadership this way: 'We have changed things fairly dramatically in the last two years. We came into a relationship that was good and fairly stable, but left a lot on the table in terms of overall value. With some concentrated effort and some key adjustments made on both sides in terms of the approach of managing the contract, with the personnel, and in terms of what we asked Accenture to do, they have risen to the occasion'.

⌇ 12.4. Key 2: Focus on business and strategic benefits beyond cost efficiencies

BP has redefined its business objectives with Accenture as the relationship matures. At BP the relationship began as a pioneering one as the world's first FAO deal shifted to an industry shared services model for BP and other oil majors, moved to extension into other BP regions and consolidation of BP M&A, while focusing on continuous cost reduction and increasingly on improvements in financial and accounting outcomes. Examples include faster closing globally, more efficient procure-to-pay, reducing costs by millions of dollars while gaining better business outcomes, better cash use and tighter debt/credit control. In a 20-year relationship there have been periods of stabilization of goals, and other periods that have seen an acceleration towards new business outcomes consequent on dynamic changes in the BP business environment. Thus since 2009 the strategic relationship has been re-galvanized as BP has re-imagined its F&A operations within a larger global business services model. For its part the service provider has stepped up to the new challenges, with both parties leveraging processes and mechanisms in the strategic relationship, that had been in place but not fully optimized in the previous 5 years. Throughout this history, both parties recognized and engaged with the fact that redefining business objectives required a further maturing of the outsourcing relationship.

⌘ 12.5. Key 3: Drive strong transition, transformational and change management capabilities

For BP, a powerful transformation, transition and change management vehicle is a robust Stabilization, Standardization, Optimization and Sourcing (SSOS) methodology introduced by the client. The overall strategic direction of BP from 2009 to 2015 has been towards a global business services model based on centralization, standardization, optimization and then strategic sourcing. Understandably, throughout the 2000s, BP's complex global structure, segregated by geographies and into strategic business units, became even more fragmented by mergers, acquisitions and strategic and more opportunistic responses to competition and events in a dynamic business environment. Process simplification, economies of scale, shared resources and better uses of fewer strategic providers have been business necessities in the difficult business climate since 2008. In this context, high business services performance using the services market only becomes possible through strategic partnering with providers, as in the case of Accenture and F&A functions.

The new BP head of shared services implemented the SSOS methodology. This provides a controlled, logical route for creating world-class shared services. The Head of BSC explained: 'I took my team through what I call the SSOS model. Stabilize what you just brought in, run it through some stabilization that included setting up process documentation and process maps and setting up SLAs between us and the businesses we support. Then standardize. When we added more businesses into our service centre, we actually were doing the same things but in different ways. I was really pushing people to come up with what are the things we could do to standardize it. Optimize is the O: What can we do with our new systems or new processes, end-to-end? For example, implementing global SAP templates. The final S in the model was Sourcing: do we continue to do things here or do it in one of our other service centres or do we do it offshore?'

The 'twist' in BP's transformation route is that the incumbent strategic provider is productively involved in the client-controlled change process. In the BP–Accenture relationship, the centralization and standardization are both facilitated by outsourcing. This point is made well by BP's commercial director of Americas BSC:

> BP is a very decentralized organization. One of the problems with decentralization is that we probably make life more difficult from the standpoint of missing opportunities to standardize the way we do things across the organization. Accenture, sitting where they do, supporting us in some key activities across many, many business units obviously have a great view and a great visibility to lots of these opportunities where we are inherently doing things inefficiently. One of the things we should be looking for from them in terms of value is that sort of insight and some suggestions of ways to continuously improve and standardize the things we do.

During this period, BP set out to transform its business services, globally, and not just F&A. It identified disjointed processes, a fragmented application landscape and high operating costs. It meant developing end-to-end processes, cost optimization and process standardization, and moving more work from the businesses to a more developed network of BSCs and OSPs. As an example let us focus on the Americas BSC, formed in 2009. Throughout 2010–2011 BP transitioned and consolidated this BSC optimizing end-to-end processes, and sorting out OSP ownership and management. From mid-2010, a key part was transforming the OSP business model with Accenture. That meant identifying joint strategies by process on Procure to Pay, Record to Report, Order to Cash and Finance operation services to enable a joint operating model.

The objectives were to raise the level of customer experience, expand BSC/Accenture business scope, reduce BP operating costs and raise productivity levels. BP and Accenture identified top joint priority initiatives for 2011 on organization structure, process approach, continuous improvement, transition and resources.[8] The change process involved working directly with Accenture, joint process ownership, engagement and teaming, acknowledgement, recognition, much more transparency and feedback and the maximum use of 'invest days' (see later). High engagement between the parties drove key business changes for BP, while Accenture expanded its responsibility for scope of services, and achieved top tier employee satisfaction, while also increasing performance levels and customer satisfaction. More strategic goals, tight deadlines for change, new transformational leadership and a practical change management tool with stretch deadlines – these set the context for further supportive changes.

⌇ 12.6. Key 4: Adopt a partnering approach to governance

BP and Accenture approach BPO governance with partnering attitudes, good governance structures and end-to-end governance of BP's KPIs:

Partnering attitudes. BP treats Accenture as a strategic partner. This can show itself in many ways. The Accenture OADM[9] talked in late 2011 of: 'an openness on their side to focus on some of the gaps in our [joint] operating model . . . it comes back to a commitment and an openness . . . looking to create a strategic plan together . . . and having transparency as to where they are going with their business and how we can help in those types of discussions . . . the whole getting the business perspective from BP has stepped up as well'. She also talked of executive behaviour on the provider side: 'Being extremely responsive and listening to where they are going. Not selling but truly becoming as I say that trusted advisor. Getting things done, taking action. That's been our strength in turning the corner with the relationship'.

Governance structures. On governance structures, BP and Accenture have joint review boards at strategic, managerial operational, process council and tactical (daily) levels. While these are designed well, we have found in our wider research that they act as hygiene factors in the sense that the absence of such structures may result in poor performance, but the presence of collaborative governance structures does not in itself necessarily lead to high performance. In practice, if not designed correctly, they can inhibit, rather than enable, high performance. What has been more salient at BP are the behaviours and objectives that have led to optimal use of such governance arrangements.

BP's commercial director for Americas BSC added to this picture: 'It's about engagement across the board, in terms of having multi-stakeholder engagement and regular governance, giving regular contact in mutually structuring metrics and scorecards that force people to focus on the right activities and outcomes. It's engagement from the standpoint of working together to understand mutual strategic objectives and making sure the activities are aligned with those objectives'. BP's commercial director stressed this high level of engagement stretches from the senior executive Joint Review Board that now meets monthly to focus on strategy and key metrics, to a monthly meeting that now focuses on continuous improvement and that encourages and rewards Accenture team leads for ideas generation. Key to the quality of the ideas generated is the great deal of contextual strategic alignment senior Accenture executives can now give their staff. For him, the top provider behaviour that contributed to success was strategic partnering: 'it is showing the real willingness to get in here and understand our strategic objectives . . . and be willing to be flexible enough and change some historic behaviours and policies to better align with our objectives. Also the quality of the people . . . we talk regularly with them, they feel part of our business, there are some rewards above the norm in some cases. There is a tremendous amount of longevity in some of the employees and dedication to BP's work and the account that is just different'.

From SLAs to end-to-end governance. According to one BP participant, BP was 'historically a bit passive as recipients of service, with metrics that were really outdated and not necessarily transparent or indicators of what BP, as the client, cares about'. Within the last 2 years, BP and Accenture have been digging deeper into SLAs and have been revisiting measures. Concerning the former, BP has recently revisited service delivery even though unproblematic, to good effect:

> That's something that was actually already strong. But again one of the transitions over the last two years we went from a set of metrics, I call [them] Green Metrics – they were the ones tied to contract that were always magically green – we went from the Green Metrics and, looking deeper, to process metrics that showed that there were other areas that needed some improvement. From the beginning, they [Accenture] have had a strong delivery. I'm not saying that we went deeper and found all the red items it was just more of finding some yellow metrics on some things that started pointing to where we could do some continuous improvement. A lot of outsourcing arrangements argue over all the process failures and breakdowns, we weren't in that state at all, even at the beginning two years ago. They always had a strong delivery. – Head of BP Americas BSC

Concerning the metrics that matter most to clients, BP and Accenture agreed on a set of metrics that better represent the actual activities that the business recipients of the service care about:

> We also created a service catalog both for the business service centre and for Accenture. This is critical, listing what you are asking them to do at an activity level, what is agreed and then putting metrics and SLAs around those activities to hold the right people – BP or Accenture – accountable, and determine whether work is new or something they're already supposed to be doing. Then we put governance around that, that connects to higher level metrics and more strategic conversations. – BP Commercial Director, BSC

BP and Accenture were clearly not settling for just 'green' service-level performance.

At BP, our research shows an evolution from a relatively simple F&A deal in the early 1990s to one that became highly complex, with dynamic changes in scope, scale, technologies and locations over time. Each change represented a recalibration of the relationship between processes, people and technology, and levels of consolidation and standardization needed. BP and Accenture managed these challenges effectively on each occasion. More recently, the relationship has been further invigorated in the face of much greater consolidation of shared service centres globally. First, BP got its own arms around its own processes, using the SSOS methodology. Secondly, BP's Head of Americas BSC told us: 'I'd say there was a shift to a culture that we all own end-in-end processes, and Accenture delivery is an integral part of those processes'. Thirdly, BP brought greater rigour to end-to-end process design and documentation which embraced what both BP and Accenture did, together with end-to-end metrics that focused not just on service but also on business process outcomes. This allowed the provider to better align their expertise and opportunities to BP's desire to stabilize and optimize certain processes:

> Accenture came to the table, and said, 'here are the processes and what other companies do' and where they do it . . . we call them process breakouts . . . and (they) realigned some of their organizational aspects to match with how we were organized . . . and brought to the table some metric methodologies, testing out some new stuff. This improved alignment allowed us to better match some of their demonstrated strengths with our areas of identified need – BP Commercial Director BSC.

12.7. Key 5: Align the retained organization, outsourced processes and provider staff

I challenge my own leadership team members by saying 'you don't just have just 20 people here you actually have 120 because 100 of your people are over in Bangalore with the provider'. You can't run a process without including your team over in Bangalore as part of your operation. – BP Head of Shared Services

World-class BPOs place as much importance on internal transformation as they place on transforming the outsourced processes. Successful BPO relationships not only are forged as a result of a world-class outsourced process, but also require transforming the retained organization in terms of roles, responsibilities and requisite skills around the new service delivery model. A successful internal transformation also empowers the business users to align the direction of the BPO relationship with organization goals. At BP, this is precisely what the leaders set about doing in order to underpin the vision and delivery of a future global shared financial services model. Part of this, as we have seen, was moving the retained staff to a more teaming, collaborative way of working with the provider. But the really powerful key for success was aligning the retained organization with outsourced processes and provider staff.

When BP engages Accenture to perform a service, it involves Accenture at all levels, including the 330 Accenture employees in the Bangalore delivery centre who are dedicated to the FAO account. The client visits the remotely located provider employees, has monthly meetings to hear their ideas about innovation and financially rewards continuous improvement and innovation from the offshore staff. This client leader said these practices have 'generated lots of good ideas that we've been able to put into practice'. One other amazing outcome is that the turnover among the provider's Bangalore-based employees is only 8 per cent – one of the lowest turnover rates for an Indian delivery centre in our studies.

Time and again in our research programmes, we have found many clients needing to recalibrate their retained processes and organization first, in order to get real added value from their service providers[10]. BP not only stepped up to this requirement but, recognizing the strategic role of the provider in the future model, and began to involve Accenture heavily in these change processes. Investing in changing the retained organization and its behaviours and practices has meant that the provider's capabilities can be leveraged to more strategic effect for BP.

We found the client also doing a good job of getting BP process owners and SMEs working with Accenture's offshore resources:

> When we make the decision that we're offshoring work, we might send 20 roles to Bangalore, and keep the team lead and add extra SMEs at BP. So from a team of 20, you now have 4 in-house. And every week and month, the team leader here is now managing an extended virtual team directly, having meetings and sharing strategic context. – BP Commercial Director BSC

We identified a further practice whereby the BP client empowered and rewarded the staff in India, through a monthly meeting specifically intended to discuss the notion of continuous improvement:

> It's an opportunity for the folks from Accenture and various team leads, to encourage and reward [the delivery teams], and we fund this reward and the generation of ideas from their folks. It's produced lots of good ideas that we've been able to put into practice. – BP Commercial Director, Americas BSC

Empowering and rewarding vendor staff also links back to practices 1 and 3, especially leadership. Asked to explain her staff commitment in India, the Accenture OADM told us: 'We have a really strong leader that has been on the account for five or six years. In addition, working with the client, coaching the, that their notes of thank you and their site visits are very important to the teams with their culture, that helps. [This is] something that BP has stepped up to and continues to do is recognition so when we do the site visits, we do team meetings, they do the floor walks. Through our governance we give recognition to continuous improvement projects, [highlighting] how the ideas were raised, and so notes are sent. I think that type of level down to the people level – that's helped tremendously. Our team members have also been on the account for quite a while and there's a sense of family. We've had a focus on succession planning and Accenture has a strong career counsellor and training opportunities. It has all added up'.

In practice, the Bangalore service centre had technically smart people who had really lacked context and strategic alignment and therefore struggled with things like judgement, critique and advancing new ideas. This had changed:

> They are getting directed by the people who really understand the things we're doing and why we are doing them. That's critical. – BP, Commercial Director, BSC

In the BP–Accenture BPO relationship, integrating, empowering and rewarding provider staff has become a key practice. One outcome is the highest employee satisfaction in the company, and a very low labour turnover at the Bangalore site:

> Our turnover on the account in Bangalore is single digit, which is almost unheard of in Bangalore. It's gotten all the way down so even the employees of Accenture at Bangalore feel far more valued and that's resulted in lower turnover and results in more effective operation. – BP Head of Americas BSC

Another BP senior manager told us that 'they seem to almost take more pride and support in BP than in working for Accenture. They view themselves as BP employees which again is unusual amount of ownership'.

⚷ 12.8. Key 6: Resolve issues together and conflicts fairly

Clearly in any large-scale BPO, there are going to be numerous points of difference and conflicts especially in fast-changing environments as at BP. Our respondents were clear that both parties handled conflicts toughly but fairly in a partnering style. The Head of Americas BSC described what he called one such Howitzer Moment involving Accenture employees working onshore. BP could not see their value, and a conflict developed for several months. However, according to the BP commercial director, 'the new contract manager . . . came on board and that was the key. We all agreed after time to transition those five remaining FTEs worth of activities to Bangalore rather than here. But it came from a partner who in the end was willing (but was not contractually bound) to be transparent and take challenge and work with you to achieve objectives that were not helpful to them in terms of revenue but more helpful in terms of partnership'. (The details of this particular conflict were discussed in Chapter 8, under the story heading, 'A client pays for bloated provider staff'.)

12.9. Key 7: Prioritize and incent innovation

BP and Accenture designed in innovation at the very start of the deal using 'Invest Days'. In the contract, BP is entitled to 150 consulting days from Accenture's top consultants for free. The contract stipulates that the content of the Invest Days has to be mutually agreed upon. The idea is that the client gets complimentary access to top consulting expertise and the provider gets an opportunity to sell additional services. When the Head of BSC came on board in 2009, BP was not using any Invest Days. As part of re-learning to be great, BP by 2011 was using 100 per cent of Invest Days. BP's Commercial Director for Americas BSC talked animatedly about the Invest Days:

> Invest Days is a great idea. One of the most mutually beneficial activities you can engage in with that kind of consulting is thinking about more things that you can potentially offshore to India that increase their scope and revenues while also saving us money because we are doing work that we need to do at a lower cost, by benefiting from the arbitrage.

The outcomes from Invest Days have been beneficial to both parties. Most recently, the parties identified two clear candidates for offshoring that had not been offshored previously. Customer master data is one example: Customer master data (as an idea) came from Accenture who said: 'This is an area that we do for other companies and we do it very effectively'. It was almost a gimme. And we went,

> Oh! . . . Don't just take our requests, you need to come and challenge us around our processes and bring in that external view. – BP Head of BSC

The provider also gains from this work, not least in working more closely and strategically with the client to identify future opportunities:

> It has resulted in mutual benefit – they are transitioning 10% of their America's service center business over to us in Bangalore. . . . Also I've actually worked with the BP commercial team (through SSOS) to look at each area and based on what we typically see outsourced where they are in their maturity . . . and we honed in on a couple of opportunities, that went through risk assessments, due diligence and that was what they decided to use their Investment Days on. We brought individuals in from our BPO capability [group] and a transition lead from mobilization and that's part of our investment that we used. – Accenture OADM

12.10. Conclusion

The BP case study is about re-learning to be great. Long-term relationships can frequently see both sides taking their eyes off the road, their feet off the accelerators. World-class BPO performers regularly revisit, refocus and re-energize targets and activities. They do so in order to release the potential of the relationship to deliver on changing and new business imperatives. In researching this case, we identified seven keys for top performance in F&A BPO. If the partnership approach is fundamental, then transformational leadership, operationalizing the SSOS methodology and strong transformational and change management capability were critical in avoiding the possible dangers of complacency in long-term partnering – and achieving change momentum. The other practices reinforce the drive towards re-learning to be great. BP's Head of Americas' BSC summarized the learning succinctly:

> Some people take the approach of my mess for less. They chuck it over the wall or say, I'm not going to mess my hands and I'm going to hire a bunch of people in Bangalore to do it for less'. My biggest advice is you really have to know what you've got, what your processes are, how you want them run end-to-end. Then start on the BPO relationship and be open to bringing things to the table that you didn't know were possible or new ways things can be done. To make it work, it truly has to be a two-way partnership.

[1] As explained in the previous chapter, a 10-point scale was used to assess provider performance during the interviews, with 1 indicating 'pitiful performance', 5 indicating 'meets expectations' and 10 indicating 'exceeds expectations'.

[2] Cross, J., Earl, M. and Sampler, J. (1997), 'Transformation of the IT Function at British Petroleum', available at http://www.iei.liu.se/indek/utbildning/ekonomiska-informationssystem/tkmm02/files/1.111562/BPXmisqpap.pdf

[3] The 1993–1998 deals and subsequent events are analysed in detail in Lacity, M. and Willcocks (2001), *Global Information Technology Outsourcing: In Search of Business Advantage*, Wiley, Chichester.

[4] For more on the HRO deal, see Adler, P. S., 'The Human Resource Business Process Outsourcing Industry: The BP-Exult Partnership', available at http://dx.doi.org/10.2139/ssrn.317502. The HR deal with Exult proved challenging. For an analysis, see: Willcocks, L. and Lacity, M (2006)., *Global Sourcing of Business and IT Services*, Palgrave, London. For an account of the Exult (subsequently Hewitt) HRO with BP, see Willcocks, L., Feeny, D. and Olson, N. (2006), 'IT Outsourcing and Retained IS Capabilities: Challenges and Lessons', *European Management Journal*, February, 24(1), 20–33.

[5] These include The Outsourcing Journal's 2002 Editor's Choice award, BP FC and A Awards 2004, 2005, 2006, and several awards from professional associations and journals.

[6] Goolsby, K. (2002), 'How British Petroleum Began Using Outsourcing to Make its Dreams Come True – See more at: http://outsourcing-center.com/2002-02-how-british-petroleum-began-using-outsourcing-to-make-its-dreams-come-true-article-38072.html#sthash.FKJNp2aM.dpuf

[7] The scope of the outsourcing is that Accenture manage systems and data management, financial accounting and reporting, most of management accounting and reporting, accounts payable and capital projects and fixed assets. BP retains capability primarily in regulatory funds and reporting, receivables and collections and approving and executing capital projects.

[8] Medium priority was also assigned to performance metrics, technology, scope, governance and contracting.

[9] Outsourcing Account Delivery Manager.

[10] See, for example, the cases in Lacity and Willcocks, *Advanced Outsourcing Practice*. Also Willcocks, L. and Lacity, M. (2010), *The Practice of Outsourcing*, Palgrave, London.

$\circ$⚿ EMC case study: Journey to world-class performance

What's Inside: EMC illustrates a typical journey to world-class performance in that the nine keys were adopted over time. Initially, service performance was uneven during the transition but performance became great in about 2 years by adopting the first six keys of world-class performance. Cost savings were delivered, service levels were green and the client was highly satisfied. But the partners didn't stop at great operational performance; they adopted more world-class performance practices like applying business analytics and more formally incenting innovation.

13.1. Introduction

EMC, a multinational company based in Hopkinton, Massachusetts, sells data storage products and services used to build web-based computing systems. EMC was founded in 1979 by Richard Egan, Roger Marino and an unidentified third person (presumably with a last name that starts with a **C**). In 2012, EMC generated $22 billion in revenues, earned almost $3 billion in profits and employed 64,000 people.

The BPO story began in 2008 when EMC decided to create Global Business Services (GBS). At that time, EMC sought to further develop their service centres in Ireland, India, Egypt and Brazil into Centers of Excellence and sought a BPO partner to help with that enormous transformation. EMC selected Accenture. The initial contract was signed in 2008 for a duration of 7 years (see Table 13.1). The initial contract size, measured by FTEs, was about 140 people. The initial scope spanned five service areas; however, three became the focus of the initial transition efforts: Global Revenue Operations (GRO), Project Accounting

Table 13.1 EMC's BPO relationship

BPO type	FAO
Initial contract date	2008
Outsourcing driver	Enable the creation of global shared service
Provider	Accenture
Number of provider FTEs on this account	300
Outsourcing outcomes	Significant cost savings, operational excellence and strategic agility

Services (PAS) and Accounts Payable (AP). GRO services process EMC sales orders and assure that those orders can be recorded as valid revenue. PAS comprises activities that support the EMC services organizations, for example, project set up, budget updates and invoicing. AP services included accounts payable, transaction processing and travel and expense reporting. Accenture initially provided these services from their delivery centre in Manila.

Initially, as often happens, service performance was uneven during the transition, but as the VP of GBS said: 'We understand that transitions can be bumpy [so] if a threshold isn't achieved or an SLA isn't met, we're not accusatory – rather we seek to address the root cause issues which are often related to training, procedural documentation and/or communication gaps'. In about 2 years, performance became great – cost savings were delivered, service levels became green and the client was highly satisfied. But the partners didn't stop at great operational performance; they sought to explore new frontiers by applying business analytics and more formally focusing on innovation. The VP of GBS summarized the value of the BPO relationship as follows: 'Our BPO partner has performed very well. Put simply – they execute. We have found that if we set the bar high, they do all that they can to jump over it. In addition to providing transactional services that exceed SLAs, they help us to think strategically about running our business'.

Initially, GBS spanned 400 FTEs across EMC, of which 100 were Accenture employees. By the end of 2012, GBS had grown to ˜1,500 FTEs, of which about 300 were Accenture employees. As of 2013, EMC had realized about 30 per cent savings as a result of GBS and the BPO relationship with Accenture. Savings have been driven by labour arbitrage and 5 per cent yearly productivity increases. The service levels were green. Beyond cost savings and operational excellence, the Accenture helped enable EMC's strategic outcomes, like quickly integrating acquired firms by leveraging GBS offerings. Since the initial agreement, EMC and Accenture have continued to evolve the agreement and the corresponding scope of services (and locations) to align with EMC's shared services vision and strategic imperatives.

EMC enmeshed keys one and two into the fabric of their BPO relationship even before sending out a request for proposal (RFP). Once it engaged the BPO provider, EMC and Accenture implemented keys three through six during the transition and stabilization periods. As the relationship matured, the partners launched practices seven through nine.

⌾⌁ 13.2. Key 1: Assign a great leadership pair

The individuals in-charge of the BPO relationship at EMC and Accenture are both experienced and respected leaders. The VP of GBS is a longtime EMC employee. She previously bought IT services from Accenture where she orchestrated the IT services among business units, the IT function and Accenture. She was promoted into the position of VP of GBS from IT based on her performance record and the value of her long-standing relationships with EMC internal customers. Accenture's Outsourcing Account Delivery Manager had previously done consulting work for EMC, so he understood EMC's unique business needs, such as the importance of EMC's end of quarter close and the business processes that are critical for success.

In addition to being strong as individuals, the VP of GBS and Accenture's OADM value and respect one another. The VP of EMC said of Accenture's OADM: 'Our Accenture account manager sits on my staff, he goes to my staff meeting, he goes to my off-sites, and he contributes to our strategic plan. He is a very valuable member of my team'. Accenture's OADM also speaks highly of the VP of GBS. He also further asserts that there are close relationships among all the leaders up and down the chain of command. He said, 'The relationship between EMC and Accenture is an important one, across several dimensions, for example as customers of each other, as partner in the marketplace, etc. This importance is reflected in the strong relationships we have in the BPO program and throughout the account. For the BPO program this includes the Vice President of GBS and her leadership team, and extends upwards through the shared services governance model. Across this spectrum, we strive to increase the strategic relevance of our services and grow the relationships across multiple dimensions inside and outside the four walls of the two companies'.

🔑 13.3. Key 2: Focus on business and strategic benefits beyond cost efficiencies

In 2008, EMC was not looking for a BPO vendor to merely reduce costs, but rather for a partner that could help them realize the global shared services vision quicker. According to the VP of GBS: 'First and foremost, we wanted a partner who could get us there faster. We had yet to establish as fully as we have now our own Centers of Excellence based in low cost regions outside of US [in India, Egypt, and Ireland] at that time. To achieve benefits quickly, establishing an outsourcing arrangement was a strategy that just got us there quicker'. EMC sent out a RFP and received responses from several global and Indian-based providers. After analysing the responses and interviewing the short-list, EMC selected Accenture. Accenture was the best fit for EMC's top three objectives. The VP of GBS explains: 'Having an ability to execute was probably the number one decision factor, and then having a good working relationship with the company was probably number two. Number three was cost, both initial and over the long-term life of the agreement'. In addition to meeting the selection criteria, EMC trusted that Accenture would be a collaborative partner based on prior successful relationships in the information technology and consulting spaces. For example, Accenture had previously helped EMC implement a global enterprise architecture that yielded great business results like reducing product design changes from 25 to 10 days and getting a new part created in minutes instead of 3 days.

13.4. Key 3: Drive strong transition, transformational and change management capabilities

At EMC, the scale of moving to global business services involved several transitions, and the partners quickly learned from early mistakes. One challenge early in the EMC–Accenture relationship was alignment on service performance reporting. The partners worked together to lock down reporting protocols, put reporting structures in place and posted reports on a regular schedule and in a format that made sense to EMC's managers. Subsequent transitions went much smoother: 'In the first phase, it took a really long time to get baselines. In subsequent phases we piggybacked on what we already had and used that as a proxy to accelerate the overall cycle', said the VP of GBS. She commended Accenture's change management capability: 'We've now done two other large scale transitions with Accenture since the inception of our partnership. I would say that we have learned along the way and now not only follow Accenture's formal methodology and approach to the onboarding of work but truly leverage the defined gates for pass/stop evaluations throughout. We have found that Accenture's level of documentation is good and their knowledge transfer approach of on-site training followed by reverse knowledge transfer really works'.

13.5. Key 4: Adopt a partnering approach to governance

The EMC executives in-charge of the BPO relationship view Accenture as their strategic partner. The VP of GBS described the relationship as: 'Accenture is a key partner for EMC on both the go to market side as well as on the service side . . . our partner is helping us to be a higher performing organization'. According to Accenture's OADM, the partnership view is very evident: 'The agreement may say that we are a BPO provider, but there really is a sense of partnership and collaboration throughout the entire organization. Accenture is part of the GBS fabric; this includes ongoing collaboration and transparency across the organization from both a tactical and strategic perspective'.

The partnership view manifests itself in partnership behaviours. The provider doesn't just care that its services levels are 'green', but that it is driving the right behaviours that matter most to business clients. On the EMC–Accenture deal, there are about 100 service areas measured and reported upon each month. About 14 critical process indicators (CPIs) are tied to potential credits if SLAs are missed, but client and provider participants affirmed that service levels are very high. In some instances, EMC no longer feels the need to randomly check certain services. Overall, the client described the performance as outstanding: 'The performance from each service area team has been high. For the past couple of years, performance from our Manila-based staff has been north of 99 percent with rare exception'. The OADM adds: 'Our SLAs are consistently green. From the CPI perspective, in the last year, we missed either four or five out of about 170; performance is now literally an afterthought. It starts to open up a different dialog with the customer of: What's next? What else can we provide? What other additional value can we bring back to EMC now because the performance is so high?'

⚷ 13.6. Key 5: Align the retained organization, outsourced processes and provider staff

EMC integrates the provider meaningfully into its organization, invites providers to key meetings and treats the provider's remotely located staff as part of the global delivery team by collaborating virtually and physically with them. About 50 EMC managers and retained team members have visited Accenture's delivery centres, the Philippines and China. Accenture's remotely located employees are clearly viewed and treated as part of the GBS team. The VP of GBS said: 'We don't treat them like a vendor. They are extensions of our team. We know the names of their staff. We treat them like they are ours. I think that's been great'. Accenture's OADM corroborated that EMC views his staff as part of GBS: 'There is a true sense of what we call 'One EMC'. So, our teams are viewed as their teams. The people who are in-charge operationally from the retained EMC perspective on a day-to-day basis, they truly believe the team in the Philippines and China are part of their staff. It is not a 'you are my service provider, I will keep pushing you until I get what I want'. There is a true sense of caring for the individuals as well as this shared sense of what it takes to get the job done'. The only downside to this close teaming is that it can restrict a service provider's ability to transfer human resources.

As a consequence of being treated as part of the GBS team, Accenture's remotely located employees have demonstrated their strong commitment to EMC. For example, early on in the relationship when a severe typhoon hit the Philippines, most people in metro Manila could not get to work, but the majority of Accenture's EMC support team still showed up and supported a successful end of quarter cycle. The perception of 'One EMC' was further strengthened as the OADM explained: 'There is a sense of 'do whatever you have to do to get the job done'. The teams in our centres have demonstrated that they are willing to do that. When the typhoon hit a couple of years ago, there was zero impact on EMC business and that was at the end of the quarter. There is a tremendous amount of respect of what our teams will do to keep the business running. That mentality is a shared mentality with the onshore team, and it's gone a very long way to extend that feeling of One EMC'.

⌘ 13.7. Key 6: Resolve issues together and conflicts fairly

In world-class BPO relationships, partners seek to resolve issues together, not to assign blame. This behaviour is certainly evident at EMC. The OADM explained, 'The relationship we have with EMC is one of 'being in the trenches' together. If there is an issue or concern, everyone knows we won't run from it, but will instead roll up our sleeves and address it together'.

During the early years of the EMC–Accenture contract, an adverse commercial situation became evident when the parties realized that the shared services business case wasn't delivering expected savings. Part of the underlying issue was the initial 'deal shape' with Accenture. To address the situation, EMC and Accenture reopened the agreement and revised key elements to mitigate the situation in a manner that left both parties comfortable.

The initial contract was priced using different rate cards for different types and complexities of work. After the initial transition and stabilization period, it was determined that EMC's business case was not being met in part due to the rate card pricing/staffing mechanism. Considering this, EMC asked to renegotiate the pricing mechanism. Accenture agreed to a flat rate card in exchange for a longer contract and an increased scope of work. The resulting structure enabled EMC to deliver the targeted business case, while Accenture was able to keep its commercial interests intact. Accenture's OADM explained: 'When the contract was reopened, it was a challenging situation however, both parties felt we landed on a revised agreement that met our mutual interests and ultimately strengthened the relationship'.

The start-up issues at the Chinese service centre provide additional strong evidence of the collaborative approach to solving issues. During the initial transition, multiple upstream challenges were encountered that eventually led to a downstream uptick in attrition (the staff turnover rate was extremely high and unanticipated), resulting in below-target initial performance and an extended stabilization period. The OADM explained the collaborative view of the issues the joint team faced: 'The root cause of the challenges was shared across the organization – it just wasn't Accenture, or GBS, or GBS' customers, it was elements of all three'. EMC and Accenture worked together to solve each issue. To ease the pain of high turnover resulting from upstream knowledge transfer processes, for example, the partners worked together to redesign the entire process, including an increased focus on redesigned language-specific training materials. As the partners worked through issues, the service delivery centre became stable and service level measures went green.

⚿ 13.8. Key 7: Use technology as enabler and accelerator of performance

Technology is clearly an important enabler of operational success for the EMC–Accenture relationship. The contract requires that Accenture will keep (Accenture-provided) technology current within one version of Accenture's most recent technology release. Accenture's OADM provided an example: 'Within accounts payable we have a workflow tool that is continuing to evolve. Since Go Live, there have been point releases. Now there is a new major release that is coming up. When we take advantage of that major release, we will be able to streamline EMC's receipt of their vendor invoices, which will reduce and possibly eliminate the current physical scanning dependency. Quite rapidly, we can deliver an in-year business case'. The team estimates that this will reduce their annual scanning-related charges by six figures, and during the life of the contract could drive a cost to serve reduction in excess of $1 million. According to the VP of GBS: 'Accenture has a great dashboard that we can access 'live' to view performance against our SLAs for the current quarter and over-time. From running a business within a business perspective that level of automation and transparency is great. The work flow tool is sound and has been very helpful to us particularly on the procure-to-pay side'.

Additionally, Accenture continues to identify opportunities and to take steps to deploy complementary toolsets to drive increased value (e.g. efficiencies, controls, etc.) within the environment. Accenture's OADM noted: 'as part of our value creation agenda, we continually review our portfolio of enabling technology assets (for example our Planning and Control tool) to determine applicability within the EMC environment. If we believe there's a compelling fit, we work closely with our EMC peers to confirm our thinking and evaluate how best to move forward'.

⚿ 13.9. Key 8: Deploy domain expertise and business analytics

In world-class relationships, the provider applies their domain exper-tise to launch rigorous analytics processes that measure the right key process indicators, deploys tools and techniques to measure and report on KPIs and applies algorithms, models and sophisticated statistics to identify weaknesses and opportunities. Then, the partners redesign processes to deliver measurable business outcomes.

In many BPO relationships, business analytics ambitions get stalled because operational people are too busy with daily activities. The real push for analytics typically happens after the relationship stabilizes. By first quarter of 2012, EMC and Accenture were ready to turn their attention to analytics. At that time, the client said: 'What we are looking for now, and where I think Accenture has a broad perspective given their extensive customer base, is in the spend analytics space. They have a fair amount of knowledge of our AP/T&E payment processes and data. As such, they are well positioned to offer a perspective on areas where we can improve cycle times, and discount achievement metrics with changes to process, policy and/or technology settings/enhancements. I would be very open to their suggestions'.

Accenture responded in 2012 by helping EMC build a business analytics capability to evolve their focus from day-to-day operational performance towards business outcomes. Accenture unleashed the power of analytics by establishing a Value Creation Team devoted to using analytics to improve the client's business performance. Importantly, the Value Creation Team is separate from the operations staff to promote a 'healthy tension' between the groups. Even more importantly, EMC and Accenture wrapped a joint governance structure around the Value Creation Team. The OADM explained the importance of joint governance: 'A Value Creation Team cannot be a provider working in a box. The client has to jointly govern them so that we prioritize opportunities, choose which ones to deploy, and sign off on the business value to be delivered'.

Additionally, Accenture is investing in an underlying technology to improve access and visibility of the key indicators of business performance. This combination of people, process and technology focused on driving outcomes is changing the conversation at senior levels within the relationship. According to Accenture's OADM: 'Instead of talking only about service levels, we now talk about key business outcomes and what additional value we can bring to the table; our teams are focused on elevating their games in this area. We've infused that mindset across our locations and are gaining momentum in this space'.

⚷ 13.10. Key 9: Prioritize and incent innovation

Initially, the EMC–Accenture contract did not have specific innovation clauses like required productivity improvement clauses in their contract. The main driver of innovation came from Accenture's desire to please the client and to grow the relationship by continuing to add value to EMC. The OADM explained: 'In our FTE based deal shape, EMC receives the benefit of productivity gains as our teams are able to 'do more with less'. This means that as EMC's volumes increase as a result of business growth our headcount grows at a slower pace based on efficiencies the centres have delivered'. As the GBS organization communicates 'value delivered' back to key EMC stakeholders, these efficiencies are then part of the overall story.

However, when EMC and Accenture expanded the scope of the agreement in 2012 to include India-based services, the partners did move beyond 'good faith' efforts, to formalize a mandatory productivity improvement clause. EMC requested the clause and Accenture obliged willingly because they were already delivering annual productivity savings. After a transition period, Accenture is now contractually obligated to deliver a double digit productivity improvement over a 4-year period. The bigger lesson, again, for other clients, is that it is never too late to implement practices that lead to world-class performance.

13.11. Conclusion

The EMC–Accenture BPO relationship is following a path to world-class performance that is typical among our cases. The partners have deployed best practices over time, with the most advanced practices like Value Creation Teams to drive analytics coming later once initial objectives have been met and the services well established. So what practices might be next? Client participants across our research have increasingly told us that the next best practice they want to see is the provider sharing metrics and practices across all their clients. The idea would be that the provider reports the client's KPI as well as the anonymized KPIs across all the provider's accounts, and in cases where a KPI is below best-of-breed, the client and provider would jointly develop an innovation project to improve the client's KPI. We see evidence that this 'raising the bar' phenomenon is already happening at selected high-performing relationships.

Chapter 14

⚷ TalkTalk case study: Transforming a vendor into a partner

What's Inside: The UK telecommunications company, TalkTalk, and its call centre provider, CCI, grew up together since both companies were founded about the same time. TalkTalk needed CCI to help enable its rapid growth. When TalkTalk finally made CCI its exclusive offshore partner, it enacted eight of the nine practices to claim world-class performance.

14.1. Introduction

> CCI's performance is just phenomenal. In terms of delivery for us, they've increased and improved dramatically. And on many levels, they're starting to give my onshore teams a run for their money. – TalkTalk's Marketing, Acquisition, and Retention Director

> This year's really seen a pioneering shift in the way that we interact with TalkTalk and the way TalkTalk interacts with us. – CCI's Account Director

TalkTalk provides pay television, telecommunications, internet access and mobile network services to businesses and consumers in the United Kingdom. In 2013, the company earned £1.7 billion in revenue and generated a net profit of £100 million. TalkTalk had over 4 million customers, representing 20 per cent of UK market share. Through its investments in own local telephone exchanges, TalkTalk can reach 95 per cent of the country's households.[1]

The TalkTalk BPO case is about a 9-year-old outsourcing relationship with its call centre provider, CCI Call Centres[2] (hereafter 'CCI').

Table 14.1 TalkTalk's BPO relationship

BPO type	Full call centre services – outbound sales, inbound calls, up-sell, cross-sell, web chat, email correspondence
Initial contract date	2005
Outsourcing driver	Enable rapid growth
Provider	CCI
Provider services located	South Africa
Number of provider FTEs on this account	1,000
Outsourcing outcomes	Critically enabled rapid growth, partnership is strategically aligned

TalkTalk initially signed a contract with CCI in 2005 (see Table 14.1). The scope included a 50-seat call centre for outbound sales. From that day forward, CCI has been a critical enabler of TalkTalk's rapid growth. When TalkTalk announced in 2006 that it would offer customers *free* broadband, the massive surge in customer calls left TalkTalk scrambling to find enough call centre seats to meet the elevated demand. CCI did its share by expanding the relationship to 200 seats. By 2008, CCI had about 400 seats dedicated to TalkTalk and about 700 seats by 2010. After CCI became TalkTalk's exclusive partner in 2011, the leaders transformed their relationship from a 'typical' BPO relationship to a world-class BPO relationship by implementing eight of the world-class BPO practices.

This mature relationship is an exemplary strategic alignment story. For BPO relationships that operate primarily in a reactionary, 'fire-fighting' mode, this case illustrates how adopting the keys to world-class performance can help turn off the hoses.

To understand TalkTalk's journey to world-class performance, we first describe the historical context of its rapid growth and then describe how it enacted eight of the nine keys to world-class performance.

14.2. TalkTalk's history

The backdrop for the TalkTalk–CCI case study begins with the founding of TalkTalk in 2002 as a subsidiary of Carphone Warehouse. In that year, Carphone Warehouse acquired the company Opal Telecommunications, a switching network provider that could access BT's fixed lines. Opportunities for the subsidiary exploded with the passing of the United Kingdom's Communications Act 2003. This Act took away the monopoly protection of BT's fixed-line assets, allowing customers to switch telecommunications providers. The Communications Act also created the regulatory body called the Office of Communications, known as 'Ofcom'. Ofcom oversees the telephone, television, radio and postal services in the United Kingdom and also plays a key role in the story.[3]

According to TalkTalk's website, its first big step while still a subsidiary of Carphone Warehouse was offering free calls between TalkTalk customers in 2004. The amount of new customer orders generated from this event was so tremendous that TalkTalk needed to engage the help of call centre service providers. They were using UK contact centres for Telesales and they brought on offshore centres in South Africa and India to reduce their cost per acquisition. One of those providers became start-up firm, CCI. This resulted partly from a chance meeting between the owner of CCI and a Director of TalkTalk. This led to TalkTalk trialling CCI and another centre in Cape Town, one in Kenya and one in India. The judgement was that none of the other offshore providers could deliver high quality sales with low cancellation rates. CCI did manage to achieve this – partly because of its investment in UK management team – and as such soon became the only TalkTalk offshore provider for customer sales, up-sell and retention. TalkTalk also selected South Africa because of its high cultural affinity with Britain and because costs were and still are lower in South Africa than in the United Kingdom. The initial contract was signed in 2004. The scope included a 50-seat call centre for outbound sales (see Table 14.1).

In 2005, Ofcom required 'local loop unbundling' (LLU), which meant that legacy telecommunications providers (most notably giant BT) had to allow other telecommunications providers to offer services through their local loops, that is, the existing physical links to customers' premises. BT eventually opened up over 2,000,000 local loops and AOL-UK unbundled 100,000 lines.[4] Ofcom's policy caused what one participant called '*a land grab environment*'. To build market share quickly, TalkTalk announced in 2006 a bold and unprecedented service: It would offer customers free broadband. This announcement caused a surge in customer calls that can only be described as explosive. TalkTalk scrambled to find enough call centre seats to meet demand. CCI did its share by expanding the relationship to 200 seats in 2006. TalkTalk filled gaps with other call centres in India, Ireland and the Philippines. TalkTalk's customers grew to 2.5 million that year.

In 2007, TalkTalk, while still owned by Carphone Warehouse, purchased AOL-UK's Broadband services. In 2009, TalkTalk purchased Tiscali. These purchases made TalkTalk among the biggest Home Broadband provider in the United Kingdom, with, at one time, 4.25 million home broadband subscribers,[5] compared with BT's 3.9 million. TalkTalk became an independent company in 2010 and TalkTalk Business was branded in 2012. While TalkTalk was growing rapidly and expanding into new services, the CCI relationship grew with it. By 2008, CCI had about 400 seats dedicated to TalkTalk, and about 700 seats by 2010. CCI's scope of services also expanded to include inbound and outbound new sales, up-sells, cross-sells, web chat, email correspondence and back-office data-processing services.

Due to TalkTalk's rapid growth and acquisitions, it ended up with 18 call centres in the United Kingdom, Ireland, India, the Philippines and South Africa, some of which were quite small. The oversight cost required to manage so many centres was absurdly high. Executives from TalkTalk's customer service division decided to rationalize their portfolio of call centre service providers in 2011. Some providers were in the United Kingdom, while an Indian provider was selected for technical support; a Philippines-based provider was selected for customer service support and CCI was selected for sales support. As one participant said, selecting CCI was a 'no brainer because the CCI site was the cheapest but delivering the best performance'. Today, TalkTalk offshore outsources a lot of its commercial sales, up-sells and retentions to CCI and also keeps a sizeable proportion of this activity onshore in the United Kingdom.

In 2012, TalkTalk's Marketing, Acquisition, and Retention Director began her new job with a mission statement for her division. Her leadership defined what TalkTalk wanted customers to be saying about TalkTalk within the next 2 years, the KPIs to define success (like campaign KPIs) and the change initiatives needed to get there. Because CCI was now TalkTalk's primary and exclusive commercial partner, she decided to share this strategic document with CCI on the phone just prior to her next 4-day visit to Durban. She explained: 'Before I got to South Africa, I had a call with CCI and took them through our mission statement because I thought it would be good for them to get their heads around the mission before we showed up'. When the CCI Account Director read it, he had a 'eureka' moment, realizing that a mission statement for CCI could be created that mirrored TalkTalk's mission statement. Both parties realized they had a wonderful opportunity to redesign the outsourcing relationship.

Over the next 8 months, TalkTalk and CCI transformed their relationship from a 'typical' BPO relationship to a world-class BPO relationship through an initiative they called 'The Front Line Operating Model'. TalkTalk and CCI aligned their missions, changed their attitudes, altered their planning and forecasting processes, approached problems differently, increased the level of trust and communication and broadened provider engagement beyond SLAs. Specifically, the attitudes about the relationship transformed from a 'vendor view' to a 'partnership view'. Planning and forecasting transformed from throwing requirements 'over the wall' to CCI to planning and forecasting together, which the partners call 'shoulder to shoulder'. The role of CCI's frontline employees expanded from post hoc implementers to strategy consultants. Their transformation has been so dramatic that TalkTalk adopted the new partnership model for their onshore call centres as well.

Our prior research has also uncovered many of these practices,[6] thus they have been proven across a variety of contexts. We believe that many companies can learn from these key practices of world-class performance, which are summarized in Table 14.2 and discussed in more detail.

Table 14.2 TalkTalk's BPO relationship transformation

Key practice	Typical BPO relationship	World-class BPO relationship
☞ 1. Assign a great leadership pair	Each protects the interests of its own organization	Each protects the interests of the partnership
☞ 2. Focus on business and strategic benefits beyond cost efficiencies	Disconnected mission and objectives	Shared mission and objectives
☞ 3. Drive strong transition and change management capabilities	Reactionary: Client informs provider after the fact	Shoulder-to-shoulder: Client involves provider in planning and forecasting
☞ 4. Adopt a partnering approach to governance	Vendor view	Partnership view
	Client holds provider accountable to operational Service Level Agreements (SLAs)	Client's involves provider in end-to-end process and provider contributes to improving the client's Key Process Indicators (KPIs)
☞ 5. Align the retained organization, outsourced processes and provider staff	Exclusion	Inclusion
	Opaque communication	Transparent communication
☞ 6. Resolve issues together and conflicts fairly	Fault-finding	Joint problem-solving
☞ 8. Deploy domain expertise and business analytics	Client only tracking KPI	Tracking Fizzback metrics together
☞ 9. Prioritize and incent innovation	Client sends provider long lists of things to fix	Client focuses provider on a few key initiatives

🔑 14.3. Key 1: Assign a great leadership pair

I don't think you should manage offshore providers with the stick approach and say, 'we'll let you figure out how you want to manage your business and we'll just beat you every time you miss your numbers'. I don't believe in that. – TalkTalk's Marketing, Acquisition, and Retention Director

Behind the successful execution of key practices are the extraordinary leaders who drive the adoption. As we were conducting research on the TalkTalk–CCI case, it became clear to us that their leadership pair as at 2013, which included the Marketing, Acquisition, and Retention Director at TalkTalk and the Account Director at CCI, exhibited nearly all of the important traits and behaviours of effective leadership pairs (see Chapter 2). Pertaining to background traits, both leaders were experienced, capable and had high levels of credibility, clout and power within their own organizations. TalkTalk's Marketing, Acquisition, and Retention Director had a consulting career before being recruited in 2009 as Marketing Director. Sales and retention were added to her responsibilities in February 2013. She brought all the client-facing, fast-paced, high-energy leadership one finds from the top consulting firms to her new post. CCI's Account Director previously worked his way up the ladder of TalkTalk and moved Continents several times before transferring to CCI. He had the respect of both sides because he knew every part of the business from both client and provider perspectives.

Our research identified the ten behaviours of effective leadership pairs (see Chapter 2). The TalkTalk–CCI leadership pair displayed most of the following key behaviours:

1. *A focus on the future:* In world-class relationships, the leadership pair focuses on where they want the BPO relationship to go, not where the relationship was or where it had been. In the TalkTalk–CCI story, we will see this behaviour discussed in terms of the leadership pair moving the relationship from reactionary to shoulder-to-shoulder.

2. *A focus on client outcomes:* An effective leadership pair always does what is best for the client organization and then settles a commercially equitable agreement. Clearly, the TalkTalk–CCI leadership pair focused on client outcomes (although neither discussed commercial implications).

3. *A spirit of togetherness:* We previously found that an effective leadership pair argued behind closed doors (sometimes frequently!), but presented a united front to stakeholders in their respective organizations and to the public at large. Certainly as outside researchers, the TalkTalk–CCI leadership pair presented a united front to us.

4. *Transparency:* In top-performing relationships, effective leadership pairs are open and honest about all operational issues. What is even more special about the TalkTalk–CCI leadership pair is that this transparency permeated both organizations down the chains of command as explained in Key Practice 5. It was not merely the pair who was transparent in this relationship.

5. *Orientation toward problem-solving:* World-class BPO performers seek to diagnose and fix problems; they did not seek to assign blame. The quote that opens this section certainly provides strong testimony to the fact that TalkTalk's leader jointly worked with her counterpart to solve problems. The TalkTalk–CCI leadership pair embedded this approach beyond the pair to include frontline employees (see Key Practice 6).

6. *Action orientation:* As stated earlier, our research found that the leadership pair is not afraid to expend their powers and that leaders acted swiftly to remove or workaround obstructions to change stemming from people, processes or contracts. TalkTalk's leader had to remove people who could not adapt to the new operating model. This was a difficult decision for her.

Because the leadership pair is so crucial to outsourcing success, the departure of either individual has the potential to erode performance. We asked TalkTalk's Marketing, Acquisition, and Retention Director, 'What happens then when the times comes when you're not there and CCI's Account Director is not there?' She responded with what every true transformational leader needs to do – she made herself redundant. She said: 'My team has taken the operating model and the rhythm beyond anything I imagined. So the amazing thing is that I'm not that relevant now. It sounds awful, but I'm basically a cheerleader for them right now. My team is very clear on the roadmap'. CCI's Account Director also confirmed that the Front Line Operating Model does not rely on just the pair. He said: 'Talent: we have the right people in the right positions with the right skills set on both sides of the business'. In academic terms, we say that this leadership pair has *institutionalized* change.

🔑 14.4. Key 2: Focus on business and strategic benefits beyond cost efficiencies

So my goal was to get them to buy into our mission and to empower them so that we could work shoulder-to-shoulder to deliver on the mission. – TalkTalk's Marketing, Acquisition, and Retention Director

From disconnected to shared missions. Initially, TalkTalk's relationships with their call centre providers were about operational urgency. TalkTalk sought partners that could rapidly fill seats and deliver good quality at a reasonable price. But after CCI became TalkTalk's exclusive offshore partner, the partners focused on more strategically aligned business objectives. Rather than TalkTalk having its own vision and CCI having its own vision, CCI decided to align its mission with TalkTalk's to create a shared mission. Returning to the moment when CCI's Account Director first received a copy of TalkTalk's mission statement, he recalled: 'So we then went away with their mission plan and said we should have our own version of their plan. As their key partner, we are responsible for 70 percent of all their activity, we need our own version of the plan. So we took exactly the same logic and said, "So what do we want TalkTalk, our client, to be saying about us as a business?"' This was one of the first big steps towards transforming the relationship from a traditional BPO relationship to a world-class-performing BPO relationship. But getting the ranks and files to embrace the new mission required the deployment of more key practices.

⚷ 14.5. Key 3: Drive strong transition, transformational and change management capabilities

We're now in a situation where we know what's coming over the next quarter, we know what the big events are, we know what we need to be aware of, and we know when they're happening. – CCI's Account Director

From reactionary to shoulder-to-shoulder planning. In the past, TalkTalk had poor transition and change management capabilities. Senior executives made quick decisions and informed CCI mostly after the fact. This led CCI to be in a nearly constant reactionary state. This process was not so much by design, but by frenetic necessity. As commensurate with TalkTalk's explosive growth, its culture was described by participants as 'fast-moving, dynamic, with really aggressive targets for growth' and 'very dynamic entrepreneurial business which is very hungry for growth'. Participants estimate that before the Front Line Operating Model was enacted, CCI's management team was 90 per cent reactive and 10 per cent planned. That was causing service problems because CCI was constantly dealing with last minute changes, such as adapting to a change in one of TalkTalk's products or services. After the implementation of the Front Line Operating Model, participants estimated that the ratio has improved to 70 per cent planned activities and 30 per cent ad hoc activities. TalkTalk had finally built a world-class transition, and change management capability.

⚷ 14.6. Key 4: Adopt a partnering approach to governance

We are all in this together and we have a partnership approach to engagement. – CCI's Account Director

From vendor to partnership attitude. Ideally, clients should approach outsourcing with a partnership view in mind, but as the TalkTalk–CCI case demonstrates, it is never too late to transform attitudes about provider relationships from 'vendors' to 'partners'.

Initially, TalkTalk seemed to hold more of this 'vendor view' attitude towards CCI. One participant spoke about the relationship initially as a 'master and slave approach to outsourcing' where the client is the master and the provider is the slave. As TalkTalk and CCI went on their journey to build the new Front Line Operating Model, most people clearly began to consider the other as a true partner. But not all people embrace changes so easily. At TalkTalk, roles were reallocated to key team members who were better able to adapt to the new model. This supports two larger points we uncovered in other cases of transformation: leaders cannot be afraid to expend their powers, and leaders must act swiftly to remove or workaround obstructions to transformation stemming from people, processes or contracts.[7] By the end of the process, CCI's Account Director confirmed that both sides successfully view the relationship as a partnership. He said: 'It's no longer a supplier/ customer relationship, it's a proper partnership. And that's been a really positive transformation'. Partnership attitudes lead to partnership behaviours, like including the provider in end-to-end process governance.

From SLA to end-to-end management. SLAs formally define who, what, where and when services are to be performed. For call centre operations, SLAs may include operational performance measures such as average time to answer a call or percentage of escalated calls. However, end-to-end KPIs are more strategic, such as conversion rates from marketing campaigns, retention rates, up-sells, cross-sells and of course customer satisfaction. What value might be unlocked if clients focused their call centre providers on these KPIs?

At TalkTalk, the client initially only held CCI accountable to its SLAs. But as one participant said, this is a naïve approach to outsourcing because the client should not absolve themselves of all the frontline delivery accountability: 'A mature client realizes that they are accountable for the end result just as much as the provider'. Conversely, the provider can also be more accountable for helping TalkTalk achieve its KPIs. During the transformation process, TalkTalk and CCI began to realize that CCI was central to nearly every customer touch point. CCI spoke to TalkTalk's customers when they first signed up for service, when they wanted to add services and when they wanted to cancel services. CCI's Account Director said that in 2011, TalkTalk and CCI began to realize they were leaving value on the table by not exploiting CCI's 360 degree customer view. He said: 'We know why customers are taking products and why they're not taking products and what happened at point of sale that resulted in this complaint or up-sell. So there are really clever things that you can leverage from having all that activity in one site'.

After the transformation, the partners clearly governed end-to-end. CCI's Account Director explained: 'We watch the net numbers after three months, i.e., are we signing customers up in the right way? Are they enjoying the service? Are they staying with us after three months? And if they are staying with us after three months, what are they saying about us? Are they promoting us to their friends? So that's the thinking end-to-end part'.

14.7. Key 5: Align the retained organization, outsourced processes and provider staff

From exclusion to inclusion. TalkTalk and CCI realized that CCI's frontline employees could provide valuable insight into TalkTalk's marketing campaigns. CCI's frontline employees speak with TalkTalk's customers every day, so they are in a prime position to assess how customers might react to new campaigns. As part of the new Front Line Operating Model, a CCI agent is assigned to any new marketing campaigns being developed at TalkTalk headquarters. Agents participate in planning meetings via tele-presence and provide frontline input and feedback. In addition to their valuable input, the frontline employees become aware of the new campaigns well in advance so they can prepare their peers. Most importantly, they feel validated and valued by their client. As far as the effect on the agents, CCI's Account Director said: 'We get their feedback, we get their buy-in and then they're part owners of the roll out'.

From opaque to transparent communication. From our past ITO and BPO research, we found that both clients and providers wanted the other party to be more transparent, but each partner had a different view on what needed to be revealed. Providers wanted clients to be more transparent about their operations and wanted to be invited inside the 'strategic tent'. Clients wanted providers to be more transparent about their profit margins, cost structure, subcontracting practices, risk profile and true attrition rates. Clients also wanted to better understand how provider organizations allocate resources to staff client accounts.[8] We learned that TalkTalk and CCI became more transparent along many of these lines.

TalkTalk certainly invited CCI into the strategic tent. TalkTalk's role in this more transparent environment was formalized by giving 15-minute structured debriefings with the CCI shift teams each day, with a specific topic assigned to each weekday. For example, TalkTalk discusses product briefs one day, compliance one day and quality on another day. The debriefings help prepare the South African team to better serve TalkTalk's customers. For example, when TalkTalk launched Dr. Who on their TV service, most of the South African agents had never seen the show. The debriefing prepared them in advance to learn about the show so they could better help clients with their orders.

CCI became much more transparent by having agents directly involved with TalkTalk's teams. This is a big mindset change for many service providers – indeed provider account managers are expected to manage client expectations and often buffer their clients from unchaperoned contact with their frontline employees. CCI's Account Director admitted to being nervous about this transparency at first. He said: 'I'm the account director, right? So my role is to manage the account but also to ensure that we are always being perceived in the best possible way. I asked myself, do we really want to put frontline people in front of senior clients? They might be overly honest, they might be completely incorrect, all the rest of it. And actually, that's been the best part of the whole process – they are more than capable'. TalkTalk's Marketing, Acquisition, and Retention Director confirmed the agents' performance. She said: 'They amaze me every day'.

One further key thing the parties changed was shifting from communicating about immediate term, directly actionable needs to also giving rolling context of what was about to happen over 4-month horizons. The concept of 'context' has been critical to both parties.

⚷ 14.8. Key 6: Resolve issues together and conflicts fairly

> We had never spent adequate time problem-solving with team managers and campaign managers regarding competitor and customer dynamics they were facing – conversations usually focused entirely on performance issues. – TalkTalk's Marketing, Acquisition, and Retention Director

From fault-finding to joint problem-solving. At TalkTalk and CCI, the partners clearly moved from fault-finding to shared accountability and joint problem-solving. Both TalkTalk and CCI participants used the phrase, 'we no longer chase shadows', meaning the partners first determine whether a perceived problem is an actual problem. If it is an actual problem, the partners looked for the root cause, which might be a client-induced problem, a provider-induced problem or a combination of both. It could even be caused by changing market forces. For example, if competitors like BT launch a big campaign, that could reduce CCI's save rate. Instead of bruising CCI for the lapse, the partners now discuss the reason and plan a response.

As part of the cycle of continuous improvement, TalkTalk's marketing leaders conduct 2-hour problem-solving sessions, called sprints, with the frontline agents whenever they visit CCI in South Africa. Sprints are conducted before the morning shift begins. TalkTalk's Marketing, Acquisition, and Retention Director explained the value: 'We'd get uninterrupted thinking and problem-solving time done in the morning and then start the chaos of the day. I think that's quite an important aspect of how we operate actually, is making sure you have the time for problem-solving in an uninterrupted environment'.

CCI's Account Director describes the before and after approach of problem-solving: 'So before, a grenade would come over the fence with the pin out, 'You haven't done this, You need to do X, Y and Z' and we'd have to man the panic stations. That's the old school of working. The new way of working is, we collectively discuss, 'Is it a problem?' 'Why do we think it's happened?' We now have the confidence to be able to be honest about our own failings and we also have the confidence to be honest about their failings, in a diplomatic manner of course'. As this last quote attests, joint problem-solving can only happen in environments of high trust and transparency.

14.9. Key 7: Deploy domain expertise and business analytics

CCI's 360 degree customer view provides deep insights into helping TalkTalk achieve its KPIs, such as net ad churn rates, up-sale rates and TalkTalk's most important KPI, 'Fizzback', its customer satisfaction score. Fizzback is the name of the company that does surveys for customer to rate their satisfaction with agent interaction. The agent satisfaction (ASAT) metric is so important to TalkTalk that it is broadcast on monitors at TalkTalk's headquarters. CCI adopted this as one of their major KPIs and even award agents' bonuses based on their individual Fizzback scores. Fizzback scores are tallied at the individual, team and campaign levels and are tracked and reported daily to all levels – agents, team managers, campaign managers, campaign directors and head of site.

14.10. Key 8: Prioritize and incent innovation

Before, we were very much 'try this', 'try this', 'try this', and 'try this'. We had so many different initiatives happening at the same time, we could never really tell which effort was driving the results. – CCI Account Director

CCI senior management team were really honest with me. They told me they were skeptical we'd be able to deliver the change initiatives, because they always have too many things to deliver in the here and now. This made me realize that I couldn't return from my visit with a list of 20 actions – it forced me to pare the list down to a 3–4 high priority, game-changing areas of focus. I was only able to do this because they took the risk to be brutally honest with me. – TalkTalk's Marketing, Acquisition, and Retention Director

From long to-do lists to focused initiatives. After visiting CCI's South African call centre, TalkTalk's Marketing, Acquisition, and Retention Director went back and wrote up copious notes from all the problem-solving sprints, listening in on calls and discussions. She was going to send detailed feedback to CCI, but decided instead to whittle the long list down to a few key points. Call centre providers are so focused on daily delivery, that assigning them too many improvement tasks will frustrate and distract them. She explained: 'I looked at all my notes and I was going to press send. And then I just took a step back. I slept on it. The next day, I decided they can only focus on three things. This is one of my biggest learnings that I would give to anyone who wants to manage an offshore service provider: If you send laundry lists of things of things for them to do, people lose the wood for the trees and don't know how to prioritize'.

CCI's Account Director noted that in the past, CCI was trying to do too many things at once. After the Front Line Operating Model went into effect, the partners prioritize their top initiatives. Furthermore, they implemented strict change control so only one team pilots a new initiative to isolate cause and effect. CCI's Account Director described how new initiatives are launched now. He said: 'So now it's very much adopt the test and learn approach. We do it in a test and learn environment so you only have one team trialling it as opposed to everyone so you can see whether actually that change had the impact or whether that was just a general change'.

14.11. Case discussion

The earlier quotation testifies that transforming CCI from a vendor to a partner has yielded a significant and positive affect on performance.

But the journey is not over. As of autumn 2013, TalkTalk and CCI had implemented about 60 per cent of their Front Line Operating Model. The partners estimated that it would take about another 6 to 9 months to fully implement the model so that every agent – all 1,000 people working on the TalkTalk account – fully embraced the new mission and new operating procedures. TalkTalk's Marketing, Acquisition, and Retention Director envisioned that eventually the entire operation would be similar to a lean manufacturing site where every machine operator would be completely bedded into the mission of continual improvement and reduced wastage.

The TalkTalk–CCI case warrants discussion of the benefits and risks of large-sized engagements first introduced in Chapter 1. The magnitude of transformation described in this and other cases we have studied requires scale. Outsourcing relationships have to be large enough to warrant the level of client attention and resources a partnership requires, but there are also additional risks from large-sized relationships.

In our research, we have studied outsourcing arrangements from very small contracts to contracts that operate in over 90 countries and comprise hundreds of FTEs. Our prior research[9] found that large engagements with bundled services offer clients significant benefits. The major advantages include simplified procurement, simplified governance, fewer transaction costs and economies of scale and scope. We see evidence of all these benefits at the TalkTalk–CCI relationship. In particular, we noted that bundled services (sales, retentions, up-sells and cross-sells) gave CCI the previously mentioned advantage of the 360 degree view it has of TalkTalk's customers. However, larger deals bring greater risks. Therefore, careful consideration must always be given to the scale and scope of work assigned to providers.

Once the CCI engagement had reached over 1,000 seats, a number of additional business benefits became possible. CCI could afford to invest in coaching, mentoring and training to build critical middle management and leadership skills. Their programme is called The Management Academy. This is precisely the type of initiative South Africa itself needed, as our prior research found that South Africa's challenges in the BPO space come primarily from its recent successes and the anticipated high levels of growth, creating a potential shortage of middle management and leadership skills.[10] We recommended that

South Africa needed to accelerate and scale the development of these skills. CCI's Account Director told us: 'we take advantage of scale and the fact we have a lot of people to work with and therefore, a lot of opportunity. We have people who have worked on TalkTalk for a good number of years and worked up the management chain. So they would be an agent, then they would be a team manager, and then they may become campaign managers. Now 50 percent of our campaign managers are South African nationals compared to before when we mainly hired UK nationals to run our campaigns'. At CCI, scale allows it to do this training in-house, leading to richer career paths, more satisfied employees, lower turnover and ultimately better service to the client.

But we do have one word of caution. Despite all the additional value afforded by large-scale partnerships, reliance on one key partner increases switching costs, creates lock-in and raises the risks of opportunism, that is, the probability that one party can be self-seeking with guile.[11] Even though TalkTalk views CCI as a partner, it keeps a competitive lever on CCI through benchmarking. Benchmarking allows TalkTalk to understand the costs and service levels it can obtain in the United Kingdom and thus holds CCI accountable for equal or better service quality while benefiting from lower offshore rates. According to CCI's Account Director, benchmarking works as follows: 'So we get a percentage of the same calls as onshore get. We get all the same data as onshore get and it's just a very clear comparison of 'Here are your results, here are their results'. So it's quite a clever set up and it keeps everyone on their toes and everything is compared apples with apples'.

14.12. Conclusion

Our broader research goal for this case was to investigate the viability of South Africa as a destination for global BPO services.[12] We believe this is best demonstrated through proven success stories. Clearly, the TalkTalk–CCI case study is a testimony to the type of deep partnership that can occur between a Western-based client and a South African-based provider. Success is driven by a strong leadership pair who can institutionalize key practices associated with world-class performance.

1   Sources: http://www.talktalkgroup.com/about-us/our-history.aspx; Wikipedia, http://en.wikipedia.org/wiki/TalkTalk_Group

2   The CCI Group consists of Communication Centres International (Group) Ltd, being the main group holding company and contracting party with TalkTalk. CCI Call Centres Pty Ltd, based in Kwa-Zulu Natal province of South Africa. It services large international customers based in the United Kingdom and Australia.

3   History of Ofcom comes from Wikipedia (http://en.wikipedia.org/wiki/Ofcom), UK Legislative http://www.legislation.gov.uk/ukpga/2003/21/contents and Ofcom (http://www.ofcom.org.uk/about/) websites

4   History of Ofcom comes from Wikipedia (http://en.wikipedia.org/wiki/Ofcom), UK Legislative http://www.legislation.gov.uk/ukpga/2003/21/contents and Ofcom (http://www.ofcom.org.uk/about/) websites

5   Source: http://www.talktalkgroup.com/about-us/our-history.aspx

6   Our prior research on transforming ITO and BPO relationships spans multiple research projects. Most recently, we have identified best practices in the context of legal, F&A, human resources, cloud and supply chain services. See Lacity et al., *The Rise of Legal Services Outsourcing*; Lacity and Willcocks, *Advanced Outsourcing Practice*; Willcocks et al., *Moving To The Cloud Corporation* and 15 practice papers written for Accenture (see our research on high-performance BPO is available at http://www.accenture.com/Microsites/highperfbpo/Pages/home.aspx

7   Lacity and Willcocks, *Sloan Management Review*.

8   See Lacity, M. and Rottman, J. (2011), 'Building a Better Outsourcing Community', *Globalization Today*, March, 29–31.

9   See Willcocks, L., Oshri, I. and Hindle, J. (2010), *To Bundle or Not To Bundle? Effective Decision-Making for Business and IT Services*, OU/Accenture, London. A newer version is also available in Lacity and Willcocks, *Advanced Outsourcing Practice*. To understand the trade-offs between bundling services and multi-sourcing, we studied over 1,850 outsourcing contracts, and carried out interviews with 69 leading clients and providers in ITO and BPO services. We identify 20 drivers to consider when deciding between bundled or unbundled ITO and BPO services. These drivers are grouped into five areas: client factors, relational factors, provider market, capabilities factors and cost effectiveness characteristics, and form the basis of a decision-making matrix designed for client use. From the research, we also distill five profiles of clients more, or less, likely to buy bundled services: Strategic Explorer, Conservative, Operational Exploiter, Experimenter and Multi-sourcer. This is a distinctive and new contribution to the understanding of clients, and how they can continue to develop their ability to harness the ever-increasing capabilities of business and IT service providers.

10 See Willcocks, L., Craig, A. and Lacity, M. (2012), 'Becoming Strategic – South Africa's BPO Service Advantage', available at http://www.outsourcingunit.org/WorkingPapers/WP12_4.pdf

11 These notions arise from Transaction Cost Economics. See Williamson, O. (1991), 'Comparative Economic Organization: The Analysis of Discrete Structural Alternatives', *Administrative Science Quarterly*, 36(2), 269–296.

12 See Willcocks, L., Lacity, M. and Craig, A. (2015), *South Africa's BPO Service Advantage*, Palgrave, London.

Research base and method

Throughout the 2011–2014 period, we participated in one BPO survey, conducted four surveys and interviewed 65 BPO clients/providers to find the key practices associated with world-class BPO performance.

The BPO survey

The survey was administered by The Everest Group, a leading outsourcing advisory firm. Our role was to comment on survey design and we had access to the survey findings. Two hundred and sixty-three qualified BPO clients responded. The initial findings are reported in Mindrum et al. (2012).[1]

The survey used two sets of criteria to identify top BPO performers. First, strong performance for three 'must-have' elements: (1) The BPO relationship meets financial objectives; (2) The BPO relationship meets service level objectives and (3) The BPO provider's service delivery is consistent and predictable with low variability in performance levels. Second, world-class relationships performed in the top quartile across seven value indicators. These were: (1) Greater flexibility to manage temporary volume fluctuations; (2) Increased speed to prepare for changing business conditions; (3) Optimized and enabled the entire process or business function; (4) Improved business performance of other parts of the client organization; (5) Created additional sources of value; (6) Delivered business outcomes which were not originally expected and (7) Enabled the organization to increase the top line.

The survey identified 20 per cent of respondents as world-class, scoring strongly on the three must-have elements and in the top quartile on seven value indicators. The survey found that levels of performance were independent of industry, geography, size of deal, tenure of BPO relationship and business function outsourced. The survey research identified eight practices that strongly correlated with world-class performance. The initial set of eight practices was:

Practice 1. Focus on benefits beyond cost reduction
Practice 2. Adopt a partnership-based approach to governance
Practice 3. Align the retained organization with the outsourced processes
Practice 4. Take a holistic approach to the scope of the BPO relationship
Practice 5. Target strategic outcomes
Practice 6. Drive strong transition and change management capabilities
Practice 7. Contextualize data through domain expertise and analytics
Practice 8. Emphasize the benefits of technology in the BPO relationship

The BPO community survey

We administered a survey at the 2011 IAOP World Summit in Indian Wells. At the World Summit, clients gathered in one ballroom (identity was verified at the entrance) and providers and advisors gathered in another ballroom for networking sessions. The survey asked, 'What is the one attitude or behavior you wish the other two communities would change in order to build a better outsourcing community?' Eighty-one people provided 121 comments on the open-ended question. Thirty-one customers commented on providers and advisors, 31 providers commented on customers and advisors and 19 advisors commented on customers and providers. We analysed the content of survey and report on the most frequently cited responses from each community.[2]

BPO innovation survey

The intention of the BPO innovation survey was to capture the similarities and differences between client and provider perceptions about the most effective innovation incentives, sources and funding for innovations and samples of innovations delivered in outsourcing relationships. We designed the survey and it was reviewed by members of the International Association of Outsourcing Professionals (IAOP). The survey was administered at the IAOP's 2012 Outsourcing World Summit. Mid-way through each session, participants were asked to fill in our paper survey. Two hundred and two delegates turned in completed surveys – 85 clients, 90 providers and 27 outsourcing advisors.[3]

Cloud services survey

At the 2013 IAOP Outsourcing World Summit, we surveyed 133 delegates during the customer only and provider/advisor only networking sessions. For cloud services we assessed the current status, perceptions and the expected and actual business value delivered. The sample captured a range of firm sizes as measured by number of employees worldwide. The average size of firm for customer respondents was 50,751 employees, for provider firms was 32,494 employees and for advisor firms was 4,201 employees. The size ranged from a very small advisory firm with only three employees to a very large customer firm with over 300,000 employees. Financial services (34%) and insurance (13%) were the most represented industries.[4]

Leadership pair survey

In our interview research (explained later), we identified ten attributes of effective leadership pairs. We sought to more rigorously explore these ten attributes. To what degree do client and provider leaders exhibit these attributes? Are certain attributes more important than others? Do clients and providers share similar perceptions about leadership pair attributes? To answer these questions, we surveyed delegates during the customer only and provider/advisor only networking sessions at the 2014 IAOP Outsourcing World Summit. The sample of 139 completed surveys comprises 72 clients, 51 providers, 6 advisors and 10 providers/advisors. Clients represent 51.8 per cent of the sample and providers/advisors represent 41.8 per cent of the sample. The average tenure for the leadership pair being assessed was 4.14 years, with 69.1 per cent having been leaders for fewer than 5 years. Thirty-three leadership pairs have been together for more than 5 years. The leadership pairs were primarily managing outsourcing for one functional area, most frequently an information technology outsourcing or call centre account.[5]

Interviews

Throughout 2011–2014, the present authors conducted interviews to enrich these survey findings. Our research question: 'How do BPO partners achieve world-class performance?' sought to elicit rich evidence that could corroborate, challenge and/or extend the survey findings. We were looking for high performers, using the survey instrument definition of best-in-class performance. We wanted to better understand the key practices that lead to and sustain performance from both client and provider perspectives.

We designed two interview guides: one for the client informants and one for the provider informants. The interview guides were designed to capture the eight best practices identified in the survey as well as a number of open-ended questions on attitudes, behaviours, processes and practices that affect BPO outcomes. For client participants, the guides have open-ended questions on outsourcing strategy, provider selection, contractual governance, transition of work, ongoing delivery, relational governance, outsourcing outcomes, client and provider capabilities, client and provider practices, outsourcing outcomes and overall lessons learned. The provider guide included the same set of questions for contractual governance, transition of work, ongoing delivery, relational governance, outsourcing outcomes, client and provider capabilities, client and provider practices, outsourcing and overall lessons learned. Research sponsors from Accenture reviewed the guides for clarity and understandability.

We conducted in-depth interviews with key informants from 32 BPO arrangements from October 2011 to first quarter 2014 (see Table A.1). For a given BPO relationship, we interviewed the client lead and the provider lead in-charge of the account. We studied many different types of business services, including financial and accounting services (FAO), human resources, legal services (LSO or LPO), procurement/supply chain, call centres and cloud services. The interviews were typically 45–75 minutes in length. Participants were interviewed by phone because they were globally dispersed; participants were located in Australia, Canada, India, Ireland, the Philippines, Spain, South Africa, Switzerland, Czech Republic, the United Kingdom and the United States. All interviews were tape-recorded by the interviewer and transcribed by a third party.

Table A.1 Qualitative data collected on BPO relationships

Context	Number of relationships studied	Number of key informant interviews	Sample cases
Financial and accounting services (FAO)	8	18	BP, Microsoft
Human resources (learning, recruiting, etc.) (HRO)	3	6	Telstra, Kimberly Clark
Legal process (LPO)	6	11	RadiantLaw, BT
Procurement/supply chain outsourcing	5	10	Givaudan, Synopsis
Customer care/call centre, outsourcing	6	12	TalkTalk, British Gas, iiNet
Cloud services	4	8	Diesel Direct, Dana Foundation
Total	32	65	

Data analysis to define nine key to world-class performance

The transcribed interviews are over 600 pages long. First, we extracted and wrote papers on the eight best practices identified by the BPO survey. Some of these practices proved meatier than others. As we were writing these initial papers, we became aware of three more strong themes emerging from the interviews on incenting innovation, the role of leadership pairs and engaging the provider's staff.

Based on all the evidence, we identified nine key practices by combining thinner practices and by adding our emerging practices. This resulted in the final set of nine keys to world-class performance:

⟳ 1. Assign great leaderships pairs

⟳ 2. Focus on business and strategic benefits beyond cost efficiencies

⟳ 3. Drive strong transition, transformation and change management capabilities

⟳ 4. Adopt a partnering approach to governance

⟳ 5. Align the retained organization, outsourced processes and provider staff

⟳ 6. Resolve issues together and conflicts fairly

⟳ 7. Use technology as enabler and accelerator of performance

⟳ 8. Deploy domain expertise and business analytics

⟳ 9. Prioritize and incent innovation

---

[1]   See Mindrum et al., 'Achieving High Performance in BPO'.

[2]   See Lacity, M. and Rottman, J. (2011), 'Building a Better Outsourcing Community', *Globalization Today*, March, 29–31.

[3]   Results were published in Lacity, M. and Rottman, J., *Globalization Today*.

[4]   Results were published in Lacity, M. and Willcocks, L. (2013), 'Cloud Services Forecast: Rain and Shine: Findings from the 2013 IAOP World Summit Survey', *Pulse Magazine* (5), 16–21.

[5]   See Lacity et al., *Pulse Magazine*.

Assessing leadership pair effectiveness

To what extent do you agree with the following statements pertaining to the leadership pair you are assessing?	Client leader							Provider leader						
	Strongly disagree 1	2	3	4	5	6	Strongly agree 7	Strongly disagree 1	2	3	4	5	6	Strongly agree 7
Focus on the future: This leader focuses on where the outsourcing relationship should go, not where the relationship was in the past or is in the present.	○	○	○	○	○	○	○	○	○	○	○	○	○	○
Transparent: This leader is open and honest about all operational issues.	○	○	○	○	○	○	○	○	○	○	○	○	○	○
Problem-solving: This leader seeks to diagnose and fix problems; he/she does not seek to assign blame	○	○	○	○	○	○	○	○	○	○	○	○	○	○
Client first: This leader always does what is best for the client organization	○	○	○	○	○	○	○	○	○	○	○	○	○	○

Spirit of togetherness: This leader does not talk poorly about the other party but instead presents a united front.	o	o	o	o	o	o	o	o	o	o
Clout within their own organization: This leader has high levels of credibility, clout and power within his/her own organization	o	o	o	o	o	o	o	o	o	o
Action-oriented: This leader acts swiftly to remove or workaround obstructions stemming from people, processes or contracts.	o	o	o	o	o	o	o	o	o	o
Trustworthy: This leader is trustworthy and has good intentions towards his/her counterpart.	o	o	o	o	o	o	o	o	o	o
Empathy: This leader understands, is aware of and is sensitive to the counterpart's feelings, thoughts and experiences.	o	o	o	o	o	o	o	o	o	o
Chemistry: This leader enjoys working with his/her counterpart.	o	o	o	o	o	o	o	o	o	o

This quick survey can be used to measure leadership pair effectiveness. The client lead, provider lead and other relevant stakeholders can assess the individual leaders and compare results.

Overall, how effective is this leadership pair at managing the outsourcing relationship?

	1	2	3	4	5	6	7	
Very ineffective	o	o	O	o	o	o	o	Very effective

Overall, how well is this outsourcing relationship performing?

	1	2	3	4	5	6	7	
Poor performance	o	o	O	o	o	o	o	World-class performance

Index

Page numbers in **bold** refer to figures/tables.